John P. Comer, A. Barton Hepburn Professor Emeritus of Government in Williams College from which he retired in 1953, is a native of Texas and a 1907 graduate of Trinity University. After spending six years in the Texas Public School System (1908 – 1914), Dr. Comer went to Southern Methodist University where he served as professor and Acting Dean (1916 – 1924). He then joined the faculty of Williams College where, after receiving his Ph.D. in Political Science from Columbia University in 1927, he occupied the chair of the Hepburn Professor in Government until his retirement. Author of several books on rule and decision making in federal and local government, he participated as a student and officer in the Institute of Politics.

THE FORGING OF THE FEDERAL INDIGENT CODE

THE FORGING OF
THE FEDERAL
INDIGENT CODE

By

JOHN P. COMER

PRINCIPIA PRESS OF TRINITY UNIVERSITY
SAN ANTONIO, TEXAS
1966

PREFACE

As early as 1938 Associate Justice Harlan F. Stone called my attention to what the Supreme Court was doing at that time to aid the poor man before the federal courts. He suggested that the investigation of its work along this line might be interesting to various persons not trained in the law. As Chief Justice he was still anxious for a non-technically trained man to make a study of what the Court had done in furthering the the betterment of the indigent by court action. He died in 1946 before I had either the time or the available resources for the investigation. Much later I decided to carry out a survey of what had been done by way of giving indigents free access to the federal courts; this survey was limited to the material which could be found within a reasonable distance from my home.

I soon found that the study of the free services in civil action would involve an enormous amount of work and I was obliged to omit all, or nearly all, of the civil action cases over which administrative tribunals had original jurisdiction; such cases would require a separate study. In the civil cases over which a federal court had original jurisdiction and in all those of a criminal nature, I found much research still had to be done and the results collated if possible. *In forma pauperis* procedure was inextricably tied up with constitutional and statutory law and with rulings and practices of the courts. I saw no way of properly handling the procedure without a careful study of court organization and jurisdiction, methods of appeal, legislative and common law, writs of *certiorari*, and other great common law writs such as *habeas corpus*. It is hoped that these various elements have been brought together in a coherent manner.

I wish to thank the Taft family for the privilege of examining the William Howard Taft Papers, Supreme Court Series (1921-1940), the Hughes family for the Charles Evans Hughes

PREFACE

Papers, Supreme Court Series (1930-1941), and Mrs. Harlan Fiske Stone for the Harlan Fiske Stone Papers, Supreme Court Series (1925-1946). I am grateful to David C. Mearns, Chief of the Manuscript Division of the Library of Congress, for his aid in securing the above permissions and in furnishing a desk in his section of the Library. I wish also to thank the officials of the Law Division of the Library of Congress for many services, and Miss Frances Farmer, Librarian of the University of Virginia Law Library, for space and assistance in checking material.

John P. Comer

Charlottesville, Virginia

TABLE OF CONTENTS

TABLE OF CONTENTS

ABBREVIATIONS

LAW REVIEWS AND JOURNALS

A.B.A.J. — American Bar Association Journal
A.B.A. Rep. — Reports of the American Bar Association
Amer. J. of L. Hist. — American Journal of Legal History
Amer. Pol. Sc. Rev. — American Political Science Review
B.U.L. Rev. — Boston University Law Review
Calif. L. Rev. — California Law Review
Col. L. Rev. — Columbia Law Review
Corn. L. Q. — Cornell Law Quarterly
DePaul L. Rev. — DePaul Law Review
F.R.D. — Federal Rules Decisions
Harv. L. Rev. — Harvard Law Review
Ill. L. Rev. — Illinois Law Review
Iowa L. Rev. — Iowa Law Review
J. Amer. Judic. Soc. — Journal of American Judicature Society
J. of Pub. Law — Journal of Public Law
L.W. — Law Week
Mich. L. Rev. — Michigan Law Review
Mid. J. Pol. Sc. — Mid-Western Journal of Political Science
Minn. L. Rev. — Minnesota Law Review
N.J.L.J. — New Jersey Law Journal
N.Y.U.L. Rev. — New York University Law Review
So. Tex. L. Rev. — South Texas Law Review
Stanford L. Rev. — Stanford Law Review
Tex. L. Rev. — Texas Law Review
Univ. of Chi. L. Rev. — University of Chicago Law Review
Univ. of Penn. L. Rev. — University of Pennsylvania Law Review
Univ. of Pitts. L. Rev. — University of Pittsburgh Law Review
Utah L. Rev. — Utah Law Review
Va. L. Rev. — Virginia Law Review
West. Res. L. Rev. — Western Reserve Law Review
Yale L.J. — Yale Law Journal

REPORTS

Comp. Dec. — Comptroller of the Treasury Decisions
Comp. Gen. — Comptroller General of the Treasurer Decisions
Ct. Cl. — Court of Claims Reports
F. — Federal Reporter
F. 2d. — Federal Reporter 2nd Series
F. Supp. — Federal Supplement
H. Rep. — House Report
S. Rep. — Senate Report
S. Ct. R. and B., L.C. — Supreme Court Records and Briefs,
    Law Division, Library of Congress
S. Ct. J. — Supreme Court Journal
Report of Director (or Director's Report) — Report of the
    Director of the Administrative Office of the United
    States Courts
Report of the Jud. Conf. — Annual Report of the Proceedings
    of the Judicial Conference of the United States
U.S. — Supreme Court Reports (appeal)

DOCUMENTS

Stat. — United States Statutes at Large
U.S.C. — United States Code
U.S.C.A — United States Code Annotated

PAPERS

Hughes Papers — Charles E. Hughes Papers, Supreme Court
    Series 1930-1941, Manuscript Division, Library
    of Congress
Stone Papers — The Harlan F. Stone Papers, Supreme Court
    Series 1925-1946, Manuscript Division, Library
    of Congress
Taft Papers — William Howard Taft Papers, Supreme Court
    Series 1921-1930, Manuscript Division, Library
    of Congress

PART I

FEDERAL STATUATORY AND CONSTITUTIONAL
PROCEDURE FAVORING INDIGENTS
CRIMINAL AND CIVIL, 1789-1922

CHAPTER I

INTRODUCTION

Frederic Maitland, the English lawyer and legal historian, once remarked that British liberty was an outgrowth of "writs not rights." This concise statement has of late been matched by Felix Frankfurter, the American jurist and legal historian, who wrote succinctly that "the history of liberty has largely been the history of the observance of procedural safeguards."[1] Were legal procedures, then, the Anglo-Saxon's first rights?

Neither of the learned gentlemen was at the time concerned with substantive law. Each in his own legal situation was referring to the judicial procedure by which the substantive law of his state was to be applied justly to each individual in civil and criminal cases. The one was properly emphasizing the role that the English judiciary had in developing the civil and criminal procedure whereby the individual would have the opportunity to protect his rights of property and liberty against those who had the monopoly of power and were not unwilling to use that power. The other was underlining the importance of procedure in America, whether developed by the courts, implanted in the Constitution, or expressed in statutory form under pressure of the legal fraternity.

In legal terms, judicial procedure is "the mode of proceeding by which a legal right is enforced, as distinguished from the law which gives or declines the right, and which, by means of proceeding, the court is to administer."[2] It might be more meaningful to the layman to define judicial procedure as the method by which a reasonable relation is secured between them and their government. Whatever the definition, procedure is, in a sense, a process which changes with time and circumstance despite the resistance of legal practitioners. To be sure it cannot be expected that procedure will advance *pari passu* with changing substantive law. At a particular time however, procedure should be as clear and definite as possible, since it determines the utility of the courts in grinding out what is called the grist of the democratic value, justice according to law.

Whenever procedure prevents a person from realizing that value, the courts are of little or no aid to him. In no democratic or near-democratic state have judicial proceedings met the needs of all persons who have come, willingly or otherwise, to the bar of the court. It is not too strange indeed that an Anglo-Indian scholar, after he had observed the working of the British judicial procedure imposed upon impecunious India, noted the gulf that existed between the results of that system, and the ''one common principle of judicial administration, [namely, that] the attainment of justice before a court of law be accessible to the poor without cost or delay.''[3]

To assert that the courts are not available, or not readily so, to all the people of a particular country (more especially the United States) is not to say that attempts have not been made to bring this about, nor that the judicial system is not moving to this end at the present time. The conscience of a particular community or its effective elements has steadily insisted that those who are financially embarrassed for a time, like those who are normally without funds to meet court costs and fees, should have access to the courts.

What procedures are there to meet this universal ideal? One method would be to have the government absorb all fees and pay all the costs of civil and criminal litigation, whatever the financial status and circumstances of the people concerned.[4] It has of course been applied in special categories of crime, but to go beyond that would require that the judicial procedures in all Western democracies would have to be rewritten — and there is some doubt that this could be done. Even if such were possible, however, the time lag — which is no part of justice and is especially harmful to the poor — would not necessarily be eliminated.

Another method for alleviating the poor man's difficulties would be to set up specialized low-cost courts and cheap, easily accessible first instance courts for all persons. Again, the indigent person's legal problems could be met by means of voluntary assistance of several kinds: the legal aid bureaus which give professional advice or actual service before the courts (either free or at a nominal cost); the private agencies which specialize in key liberty cases; and, the numerous economic and "ism" organizations which seek to protect their members or their own ideologies, or both; finally of course, private attorneys or bar associations whose main interest is in furthering justice. With the exception of the first (so to speak, the "free-for-all") method, modern democracies have or have had one or more of these devices in practice.

The present study will attempt to indicate in what ways indigent *citizens* (more recently, *persons*) have reached an approximate equality before the national courts in the protection of their fundamental rights. A concomitant of this attempt will be a limited consideration of the judicial procedure used in approaching a particular federal court, the securing of a judgment, and if desired the condition of appeal. This procedure does not differentiate the rich from the poor in the eyes of the court; rather it is with the aid of the Supreme Court that the poor man accomplishes his legal aims.

The care of the impecunious man before the federal courts ultimately assumes the character of what is known as *in forma pauperis* ("IFP," new style) procedure, according to which he may enter any federal court and pursue his case to the court of final jurisdiction, if necessary at little or no cost to him. On the other hand, if he has already begun his case on a paying basis he may switch to the non-paying when his funds run out. Where federal jurisdiction can be shown or a good argument therefor is made, appeal in some form may be made to the national courts. An indigent person may then sue and defend in the form of a pauper. In this event the person has 1) the legal right to sue and defend without having to pay fees (money paid to a court officer, *e. g.*, a court clerk, for services rendered in the progress of the case) and costs (allowance to a party for expenses incurred in conducting his case, or security therefor);[5] and 2) the right to free counsel. Fees and costs may be greater in civil cases than in criminal cases, but in the latter they can still be a decided burden even if the accused is not convicted.

Despite man's inhumanity to man in the medieval and early modern history of England, a humanitarian urge appeared peri-

odically in the actions of the executives, the legislature, and
the courts. The poor man's predicament in civil cases was
relieved somewhat by the English Parliament during the reign
of the first Tudor, Henry VII. The affirmation, "That writs
shall be given and counsel assigned to speed poor persons in
their suits," seems to have been the earliest Anglo-Saxon
attempt to institute civil *in forma pauperis* proceedings for
the indigent.[6] After the Restoration criminal procedures began
to exhibit (in statute and court administrative theory, as well
as in judicial decisions) a tendency to give the accused a
chance to defend himself; and by the end of the 18th century
the legal fraternity had been coming to the rescue of those
criminally charged.[7]

In North America the thirteen units of government as British colonies, as "independent" commonwealths, and as individual parts of the Confederation, had absorbed the common
law of England and had written many of the English statutes
into that law. They also had observed the good and bad practices during the "time of troubles" in England and had determined to protect the individual from state arrogance by judicial
decision, statute and constitution. By 1789 there were provisions for aiding the poor before the courts and evidence of
private legal aid.[8] The most powerful group in framing the
national Constitution, its amendments, and the early national
statutes consisted of men trained in the common law; that
group monopolized the national bench. Massachusetts attorneys in the first part of the century argued the point that both
in her Constitution and in common law there was not a single
reason why a person without means could not sue or defend as
an indigent person, since there was no state law against it.[9]
As late as the 1940's at least one of the commonwealths,
California, had allowed poor persons to proceed *in forma
pauperis,* not on the basis of her Constitution but on that of
her common law.[10]

Since the federal Constitution is one of delegated powers,
the document itself (or statutes passed under its terms) should
determine policies and judicial procedures. This does not ex-
clude interstitial or wholly made court procedures; it does not
prohibit contingent legislation by the judiciary in the field of

procedure when permitted by Congress. The courts have at
times insisted on inherent powers, which derive from the common law of England, and there have been cases in which the
Supreme Court has come close to sanctioning this doctrine.
For example, a court has provided for the payment of expenses
of a trial without statutory permission. After 1791 the Fifth
and Sixth Amendments, together with two or more parallel
statutes, have served as the chief procedural protection in
federal criminal cases where protection of the poor could be
expanded. The Fourteenth Amendment of 1868, viewed from
the perspective of 1965, has by statutory and judicial interpretation absorbed many of the essential elements of state
procedures in both civil and criminal areas.

Although a deep sense of justice underlay one or two procedural provisions of the original Constitution, it was the
sentiment of the more articulate group in the reorganized
national government which focused particular attention on procedural due process for all who came to the courts. Nevertheless, provisions soon appeared for those who were without
funds to sue or defend. More specific laws were passed to
assist everyone in a particular category (therefore aiding the
poor man), but changed conditions finally brought about legislation intended specifically for the indigent. In 1948 with one
or two exceptions the poor man found himself blessed with the
procedural process (both criminal and civil) under which he
could face the courts with at least theoretical equality with
others. It should also be noted that these procedures included
methods of preventing the indigent from plaguing the courts
with cases that had neither rhyme nor reason. The Supreme
Court has, since 1948, been moving toward the extension of
free service, not only to the poor but to everyone charged
with crime.

NOTES TO CHAPTER I

[1]McNabb v. United States, 318 U.S. 332, 347, 1945.

[2]Black's Law Dict. (4th ed., 1951), pp. 1367-68. Bouvier gives about the same definition, but would add court practices. He states that the Supreme Court admits the impossibility of an exact definition. Law Dict. (3rd ed. 1914), Vol. 2, p. 2730.

[3]N. N. Panda, "Justice and the Poor in India," 30 Law. J. Amer. Jud. Soc. (April, 1947), pp. 190-192.

[4]Albert C. Malone, Jr. in "The Soviet Bar," Cornell L. Q., Vol. 46 (Winter, 1961), pp. 258-289, seems to prove that Russia has no such system.

[5]Bouvier, Law Dict. (3rd ed., 1914), Vol. I, p. 689; A. L. Goodhart, "Costs," 38 Yale L. J. (1928-1929), pp. 849 ff.

[6]11 Henry VII, c. 12, 1495.

[7]W. S. Holdsworth, History of English Law (1924), IV, p. 538, VI, p. 518, IX, pp. 229-35; J. M. Maguire, "Poverty in Civil Litigation," 36 Harv. L. Rev. (1922-23), pp. 361-404.

[8]W. H. Beaney, The Right to Counsel in American Courts (1955), Chapter II.

[9]31 Har. L. Rev. (1917-1918), p. 485: Notes on State IFP.

[10]31 Calif. L. Rev. (1943), pp. 207-10: Notes on State IFP.

CHAPTER II

FEDERAL INDIGENT CRIMINAL
PROCEDURE TO 1910

The investigation of federal judicial procedure during the years before the Civil War indicated that rather few criminal cases were decided in the federal courts. This relative lack of criminal jurisdiction could hardly be explained in terms of the Constitution, but rather by considering the historical position of the states and the prevailing political theory. Consequently the rule of practice was to leave to the states as much of the criminal jurisdiction as possible. This rule of course limited the application of any indigent procedures. Mr. Justice Gray reviewed, and perhaps overstated, the practice in a decision of 1892:[1]

> For a long period in the history of the country, no attempt was ever made to get any criminal jurisdiction for the United States courts except of the high seas and at certain places under the special jurisdiction of Congress. As was said by Chief Justice Marshall[2] — it is not the offense committed but the place in which it is committed, which must be out of the jurisdiction of the State —. Outside of the places named, it was conceived the States could very well take care of all crimes committed within their territory; that their peace and dignity were offended by all such crimes outside of those places, and, in fact, there was no peace and dignity of the United States to be offended save and except in such places.

The Justice then noted the first important departure from the rule of practice, which Justice Strong pronounced in Tennessee v. Davis.[3] Despite the objection of Justices Field and Clifford, this new rule established the power of Congress to make effective the all-national jurisdiction of the federal courts as outlined in Articles III and VI of the Constitution.

Fortunately there was sufficient federal criminal jurisdiction to interest Congress in passing legislation in 1790 to mark a beginning of procedure which was of benefit to the poor man accused of a capital crime.

Shortly before the first ten amendments became effective Congress enacted a law which provided for a special procedure for all persons indicted for the constitutionally named crime of treason and other capital crimes enumerated in statutes. Since the law did not mention appeals on merits, it was probably assumed that the accused were obliged to limit their actions to the courts of the first instance, that is, to the circuit courts or their equivalents.[4] This was an early attempt to give more concreteness to the terms of the Sixth Amendment, which in turn was a statement of the common law principles existing in the commonwealths of the country. As Justice Brown enunciated in 1891,

> There is, however, no general obligation on the part of the Government either to furnish copies of indictment, summon witnesses or retain counsel for defendants or prisoners. The object of the constitutional provision was merely to secure those rights which the ancient rules of the common law had denied to them, but it was not contemplated that this should be done at the expense of the Government. . . .[5]

The procedure for those indicted for capital crimes was applicable to rich and poor alike. The accused was to have a copy of the indictment,[6] a list of jurors and witnesses for the prosecution, together with their addresses, and two or three days before trial; he was to have compulsory process for securing defense witnesses, and the right to make full defense by counsel learned in the law. To emphasize this last right the law went on to assure the accused that if he wanted, but could not provide, counsel for himself, the court would *upon his request,* immediately assign not more than two counsel who would have access to him at all reasonable hours. This last provision touched the poor man directly. As both a constitutional "ought" and a specific statuatory provision, it was a potential support of the indigent man. Without much change in wording, however, it was later to take on a much deeper meaning.

This early statute in its unamended parts was interpreted by the courts to mean that the condition precedent to the enjoyment of the rights given was the making of a definite request for them; and that when the accused asked for legal advisors, counsel would have the pleasure of paying the mileage and fees for the defense witnesses, if summoned. In other words counsel would have on his broad shoulders the witness burden, as well as the loss in unpaid time spent and other court expense. Only the humanitarian, the socially wise, or self-advertising attorneys would willingly sacrifice their time and money, and then usually only in outstanding cases. Thanks to the common law and the early statutes, accordingly, a defendant had obtained the right to defend himself! Unhappily, however, he could not know, unless he had some legal training or got advice from an attorney, that he must ask for copies of the indictment or list of jurors and witnesses for the prosecution.

Perhaps this system worked fairly well in rural America, but as urban centers developed it became the exception that court-appointed lawyers were of high caliber.[7] This was true in the lower courts before appeals were allowed; but after appeals were permitted, the caliber of counsel appointed by appellate courts rose to a higher standard. The Supreme Court gave particular attention to such appointments, especially after the 1890's.

It took Congress a good half-century to advance the protection of the indigent through criminal procedure. In the Act of 1790 methods to meet the need for government-compelled witnesses for the defense seemed sufficient, even if limited to those indicted for treason or other capital crimes. The general provision of the Sixth Amendment permitting a defendant in a criminal case ''to have compulsory process of obtaining witnesses in his favor'' was not limited to crimes in which the extreme penalty was death. Based partly upon the constitutional provision and partly upon the unsatisfactory results obtained from non-publicly paid witnesses for the defense, an act was passed in 1846 which not only allowed for government-paid witnesses in capital cases but extended indigent coverage to all indictable crimes.[8] This law was the first procedural federal statute passed in aid of the strictly indigent criminal. It set up among other things the form of proof which the self-styled poor man had to make before being allowed to proceed *in forma pauperis* in securing witnesses.

In order to enjoy free witness service, an indicted person had to make an affidavit setting forth that there were witnesses whose evidence was material and that he could not safely go to trial without them. He also had to state what he expected to prove by each of them and that each witness was within the judicial district or within 100 miles of the place of trial. Finally he had to swear that he had insufficient funds to pay the fees of such witnesses, with perjury the charge for false swearing. It is to be noted that as no standard was set for poverty, the proof for it was the sworn affidavit. The court might in its discretion, after considering the affiant's statement, order all or some of the witnesses within the legal area to be subpoenaed. For service rendered they were paid from federal funds on order of the court.

Cases *listed in the books* as dealing with this law seemed to center around the period 1890-1910, although some appeared earlier or much later. One matter of real importance stressed in the decisions was that the trial judge had that venerable, non-reviewable discretion, if exercised judicially, to recognize the affiant as an indigent or to subpoena witnesses at federal expense. In fact, during these years and much later, the author failed to find a single instance where a trial judge was overruled in his use of discretion. Apparently the lawmakers did not care to give the criminal "as of course" rights, and the judges preferred the age-old discretionary power to act after reviewal of the record of the individual accused and all the circumstances of the case.[9]

In 1803 two men (one an aspirant to the office of justice of peace in the District of Columbia, the other a holder of a similar office) asked the Supreme Court to interpret Article III, Section 2, Paragraph 2 of the Constitution. Both cases seemed of little importance at the time. The Judiciary Act of

1789 had bestowed upon the Supreme Court the original jurisdiction to issue writs of mandamus to compel the national officers to carry out specific duties. In the one case, Marbury, in a non-criminal action, wanted to force the Secretary of State to issue his signed commission as justice of the peace. The Court refused on the ground that Congress could not add to the original jurisdiction assigned to it by the Constitution, and as a result judicial review of congressional action (and finally that of executive) resulted.[10]

In the other case Simms, a justice of the peace, had been accused of embezzling certain fees. He was tried and convicted, and then he appealed to the Supreme Court, which accepted jurisdiction and affirmed the conviction.[11] The two cases seemed to be contradictory in principle: the Marbury case held that Congress could not add to the Supreme Court's original jurisdiction as laid out in the Constitution; on the other hand, the Simms case was accepted on appeal contrary to the specific terms of the Constitution.

Chief Justice Marshall, speaking for the Court two years later in United States *v.* More,[12] repudiated the Simms case as precedent and erased the Court's error with the remark that the question of direct appellate jurisdiction had been passed over by the opposing counsel *sub silentio.* In this case the Court held that there could be no appellate jurisdiction in any United States court without specific statutory authority, although in the Simms case Congress had not granted Supreme Court jurisdiction. A lawyer trained in the common law should have known that such law had never lifted criminal cases above the court of original jurisdiction; a United States constitutional lawyer should have known, even as early as 1803, that statutory authority alone could give appellate jurisdiction to the Supreme Court under the Constitution.[13]

It should be added, however, that Congress did provide a minor departure from the common law system in 1802 by giving the Supreme Court appellate jurisdiction over criminal cases "on certificate of divided opinion."[14] According to the statute, there could be a difference of opinion on one or more points between a Supreme Court Justice on circuit and the local federal judge. There was no statement as to what the form of decision of the divided court should be, but whatever it was had to be "held in escrow" if either party cared to appeal to the Supreme Court. Certainly the decision had to be either for or against the accused. The assumption seemed to be that the presiding Justice on Circuit should have final decision until the other members of the Supreme Court passed upon the point or points of disagreement. This situation was clarified by Congress in 1872.[15] According to Frankfurter and Landis,[16] the circuit courts began to be manned by a single district judge for some twenty years before 1889. This would of course make such appeals on certification of little use.

Despite the Simms case and the certificate of divided opinion, it took Congress half a century to make up its mind to go beyond the common law rule of "one crime/one court" as a matter of statutory right. In 1889 a law was passed which provided that a person convicted of a capital crime and sentenced to death in any United States court[17] could, by making a timely petition, have his case directly reviewed on its merits by the Supreme Court by writ of error.[18] The High Court was empowered to re-examine, reverse or affirm under its own rules. The defendant in error, whether poor or rich, was not obliged to pay costs or put up security and the clerks of the trial court had to send up the transcript of each case to the Supreme Court (the Clerk of which was required to receive, file, and docket the transcript without guarantee of fees).

This statute contained an unusual bit of procedural legislation, for it affected what the Supreme Court, as a separate division of the Federal Government, considered to be its own constitutional area. Since Congress had obeyed the constitutional command to set up "one Supreme Court," name the majority of justices for decisions, establish judicial salaries, provide funds for carrying on its necessary powers, and name its appellate jurisdiction, the Court judged that it could or should be able to carry on its internal activities without further direction. Of course, the Court held itself high above the lower federal courts, which were to be established, if at all, at the option of Congress. The Supreme Court did not attain this high and independent position to the fullest extent, but by 1963 it had in fact established itself with the consent of

Congress as a powerful part of the federal government. The law applied to a small category of persons, but the poor man had privileges equal to those of his brother, with the possible exception of able counsel.

The Court of Appeals Act of 1891[19] extended direct review by the Supreme Court to cover all cases involving infamous crimes without *specifically affirming* the privilege already granted to those convicted of capital crimes. The statute added another level of courts to the judicial hierarchy (namely the circuit court of appeals) and limited the old "circuit courts" to the trial of serious criminal cases. Misdemeanors tried in the original district courts could be reviewed by the newly established circuit courts of appeals, the judgments of which could be lifted, under limitations, to the Supreme Court by the discretionary writ of certiorari. Serious criminal cases, however, were short circuited to the Supreme Court.

One result of the extension of review by the High Court of infamous non-capital crimes was the clogging of the Supreme Court docket. Consequently, Congress was persuaded in 1897 to withdraw from the Supreme Court non-capital cases on writ of error and to confer such jurisdiction upon the circuit courts of appeal, subject to writ of certiorari by the Supreme Court.[20] This was the situation until the new Judicial Code of 1911 was enacted into law.[21] Section 238 of the Code completed the retrenchment by eliminating direct review by the Supreme Court of capital cases.[22]

Two cases decided in October Term, 1891 have proved to be of value in aiding destitute persons in criminal trials. Both involved the power of the Supreme Court to approve a court order directing the expenditure of government funds. A man named Van Duzee had been indicted for a non-capital crime and had asked for a copy of the indictment. Upon order of the trial judge the clerk had supplied the copy, the fee for which was charged to appropriated funds of the federal courts. The Comptroller of the Treasury had refused to allow the charge on the ground that existing law provided for a free copy only to persons accused of capital crimes.[23] In the resultant legal squabble, the case reached the Supreme Court. Mr. Justice Brown agreed that the 1790 Act contained a "negative pregnant" and that accordingly, in non-capital cases, the accused was not entitled as *of right* to a copy of the indictment at government expense. He then made the following statement:[24]

> We have no doubt, however, of the power of the court to order a copy of the indictment to be furnished upon the request of the defendant, and at the expense of the government; and, when such an order is made, the clerk is entitled to his fee for the copy. In many cases, however, the defendant does not desire a copy, or pleads guilty to the indictment upon its being read to him, and in such cases there is no propriety in forcing a copy upon him and charging the government with the expense.

The "negative pregnant" in this case might have been turned into an affirmation of the exclusion of non-capital crimes entirely, but the Supreme Court apparently would have had to have a more positive statement forbidding the use of public funds in behalf of the indigent before it would have given up what might be called the common law right to see that justice should be done. If this was not such an inherent right, it approached it.

After passage of the Appellate Act of 1891 and the Poor Man's Act of 1892, which applied only to civil cases, the Supreme Court, speaking through Chief Justice Fuller, approved a charge of some $400 for transcribing the entire record by the clerk, a record that included the testimony and the transcription of the stenographer's minutes of appeal. The Treasury had challenged in the Court of Claims the charge against government funds, insisting that the sole liability of the Government to aid an indigent in a non-capital case was found in the terms of the free witnesses law of 1846.[25] Said the Court:[26]

> Section 878 (Rev. Stat.) was originally enacted in 1846, and should not be held to operate as a prohibition to the extent contended. The indigent defendant ought not to be deprived of availing himself of his writ of error because of his poverty, and, *when the court has ordered the transcript in the*

interest of justice, the clerk ought not to be deprived of compensation. (Emphasis supplied.)

It seems that all arguments for the inherent power of the trial courts, or at least the power to act in the absence of absolute prohibition in connection with criminal cases before 1910, came back to the proper action of the courts in seeing that justice was properly meted out. Where expenses resulted from convenience to the courts and at the same time saved the rights of human beings charged with criminal acts, Congress had early provided a special fund to cover contingent expenditures over and above normal demands in the federal courts. After the establishment of the Department of Justice in 1871,[27] the Attorney-General had been invested with discretionary power to approve acts or orders of clerks and trial courts allowing charges against such a fund, usually designated as "Miscellaneous Expense Fund," in the general appropriation for the federal courts.[28] The Comptroller of the Treasury accepted the law but frequently refused to allow specific charges because they were contrary to the will of Congress. When justice was to be served, and the Supreme Court so held, "inherent power" and "legislative will" were reconciled. But judicial approval in the absence of specific legislative prohibition was still possible.

The Supreme Court not only had something to say about procedure in the lower federal courts during the period before 1910, but provided additional procedure in its own jurisdiction that affected the impecunious man who appealed from a conviction of a serious offense. The opportunity was furnished for the first time by the 1889 Act noted above, which authorized appeal to the Supreme Court as a matter of right by persons convicted of crimes for which the expreme penalty was death. That law was a most important development in the interest of both indigent and non-indigent persons convicted of serious criminal acts. This was so for three chief reasons: 1) it introduced at least one review of criminal convictions, together with the introduction of the principle of free services for the poor in reaching appellate courts; 2) it anticipated the placing of the great Constitutional Court as the final protector of the convicted man's rights, substantive and procedural; 3) it foreshadowed an effective supervisory power of the Supreme Court over the federal (and state) courts in criminal matters.

The Supreme Court's criminal appellate jurisdiction as of 1889 applied to a very small category of the convicted—namely, those convicted under capital punishment statutes—and included the indigent and placed them on an equal basis with the well-to-do, with the possible exception of the quality of counsel. After the Clerk of the Supreme Court had obeyed the terms of the statute by filing all the necessary papers and finally docketing the case without expense to the appellant, the Court's rules and practices took over. Transcripts of the record furnished to the Clerk from the lower level were usually in typescripts, although some were printed. The rules of the Court provided for the payment of the Clerk for work which the 1889 law insisted should be free. Thus the Clerk was paid from certain funds taken in by him (such as fees charged for joining the Supreme Court Bar).[29] But the rules of the Court again demanded that all transcripts sent up to the Court must be printed. Although few came up in such form, the Court did not "forgive" the requirement, whether the appellants were rich or poor.[30] Consequently those appellants who had funds to pay for printing of transcripts had to pay for them; those who could not pay because of lack of funds supported their claim of indigency by taking an oath.

The 1891 Act, which added the courts of appeals to the federal judicial hierarchy, expanded the category of criminal convicts that were allowed to go *as of right* to the Supreme Court on writ of error, that is, those who had been convicted of any infamous crime. The statute, however, was silent on whether the procedure allowed in capital crimes, insofar as poor persons were concerned, was to be inferred. The practice seemed to extend the provisions of the 1889 Act to the larger class of criminals. When the Act of 1897 removed the large non-capital criminals from the Court's jurisdiction and transferred that group to the circuit courts of appeal, the Supreme Court could still use its 1889 and 1891 procedure when it issued the writ of certiorari to the courts of appeals. Certainly there was nothing in the 1897 law itself that gave the 1889 procedure to all those convicted of infamous crimes, although in practice all such cases seemed to be included.

The Supreme Court, then, used certain funds taken in by the office of the Clerk to pay him for doing what the 1889 Act required of him but used the affidavit to separate the indigent from those who had funds when it was necessary to print the transcript. The poor man was not obliged to pay the costs of such printing, while the others were. The usual formula in an indigent case ran: "The affidavit of K, the motion to proceed *in forma pauperis* and to print the record at public (or government) expense were filed." If the Court was satisfied, the record was ordered "to be printed at public (or government) expense."[31]

Since the rules of the Court demanded a printed record, and since the Court had no specifically appropriated fund for such printing, how was it to be paid for? Of course, the Court could have waived its own rule, but it did not in the cases noted. It could have used the income from fees charged for admission to the Bar, but that would have somewhat strained the meaning of "public (or government) expense." It could have requested the court below to ask the Attorney-General to approve the printing of the records before they were sent up to the Clerk of the Supreme Court, but begging favors from an inferior court or an executive officer would have been considered below the dignity of such a supreme body. Finally, it could have charged the printing to the funds appropriated to itself for printing dockets, journals and decisions, both preliminary and final. This last source seemed to the author to be a reasonable interpretation of the formula, especially since he had been informed by men in the Comptroller's Office that the auditing of expenditures of the Supreme Court never went further than checking whether the report had been signed by the Chief Justice or a Justice designated for the purpose.[32] This view was hinted at in a decision by the Comptroller of the Treasury:[33]

> If records in such cases pending in the Supreme Court...are printed at the Government Printing Office by order of the Supreme Court, it was only

because the Public Printer has an appropriation for printing for the Supreme Court, the character of which printing is not subject to the examination of the accounting officers of the Treasury.

From the above discussion, the conclusion must be that for the period, 1789-1910, there was no complete and all-embracing code of criminal procedure for the accused or convicted poor man. The Constitution, as amended, guaranteed a number of rights (substantive and procedural) to anyone accused of infamous crime, but only one applied to the poor man: the appointment of counsel, apparently if he wanted and asked for such aid.

Congress had passed piecemeal bits of legislation approaching equality in procedure, and the judiciary had extended procedural rights to aid the indigent. All this, however, had not added up to a code of criminal procedure for the impecunious man; the principle of equalizing the chances of the indigent with those with funds to pay their way had been too deeply implanted in the judiciary, especially in the members of the Supreme Court and in the tendency of the Congressmen to put off the making of a code that would seemingly include all types of persons unable to pay their way.

NOTES TO CHAPTER II

[1]Logan *v.* United States, 144 U.S. 263, 272, 277, 282, 1892. Murder of federal officers, jail deliveries, counterfeiting of money bills, government bonds, and other obligations, treason, etc., called for general federal laws to assure the existence of the United States, but states covered many of the crimes. Did he overlook Amendments XIII-XV and enforcing legislation?

[2]United States *v.* Bevans, 3 Wheat, 336, 388, 1818.

[3]100 U.S. 257, 1879, which applied one part of the "transfer law" of 1875, R.S. Sec. 643. Justice Strong seemed to be a "strong" nationalist, for in the same year he spoke for the Court in connection with exclusion of Negroes from juries, giving jurisdiction to federal courts whenever he could. Strauder *v.* West Virginia, 100 U.S. 303, 1879; Virginia *v.* Rives, 100 U.S. 313, 1879; *Ex Parte* Virginia, 100 U.S. 339, 1879.

[4]1 Stat. 118, 1790.

[5]United States *v.* Van Duzee, 140 U.S. 169, 1891. The case arose over payment of monetary claims charged against the government. *Cf.* United States *v.* Allred, 155 U.S. 591, 593, 1894.

[6]44 Stat. 1023, Ch. 50, Sec. 2, 1927, extended right of securing copy of indictment to all accused of any crime, if accused asked for it. A court could charge it as cost in the case. Taylor *v.* Hudspeth, 113 F. 2nd 825, 1940.

[7]More recent forms of the 1790 statute: Rev. Stat., Secs. 1033, 1034, 1875; 18 U.S.C.A., Secs. 562, 563, 1936 and Secs. 3005, 3432, 1948. Cases cited: United States *v.* Shive, 27 Fed. Cases No. 16, 278, 1832; Nabb *et al v.* United States 1 Ct. Cl. 173, 1863; Thompson *v.* United States, 159 U.S. 268, 1895; Stevenson *v.* United States, 162 U.S. 313, 1896; Anderson *v.* Treat, 172 U.S. 24, 1898; O'Hara *v.* United States, 129 Fed. 551, 1904; Dupuis *v.* United States, 5 F. 2nd, 231, 1925; *see also* A. Holtzoff, "The Right of Counsel under the Sixth Amendment," 20 *N.Y.U.L. Rev.*, 1-22, 1944.

[8]9 Stat. 74, Sec. 11, 1846, and more recent forms, Rev. Stat., Sec. 878, 1875; 28 U.S.C.A., Sec. 656, 1926.

[9]Crumpton v. United States, 138 U.S. 361, 1891; Goldsby v. United States, 160 U.S. 70, 1895; United States v. Falshaw, 4 Ariz. 330, 1895; Gates v. United States, 122 F. 2nd. 571, 1941; certiorari denied, 314 U.S. 698, 1942.

[10]Marbury v. Madison, 1 Cr. 177, 1803.

[11]United States v. Simms, 1 Cr. 252, 1803.

[12]United States v. More; 3 Cr. 159, 1805.

[13]Yet, C. J. Jay, in 1794, charged a grand jury while on circuit: "The principle... is, that by the common law, independent of any statute, the Federal courts have power to punish offences against the federal sovereignty." This principle was repudiated in United States v. Hudson, 7 Cr. 32, 1812. The Supreme Court held that a common law offense, not specified by statute, was not indictable in federal courts. G. Van Santvoord, Lives and Service of the Chief Justices of the United States (New York, 1854), pp. 55-59.

[14]2 Stat. 159, Sec. 6, 1802. See Note in United States v. Sanges, 144 U.S. 310, 319-22, 1892, and specific cases: United States v. Eaton, 144 U.S. 677, 1892; Struther v. United States, 171 U.S. 690, 1898.

[15]17 Stat. 196, 1872. The poor man, of course, had whatever advantages there were under the general law.

[16]Frankfurter and Landis, Business of the Supreme Court (New York, 1927), Chapter I.

[17]District Courts in unorganized territories had circuit court jurisdiction, 26 Stat. 81, 1890.

[18]25 Stat. 656, 1889. Potential death penalty determines status under this law: Logan v. United States, 144 U.S. 263, 1893; Fitzpatrick v. United States, 178 U.S. 304, 1900; Good Shot v. United States, 179 U.S. 87, 1900. (District of Columbia cases were excluded until 1897.)

[19]26 Stat. 827, 1891. The circuit courts were abolished in 1911, 36 Stat. 1167, leaving a hierarchy of three courts. See also Charles Fairman, *Mr. Justice Miller and The Supreme Court* (New York, 1939), Chapter XVII.

[20]29 Stat. 492, 1897; 29 Stat. 692, 1897.

[21]36 Stat. 1157, 1911.

[22]See Stephan *v.* United States, 319 U.S. 423, 1943, and Note 9 of C. J. Warren, Carroll *v.* United States, 354 U.S. 394, 1957.

[23]1 Stat. 118, 1790.

[24]United States *v.* Van Duzee, 140 U.S. 172-73, 1891.

[25]9 Stat. 74, 1846; Rev. Stat. 166, Sec. 878, 1878, 2nd ed.

[26]United States *v.* Gildersleeve, 193 U.S. 528, 530, 1904.

[27]18 Stat. 494, 1871.

[28]*E.g.*, 28 Stat. 444, 1894. Evidence of similar provisions were traced back to the early 1880's.

[29]The legal question as to what could or could not be done with money coming into the office of the clerks of the courts was reviewed by the Supreme Court in 1910. The gist of the matter was that the clerk received the money not as property of the United States but as a fund from which he received his compensation and expenses, as ordered by his court, for the surplus for which he must account. He was a trustee and not a debtor. Refinement of the use of this intake went on for some twenty years; the process will be touched upon later.

[30]See Alexander *v.* United States, 138 U.S. 353, 1891; Crumpton *v.* United States, 138 U.S. 361, 1891; Goldsby *v.* United States, 160 U.S. 70, 1895.

[31]Examples: Cross *v.* United States, 145 U.S. 571, 1892; Graves *v.* United States, 150 U.S. 118, 1893; Tucker *v.* United States, 151 U.S. 164, 1894; Mattox *v.* United States, 156 U.S. 237, 1895; Anderson

v. United States, 170 U.S. 481, 1898; Ball *v.* United States, 140 U.S. 118, 1890; and 163 U.S. 683, 1896; Stevenson *v.* United States, 162 U.S. 313, 1896; Horton *v.* United States, 175 U.S. 727, 1899.

[32]Later, Chief Justice Taft was willing to go through the motions because he believed in having all the great Department's accounts sent to the Accounting Office. *Taft Papers*, 1-24-A2, January 9, 1926.

[33]Comp. Dec. 17-18, 1894. This same procedure in handling business connected with criminal matters reaching the Supreme Court was attested to in specific cases: in original writs of habeas corpus, *In re* Mills, 135 U.S. 263, 1890; writs of certiorari to appellate courts, Struther *v.* United States, 171 U.S. 690, 1898, and Horton *v.* United States, 175 U.S. 727, 1899; on certificate from circuit courts, Good Shot *v.* United States, 179 U.S. 87, 1900.

CHAPTER III

FEDERAL INDIGENT CIVIL
PROCEDURE, 1892-1910

By the category, "indigent civil procedure," is meant indigent procedure which does not involve the trial of criminal charges on their merits or the appellate proceedings in such trials where the charges have resulted in convictions. The federal judiciary's early assumption of jurisdiction over civil matters in accordance with the Constitution and legislation was in contrast with the original hesitation to assume such jurisdiction over criminal cases under similar terms. While jurisdiction over civil matters, from the establishment of the Constitution, was general (trial and appellate), direct criminal appeal at the will of the convicted was not permitted until 1889, and then only for a limited category. Again, *in forma pauperis* procedure in civil matters did not appear until 1892, although the principle of equalizing the opportunities of the poor and the man of means definitely was found in the first Judiciary Act passed by Congress. Interestingly enough the period, during which the statutory privilege of those criminally charged or convicted reached a point just short of a code, almost coincided in time with the special privilege of *in forma pauperis* civil procedure.

There were rumors among federal judges to the effect that persons had been allowed to sue as poor persons in non-criminal cases before the year 1892. Nevertheless, the official record of reported cases is almost bare. The only case found in the records of the federal courts was Bradford *v.* Bradford (2 Flipp. 280, 1879) in which the United States Circuit Court for the Western District of Tennessee, speaking through Judge Baxter, permitted a suit in admiralty without requiring surety for costs. The judge rightly said that there was neither a United States nor a state law requiring the plaintiff to give bond; there was only a court rule. He was aware, too, that there was no statutory provision for suits *in forma pauperis,* and that federal courts were not controlled by the *in forma pauperis* statute existing in Tennessee. These were the words of the judge:[1]

> But cases may arise possessing merits in favor of persons too poor to secure costs. For such cases some provision ought to be made. The rule of the English courts, *adopted and acted on by some of the American courts*, commends itself to our judgment as being the best calculated to protect this court as well as defendants against frivolous and harassing litigation. If the applicant will supplement his affidavit (of poverty) by the certificate of any reputable attorney of this court, to the effect that he has investigated the case and believes the applicant has a good cause of action, he will be permitted to bring and prosecute his suit *in forma pauperis*. (Emphasis supplied.)

This rule was not followed in a tort case[2] in the same district later by Judge Hammond, who had thoroughly covered the historical ground and insisted that the status of the pauper in civil cases had to be found in written law. This seems to have been the last of the matter until agitation began to appear for legislation providing for a poor man's civil procedure.

It was previously suggested that the laws of 1790 and 1846 had been put to the test of the courts within a quarter-century period, the core of which was the 1890's. The attempt of the Tennessee federal judge in 1879 to engraft the English inheritance as to proceedings *in forma pauperis* in civil cases upon the United States law and the strong court resistance set up in the same jurisdiction in 1888 were reconciled during this same crucial period in the 1890's. The 1893 Depression was almost on hand when Congress passed the Act of July 20, 1892,[3] which gave to the man without money the privilege of going to court on a more equal basis with the man supplied with resources.

The Act was potentially of far-reaching importance to the vast underlying population gradually being absorbed into an ever-expanding industrial system. Were the indicted poor man and the economically dispossessed man somehow entrapped by

this time in an enviornment that called for all possible government aid in the protection of life and property? One need only
recall agrarian and labor political agitation in and around this
period, the passage of the Interstate Commerce Act and the
Sherman Act, to characterize this era as one of economic
strife in which the corporation was reducing the individual to
economic dependence under the liberal laissez-faire banner.
It was the period of the self-nationalization of business just
as the period since 1933 has been one of self-nationalization
of labor — even though both groups had received much help
from the national Government.

The record of the passing of the poor man's legislation of
1892 has some material of value outside the law itself. The
House Report No. 1070⁴ was made by T. R. Stockdale of
Mississippi for the Committee on the Judiciary and contained
a bit of philosophy and argument that had begun to appear in
the country generally. "[T]his bill," according to the Report,
"presents the question whether this Government, having established courts to do justice to litigants, will admit the
wealthy and deny the poor entrance to them to have their
rights adjudicated." Even if this bill passes, the poor "will
not have an equal chance with other men, for men able to
prosecute gain causes that would be dismissed by the court
had it the power.... The Government will not determine questions involving the liberty of the citizen in criminal cases
without furnishing him with his witnesses on his demand.
Property is next in importance, and the less a man has the
more important it is to him, and the more reprehensible to
deprive (him) of it unjustly."

The Report stated that the bill should be passed for two
reasons. First, there should be little actual expense accruing
to the Government, since people who could not pay in advance
or secure costs would seldom litigate about property over
$2,000, which in 1892 was the minimum for diversity suits and
for those arising under United States law and treaties. State
and territorial courts handled all suits having money value of
$2,000 or less. Second, this limitation would not affect the
essential justice, or the need for it, implied in the bill.
"People who had claims of property by inheritance or devise

or by purchase worth over $2,000, and it may be their only possession," would be advantaged by it, although they could not use it to secure bondsmen or money to meet the demands for costs by reason of the fact that it was in dispute. "These persons with honest claims can be defeated, and doubtless often are, by wealthy adversaries. Corporations may destroy the head of the family, and his heirs, who have a right of action for support, will be deprived of justice by the demand for costs. Pauper procedure in State courts would be no help in such cases, for the moneyed man would transfer to the federal courts, where there was no pauper advantage."

The more articulate proponents of the *in forma pauperis* bill were obsessed with the idea that the great enemy of the little man was the corporation. That legal entity stood for "Wall Street" and for any exertion of power built upon wealth. It was thus to be expected that this animus would be stressed in putting over a bill that had to do with building up a partial equality before the courts of poor and rich. The proposed measure provided for a "free ride" only for civil "commencers" or plaintiffs; its proposers apparently could not conceive of poor defendants. The privileges of *in forma* prosecution were to be enjoyed only by *citizens*, for the increasing numbers of the "riffraff" from foreign lands were not permitted to participate, although they needed the help more than the native born and law-made citizens.

To ease the opposition of the well-to-do, the Report then insisted that the bill took care of all the evils that might spring from free litigation for the indigent. The proposed measure gave the trial judge, sitting as a court, judicial discretion to kill any potential evil before it spread to the moneyed classes. He could refuse to appoint an attorney to represent the poor plaintiff, if he deemed the cause unworthy of a trial. And he might dismiss any such cases, if it should be made to appear that the allegation of poverty was untrue or if he was satisfied that the alleged cause of action was frivolous or malicious. The proposal "will not permit of vexatious litigation for it is well guarded. In order to get the privilege of the courts which litigants with money can demand without question and compel the court to hear their cases, any one of these people who desires to enter the courts without money must first file in the court a statement under oath that because of his poverty, he is unable to pay costs of said suit or action or to give security for the same. He must also state that he believes he is entitled to the redress asked, and must set out the nature of his alleged cause of action." Under the general rule that the victor in a civil case makes his opponent pay him out-of-hand costs, the bill, in order "to avoid the possibility of imposition," provided that "judgment may be rendered for costs as in other cases, so that if the party succeeds in a suit, or failing, should afterwards acquire property, the costs may be made out of him."

David B. Culberson of Texas, chairman of the House Committee on the Judiciary, steered the bill through that body, admitting only two amendments to make more certain the protection of the Government from frivolous litigation and above all from any money obligation (which, by the way, the Report seemed to assume might be a burden on the Government, even though a small one).[5] Because of the permanence of the framework of this bill as passed,[6] it will be given in its entirety and any amendments thereto should be referred to it.

> Sec. 1. That *any citizen* of the United States, entitled to commence any suit or action in any court in the United States, may commence and *prosecute to conclusion* any such suit or action without being required to prepay fees or costs, or give security therefor before or after bringing suit or action, upon filing in said court a statement under oath, in writing, that, because of his poverty, he is unable to pay costs of said suit or action which he is about to commence, or to give security for the same, and that he believes he is entitled to the redress he seeks by such suit or action, and setting forth briefly the nature of his alleged cause or action. (Emphasis supplied.)

> Sec. 2. That after any such suit or action shall have been brought, or that it is now pending, the plaintiff may answer and avoid a demand for fees or security for costs by filing a like affidavit, and

willful false swearing in any affidavit provided for
in this or the previous section shall be punished
as perjury as in other cases.

Sec. 3. That the officers of the court shall issue,
serve all processes, and perform all duties in such
cases, and witnesses shall attend as in other
cases, and the plaintiff shall have the same remedies as are provided by law in other cases.

Sec. 4. That the court may request any attorney of
the court to represent such poor person, if it deems
the cause worthy of a trial and may dismiss any
such cause so brought under this act if it be made
to appear that the allegation of poverty is untrue,
or if said court be satisfied that the alleged cause
of action is frivolous or malicious.

Sec. 5. That judgment may be rendered for costs
at the conclusion of the suit as in other cases:
Provided, that the United States shall not be
liable for any of the costs thus incurred.

During the life of the 1892 Act, as unamended, indigent
cases of a non-criminal character began to appear fairly frequently in written form. Federal courts were available to
persons pleading under United States laws in cases above a
certain dollar value; such courts were open to persons suing
under state laws for amounts over $2,000 under the diversity
rule. As the advocates of the law anticipated most of the
cases were suits for damages for personal injuries against
corporations. States gave birth to most of the corporations
and by the 1890's such institutions were doing business in
one or more states other than the mother state. Diversity
cases were common since the respondents usually chose to
try their cases before the United States district courts. Before
1910 the federal judiciary had some eighteen years to construe
the five sections of the 1892 Act. A few of the constructions
were made by the circuit courts but the district courts seemed
to have played the widest role of interpretation; indeed, the
Supreme Court entered only twice during the period and in

doing so put an end to appeals. Federal trial courts had to give some specific meaning to the various words and clauses of the Act and often looked elsewhere for suggestions as to the construction of the law.[7]

United States citizenship was a condition precedent for enjoying the privilege of *in forma pauperis* procedure. The oath, the violation of which involved "soul searching" as well as pains of perjury, kept the records, scant as they were, formally correct. This was true regardless of the ignorance of many as to the conditions of citizenship, of the lack of vital statistics areas, and the unwillingness on the part of actual citizens to bother about who were and were not citizens.[8] Sections 1, 2 and 4 were replete with problems requiring interpretations of vital concern to the poor man. Most constructions of the original law are still a bit hazy regardless of later amendments, and only one was definitely settled by the High Court during this eighteen-year period. A few of these problems were:

a) Who had to make affidavit that "because of his poverty...he is unable to pay costs... or give security therefor," if he wishes to initiate a suit or action, carry on a pending suit or finish a suit already begun, in conformance with *in forma* procedure?

b) What is the measure of poverty?

c) In the affidavit under a) or in an additional one, what facts are sufficient to show that the cause of action "is not frivolous or malicious?" What is the meaning of "frivolous?" Of "malicious?"

d) Does "to prosecute to a conclusion" include one or two appeals or none?

e) How wide is the over-all discretion of the lower courts in applying the law?

It can be asserted definitely that the fifth question was answered inasmuch as "judicial discretion" was almost without limit during the first eighteen years of the Pauper Act; that the fourth question was judicially settled; that "frivolous" and "malicious" were not too often touched upon in written opinion; that especially the first but also the second questions were treated during this period, and that the interpretation has gone far into the twentieth century.

The first rule enunciated by the lower federal courts followed closely on the heels of the effective date of the Pauper Act: every person pecuniarily interested in the outcome of a civil case must file his or her affidavit of poverty, if the suit is to be prosecuted *in forma pauperis*. The rule was enunciated in an "old circuit court" to establish an interest in certain lands and to have the same partitioned.[9] Plaintiffs were trying to save their rights by appealing to a circuit court of appeals, whereas the respondents noted that only one of the plaintiffs had signed an affidavit of poverty. The rule however did not state that every person interested in the results of the suit had to sign an affidavit before any further action could be taken; only those who did sign could be in on the "wins." Circuit Judges William Howard Taft and Horace H. Lurton of the 6th Circuit approved this rule in 1898 in connection with a personal injury case.[10] The statute itself was silent as to the exact persons who were to be included among the oath takers.

Two years after the Fuller case a western district judge proceeded to give a morally indignant oral opinion that included certain attorneys in the group of people that were to take the oath in poverty cases.[11] His second reason for rejecting a plaintiff's motion for *in forma* procedure was that he (the plaintiff) had not included his attorney. The defending railroad had charged that the attorney had contracted to conduct the case on a contingent basis. In the opinion of many judges and not a few lawyers, it was (and still is) immoral for an attorney to buy into the economic results of his own client's case, especially if he secured more than a reasonable fee from a successful prosecution. This meant that a well-qualified and successful lawyer would have to give security for costs or drop the case, if the evidence obtained in advance was largely against the success of the plaintiff. Only the "ambulance-chasing" lawyer would pick up the case, hoping to force a compromise. "A person who acquires by contract an interest in any litigation, and a right to share in the fruits of recovery, and who is not entitled to sue *in forma pauperis*, cannot be permitted, under cover of the name of a party who is a poor person, to use judicial process and litigate at the expense of other people."[12] A different approach appeared in an 1898 district decision.[13] The judge stated that when a person had shown (by proper affidavit) that he had the right to sue as a poor person, the court would appoint an attorney for him, whose fee would be contingent upon success; and in any case would not be larger than the "quantum meruit." Continued the judge:

> The attorney assigned by the court, in the event of non-success, will, of course, receive nothing; in event of final success, he may apply to the court for an order fixing a fair compensation for services he may actually render, which will be paid him out of the fund recovered, and the balance only paid over to the plaintiff. If the attorney who brought the action is willing to continue on these terms, he will be assigned to represent the plaintiff; if not, the court will find another attorney.[14]

As late as 1907 the Whelan decision was backed as an alternative method of handling attorneys who took over the prosecution of indigent cases on some kind of contingent contract.[15] The railroad corporation had disclosed that the plaintiff's attorney was in possession of a written contract to prosecute the case for one-third of the money gained as damages, if successful. The court refused to permit the plaintiff to sue *in forma pauperis* without a showing that his attorney was also unable because of poverty to pay the costs or give security. Section 4 of the Pauper Act authorized the court to appoint counsel for an indigent suer. The plaintiff in the case asked whether he could change horses in the middle of the stream, that is, discharge his attorney and have the court appoint one for him, and name the fee in case of recovery. The court refused on the ground that the progress in the trial had gone too far. He forced the plaintiff to secure costs. While the alternative was lost to the particular indigent, it was saved for future litigants should they care to use it.

If all persons who had a monetary interest in the results of a suit should be obliged to make affidavits of poverty, drop out of the suit, or put up security for costs, the question of what should be the general measure of the "poverty" that would enable one to prosecute his suit *in forma pauperis* would not have been solved. Would the taking of the oath be all that was necessary? If so, the penalty for swearing a lie, if somehow found out, would have had to be the safeguard. Further, did the judges legally have wide discretion in accepting affidavits, if plaintiffs were not to be the sole judges of their respective financial status checked only by the fear of the pains of perjury? The Act of 1892 named the oath as the basis for indigent procedure, with the reservation in Section 4 that such procedure could be stopped if the plaintiff had been found to err in believing that he was a poor person in terms of the law or that he had committed perjury.

The answer as to what really constituted poverty could not have been successfully stated in terms of a permanent law, for the courts could not posit a definite amount of this world's goods that would always constitute the legal condition of poverty.[16] Trial judges were wary of allowing indigent procedure even to widows with young children, and used unnamed methods at times for getting at the property value of the plaintiff's holdings. Only one reported case was found for the period in which a plaintiff with small children had sufficiently small resources to entitle her and her dependents to sue as indigents.[17] In her affidavit the plaintiff stated that her property consisted of a lot valued at $1,800 and that there was a mortgage on it of $1,300. The court was kind enough to rule that if she would sign another affidavit for the small children, she could secure free judicial service.

Most of the determinations of poverty were negative in character — that is, the courts ascertained from the affidavit or otherwise that there was too much wealth for free judicial service. In one case it was held that *in forma* procedure did not apply to a person whose salary was $20 per week and whose house rent was $200 per year.[18] The court had appointed a master to find out the plaintiff's financial status. As a result of the master's findings the court concluded that the signing of an affidavit was not enough, even though there was no hint of perjury. A bankrupt person was refused indigent procedure because he had been able to hire a lawyer of his own choosing and was receiving $30 per month, which by state, not federal, law was free from execution.[19] Again, it was stated that the mere oath was not enough to enjoy the privilege of pauper procedure.

At the turn of the century an administratrix asked the trial court for permission to appeal as a pauper.[20] Her request was refused, not because the Indigent Code of 1892 did not allow appeals but because the court found from her affidavit that she had $600 let out at interest to various persons and some $200 in a savings bank. She asserted that she could not use the listed funds for the purpose to which this petition related because they were all she had with which to provide for sickness and old age. The court said that the security for costs would call for a very small amount of money and that the administratrix, a laundress, had sufficient funds to pay the costs or provide security therefor: ability to pay was the test, not inconvenience or hardship — logical thinking, this, from a rock-bound New England judge!

The Attorney-General, as auxiliary administrator for the federal judiciary, was asked in 1894 by a circuit clerk to approve from the fund an account for printing a record in the Circuit Court of Appeals, First Circuit, for an indigent suitor who without doubt had the qualifications demanded under the law of 1892. The Attorney-General, being in doubt, asked for instructions from the Comptroller of the Treasury.[21] The court rules provided that the costs should be taxed against the party "to whom costs are given," and Section 5 of the 1892 law directed that judgment might be rendered for costs at the conclusion of the suit, with the proviso that the United States should not be liable for any of the costs thus incurred. This was the intention of Congress, said the Comptroller, and the fund could not be spent for costs. The law simply imposed an additional burden upon the officers of the courts and did not transfer that burden from the litigant to the United States, although the fundamental purpose of the law was to enable the poor litigant to have the services of the courts and of their officers. He then made this statement:[22]

> I am of the opinion, therefore, that the expense of printing the record, in the case of a party who is entitled to the benefit of the act of July 20, 1892, is not properly chargeable to the appropriation "Miscellaneous Expenses, United States Courts," *although but for the implied prohibition contained in the proviso to Section 5 of said act the expense of printing a record which is for the convenience of the court, would be a proper charge against said appropriation.*   (Emphasis supplied.)

The administrative decision was the first one found on this matter and the later court decisions dealing with the same question never overturned it during the period under review. The irony of the "dictum" as regards what he would have done had the proviso not been placed in the original House Committee bill in 1892 indicated how little coordination of legislative thinking there was in it for the indigent plaintiff in trading fees for costs! Eleven days later in the same year the Comptroller of the Treasury rendered another decision on eligibility under the law of 1892.[23] The Attorney-General had approved, in a private concern's account for printing, a number of records of indigent criminals who had appealed from the trial court to the appellate court. It was erroneously claimed by the Justice Department that the Poor Man's Act of 1892 was justification therefor. The Comptroller said that the printing charged for in the account took place before the 1892 Act had been passed and therefore in the instant case this Act could not be the basis. However, he insisted that in general the Poor Man's Act did not apply to criminal cases "to which the United States are a party as to the prosecutor." He then stated:

In criminal cases it seems to me the Government may owe the duty to a poor defendant of having the record printed at its expense if that is necessary for him to have the benefit of the decision of the reviewing court, *the printing being required by the court for its own convenience,* and that policy seems to be fairly implied from the provisions of Section 878, Revised Statutes (1846), which require in criminal cases that the costs of obtaining the witnesses for a poor defendant shall be paid by the United States, *whereas in civil cases between poor litigants, provided for by the Act of July 20, 1892, no costs are to be charged against the Government* ... The claim is, therefore, a proper charge against the appropriation, "Miscellaneous Expenses, United States Courts," and will be allowed. (Emphasis supplied.)

It should be noticed again that, in the discussion of the printing of the record on appeal, nothing was said about appeals in the 1892 Act. The First Circuit and the District of Columbia courts had assumed that the privilege of appeal existed and the only question raised was the payment of costs. In a few federal jurisdictions the question arose as to the meaning of the phrase, "commence and prosecute to a conclusion any suit or action." In 1896 a federal trial court in Massachusetts permitted a poor person to appeal and the Circuit Court of Appeals of the First Circuit accepted jurisdiction and passed upon the main question.[24] Judge Lurton of the Sixth Circuit, who became a member of the Supreme Court eight years later, climaxed a series of rulings in Reed *v.* Pennsylvania Company,[25] wherein he held that the poor man could appeal under the 1892 law. Few decisions denied appellate power under the law and the confusion could only be ended by the Supreme Court.

The tenure of Mr. Chief Justice Fuller, who presided from 1888 to 1910, in the main spanned the important period under consideration. A "personal liberty" liberal, he was ever ready to aid those, especially the indigent, who ran afoul of criminal law. An "economic liberal" also, he believed strongly in the economic initiative of the individual, whether he was natural or fictitious. Consequently, he had little patience with those who were unable to meet competition in the market place. He spoke for the Court in the Fort Worth Bank Case,[26] wherein an indigent plaintiff in error was denied the right of prosecuting a writ of error from the highest Texas court. The Chief Justice insisted that security be given for costs because that was the specific demand of the law in such a case[27] The brief statement of the Court was as follows:

> Our ruling has uniformly been, and has been enforced in repeated instances, that the Act[28] has no application to proceedings in this court.

The Chief Justice was technically correct in his decision in that the Court had no jurisdiction because there was no statute providing for appeal *in forma pauperis* from a State Court to the Supreme Court. The obscurity of the opinion lay in the fact that he cited no specific cases to guide lower courts in similar cases. The rule he had in mind, was, doubtless, the ancient one reasserted by Chief Justice Warren as recently as 1957:[29]

> It is axiomatic, as a matter of history as well as doctrine, that the existence of appellate jurisdiction in a specific federal court over a given type of case is dependent upon authority conferred by statutes. And since the jurisdictional statutes prevailing at any given time are so much a product of federal-court jurisdiction since the First Judiciary Act, 1 Stat. 73, they have always been interpreted in the light of that history and of the axiom that clear statutory mandate must exist to found jurisdiction.

In giving precedents to prove his general statement, Chief Justice Fuller cited four cases before 1910, three of which had been decided by his court.

Two years later Chief Justice Fuller again had the opportunity to apply this general principle to the poor man's civil procedural rights.[30] A federal circuit court in Tennessee, in a "diversity" tort case, had permitted a writ of error *in forma*

pauperis. The appellate court had begun to have doubts as to
its earlier interpretation of the pauper law proceedings on appeal, due to contrary interpretations in other circuits, but it
was anxious to help in some way a case with so much merit.
It therefore ordered all the facts to be certified to the Supreme
Court and that the instructions of that Court be requested for
the proper determination of the following questions:

> 1. Does the act of July 20, 1892, providing when
> a plaintiff may sue as a poor person, apply to the
> prosecution of a writ of error from this Court?
>
> 2. If the act does not apply to appellate proceed-
> ings, had this court any authority to permit the
> prosecution of a writ of error *in forma pauperis*?

In this case[31] the Chief Justice gave the proper setting for
the decision by summarizing the railroad counsel's background
statement:

> It is well known that the courts are crowded with
> damage suits of every imaginable description
> against railroads and other corporations and that
> more than 90 per cent of these cases (state and
> federal) are brought on pauper's oath. Even if the
> defendant is successful in its defense of such
> cases, it is required, as a matter of law, to pay a
> proportion of the costs, that is, such as are in-
> curred on its own behalf.

These words definitely set up the economic conflict between
the impecunious and those with funds. The old rule or axiom
had run to the advantage of the non-pecunious. In answering
the first certified question the majority speaking through the
Chief Justice recalled the Fort Worth Case.[32] Asserting that
just as it had ruled against a pauper proceeding in prosecuting
a writ of error to a state court, so would the prohibition lie
had there been a review of a judgment or decree of a lower
federal court, because the statute referred only to the court of
original jurisdiction; that is, it gave no specific authority for
appeal.

This extension of the prohibition was partly based upon the interpretation of recurring words or phrases in the law of 1892. "To a conclusion" meant a termination in the court where the suit or action commenced. Chiefly on the authority of seventeenth century Lord Coke, "action" was a "cause of action" ordinarily inapplicable to writs of error. Partly, also, the application of pauper procedure could be limited to the original court on the basis of the judicial wisdom of the ages as found in the general rules of interpretation. In the present case the rule of strict construction should apply since the pauper would always come to litigate at the expense of others. "He thus enjoys a great privilege and exemption from the common lot of men, whereby, in respect to causes of action, he becomes," as Lord Bacon says, "rather able to vex than unable to sue." Lord Bacon was referring to the fifteenth century Statute, 11 Hen. VII, ch. 12, and his language was elsewhere translated to mean "that the charity of the legislature thought it better that the poor man should be able to vex than that he should not be able to sue."[33] This strict construction denied that the 1892 Act was a remedial one and, therefore, to be liberally construed, as a number of the lower courts had tried to maintain for a decade. It raised the decision in effect, to the lofty level of the railway counsel's outlook.

The last basis for the negative answer to question No. 1 was also a negation of question No. 2: appellate procedure had no origin in common law and had to have an explicit statutory basis before the court could sustain it. There was no such law on the statute book and therefore the Court of Appeals could not entertain the poor man's appeal.

Chief Justice Fuller seems to have been indirectly aware of English precedent as to appeals *in forma pauperis*. Lord Chancellor Eldon, in connection with a civil case, permitted an appeal after remarking that it was a singular proposition and that he could not see why because a party was poor, the court should not set itself right.[34] On this theory the brief for Bradford argued as follows:

> Independent of any statute, the Circuit Court of
> Appeals possesses inherent power to allow the

prosecution of a writ of error *in forma pauperis* in any case wherein there might be a failure of justice...if the Act of Congress[35] does not apply to appellate proceedings, it is nevertheless within the discretionary power of the Circuit Court of Appeals to allow plaintiff in error, for cause shown, to prosecute her writ of error *in forma pauperis*.

NOTES TO CHAPTER III

[1]Bradford v. Bradford, 2 Flipp. 280, 281, 1879.

[2]Roy v. Louisville N.O. and T.R.R. Co., 34 F. 276, 1888.

[3]27 Stat. 252, 1892. See Appendix A-I.

[4]H. R. 8153, 52nd Cong., 1st Sess., 1892.

[5]*Supra.*, p. 25. See also Appendix A-I.

[6]27 Stat. 252, (July) 1892.

[7]The judges often turned to the interpretations of similar laws by state judges, especially those of New York State (See *Cent. Dig.*, Secs. 502 and 508, under "Costs"). In a letter to James R. Garfield (Washington, D.C.), Frederick Howe of Cleveland asked the former to help in appointing a good man to fill the position of district judge for the Northern District of Ohio. His reason was that the Cleveland area had so many foreign corporations doing business there that personal injury cases fell largely to the federal district courts on the basis of "diversity," much to the economic disadvantage of the poor man. Evidently the appointee had to be an experienced liberal to offset the usual harshness of the general run of the federal judges. See the *James R. Garfield Papers*, Library of Congress.

[8]See Appendix II, Note 2. for ammendment deleting the word "citizen" and putting in its place that of "person." Interpretations of treaties and decisions of the Supreme Court on the rights of persons and just common sense demanded the charge.

[9]Fuller *et al. v.* Montague *et al.*, 53 F. 206, 1892.

[10]Clay v. So. Railway, 90 F. 472, 1898. See also Reed v. Penn. Corp., 111 F. 714, 1901, where a widow, suing for herself and infant children, had to double her oath of poverty.

[11]Boyle v. Great Northern Railroad Co., 63 F. 539, 1894.

[12]*Idem.*, p. 540. This case occurred in a State where contingent

contracts were void. Similar views found in *The Bella*, 91 F. 540, 1899 and Feil *v.* Wabash R. R. Co., 119 F. 490, 1902.

[13]Whelan *v.* Manhattan Ry. Co., 26 F. 219, 1898.

[14]*Ibid.*, p. 221

[15]Phillips *v.* L. and N. R.R. Co., 153 F. 795, 1907.

[16]Under the Discharge of Indigent Prisoners Act of 1872, 17 Stat. 198, a convict, if held only for a fine or fine and costs, could by swearing that he possessed only $20 be released after 30 days. The law, amended in 1940, 54 Stat. 692, gave the Attorney-General power to forgive any excess over the $20, if the convict needed it for his own support. In 1946, by 60 Stat. 524, the excess allowed was forgiven, if it was needed to support the convict and his family; $20 was not a standard for long.

[17]McDuffie *v.* B. and M. R.R. Co., 82 F. 865, 1897.

[18]Winkelman *v.* Dick Co., 85 F. 851, 1898.

[19]*In re* Collier, 93 F. 191, 1899.

[20]Volk *v.* Sturtevant Co., 99 F. 532, 1900.

[21]1 Comp. Dec. 17, Oct. 16, 1894. The expense fund was in aid of the court and only incidentally to help certain litigants.

[22]*Ibid.*

[23]1 Comp. Dec. 26, Oct. 27, 1894.

[24]Columb *v.* Webster Manufacturing Co., 76 F. 198, 1896, and on appeal, 84 F. 592, 1898.

[25]Reed *v.* Pennsylvania Co., 111 F. 714, 1901. The court stated that the 6th Circuit (Tenn., Ky., Ohio, Mich.) had allowed appeals in a number of unreported cases; that in reported cases, *in forma pauperis* appeals had been allowed in Fuller *v.* Montague, 53 F. 206, 1892. In this case, the court stated that "the plaintiff can hardly be said 'to prosecute to a conclusion' unless he be allowed to take it

by appeal to the court of appeals." The court in Brinkley v. L. and
N. R. Co., 95 F. 345, 1899, though it denied appeal for other reasons,
remarked that appeal under the 1892 Act was a proper construction
of that Act despite the fact that the 5th Circuit, as well as other
circuits, had ruled against appellate jurisdiction under the 1892
Act, as in The *Presto*, 93 F. 522, 1899. Other cases sanctioning
appeal: Winkelman v. Dick Co., 85 F. 851, 1898; Clay v. So. Ky.,
90 F. 472, 1898, W. H. Taft and H. H. Lurton, judges; Volk v.
Sturtevant Co., 99 F. 532, 1900.

[26]Galloway v. State National Bank of Fort Worth, 186 U.S. 177,
178, 1902.

[27]Sec. 1,000, Rev. Stat.

[28] 27 Stat. Sec. 5, 1892.

[29]Carroll v. United States, 354 U.S. 394, 399, 1957, citing United
States v. More, 3 Cr. 159, 1805; United States v. Sanges, 144 U.S.
310, 1892; *in re* Heath, 144 U.S. 92, 1892; Cross v. United States,
145 U.S. 571, 1892. *Cf.* Rathner, 109 *Univer. of Penn. L. Rev.* 157,
1960, as to power of Congress to control appeal on constitutional
questions.

[30]Bradford v. So. Ry. Co., 195 U.S. 243, 1904, and accompanying
briefs.

[31]*Ibid.*

[32]186 U.S. 177, 1902.

[33]Bradford Case, 195 U.S. 249-250, 1904. The Chief Justice re-
lied upon Judge Cowen's historical interpretation in applying an
1836 New York State law governing a poor man's power to sue,
Moore v. Cooley, 2 Hill 412, N.Y.

[34]2 Jac. and W. 402, 1820; 37 English Reports 680, cited in
Brinkley v. L. and N. R.R. Co., 95 F. 345, 354, 1899.

[35]27 Stat. 252, 1892.

CHAPTER IV

FEDERAL INDIGENT CODE OF
CIVIL AND CRIMINAL PROCEDURE,
1910-1922

Between 1892 and 1922 industry and finance had become well organized nationally. While farmers and laborers had gone far toward establishing themselves as major economic groups, the general population was not very content physically or spiritually. Theodore Roosevelt had taken over the leadership of the Progressive Movement and had used the White House and the political stump as forums to arouse his fellow Americans to the dangers of "dishonest success," to inform them of the increasing miscarriage of justice by some of the courts of the land and to warn them, like the Hebrew prophets of old, of the results of the failure to make the average man "get into his soul the belief that he will not only receive justice but will have a part in meting out justice."[1] During this period Congress began to respond to the demand to help the poor person to regain what he had lost by the 1904 decision of the Supreme Court. That was the moral obligation.

A law passed in 1910[2] amended section one of the Act of 1892.[3] *In forma* procedure was open to both *plaintiff* and *defendant*. "To a conclusion" was left at the trial court level, but indigents could use it in civil and criminal cases; appellate processes became open to the poor in both types of cases all the way to the Supreme Court, and printing of the record on appeal became a part of costs that could apparently be avoided or delayed. An important characteristic of the amended section was the *wide discretion of the trial court in refusing appeals from its judgments.*

This law had its origin in a majority Republican Senate, and according to the Senate Report on the bill the proposers merely intended to correct the measure to the extent that the Supreme Court had damaged it in 1904.[4] Senator Overman of

North Carolina admitted this was the case and said that by
adding "two or three words" the trick could be accomplished,
much to the disgust of Senator Kean of New Jersey. Senator
Bacon of Georgia then took up the discussion:

> The evident intent of Congress was that it [the
> Act of 1892] should relate to all the courts. But a
> case which had gone through the court of original
> jurisdiction afterwards went to the Circuit Court
> of Appeals and then went to the Supreme Court...;
> and the Supreme Court decided that the word "con-
> clusion" used in the statute meant simply the
> original court. There was a purpose, and the well
> conceived purpose, of Congress to let a man who
> had a cause for action, but was unable to pay the
> cost of the suit to pursue his case *in forma pau-
> peris,* and by the construction of the word "con-
> clusion"...that purpose of the law is defeated.
> The sole purpose of this bill is to enlarge the law
> as it now stands...so that one who is unable to
> pay the costs of a suit shall not only be permitted
> to pursue it in the court where it originates but
> also in the appellate courts.

Senator Rayburn of Idaho, evidently suffering from a six-year
blindspot, remarked that he was not aware that any necessity
had risen for further legislation for the poor man, since under
the existing law it was always within the power of the court,
by order, to allow appeal.

Senator Clarke of Arkansas approved pauper proceedings
in the trial court but believed that, if permission were given
to paupers to appeal as in the bill under consideration, no trial
judge would dare use his discretion to refuse an appeal after
he had tried the case. The Senator thought that a more serious
check on appeals should be imposed lest "great expense and
time will be suffered by the Government wholly upon the initiation of an unsuccessful litigant and his lawyer....There
is no use overlooking the fact that many cases presented *in
forma pauperis* are gotten up by ambulance-chasing lawyers,
whose business it is to trump up personal injury cases against
corporations."[5]

When the Senate handed the bill over to the House, the

Committee on the Judiciary of that body proceeded to expand the measure to include both civil and criminal cases. Its Report was adopted by the House and returned to the Senate where the amendments were concurred in. Public debate played little part in the entire legislative process.[6]

Congress as a whole glided without serious reflection into the major changes in the 1892 Act. This movement, however, might well have been justified on the moral grounds of the Progressive Movement — which had not only been advancing openly under Theodore Roosevelt, but was to be emphasized by President Wilson, to take cover in the Golden Decade of the twenties, and to reappear with renewed strength under the second Roosevelt. Likely, too, the correlation of the two general types of cases under a formal indigent law gained acceptance without much debate inasmuch as the inclusion of appellate proceedings simply achieved what the informed public and the members of Congress thought had been accomplished in 1892. To be sure the eighteen years of practice in applying civil procedure was largely the work of the lower courts.[7] Not until attempts were made to appeal to the Supreme Court did that agency of government put an end to all appeals until Congress could give the proper jurisdiction.

Apparently the lawmakers thought that the 1892 statute, as amended in 1910, had consolidated the procedural privileges of the impecunious in civil and criminal matters and that effective safeguards against abuse by indigents in initiating litigation and in prosecuting appeals had been set up. It was discovered, however, that the poor person was at a disadvantage because of the existence of another law which had either no relation to the main pauper statute or was entirely uncorrelated with it. In other words Congress had passed, or would pass, specific legislation that had affected or would affect the indigent plaintiff or defendant without taking into account the existing legal environment. The national judiciary did not have within itself any agency for directing and coordinating judicial administration, that is, the handling of the business of the courts. Had there been such an agency, it would at least have endeavored to promote the passage of a more logical set of statutes for the protection of the indigent.

The judiciary did have the Attorney-General as an auxiliary agent, but his activities seem to have been as unplanned as that of the legislature and the judiciary. One of the inconsistencies of the law had to do with the required printing of the records on appeal in criminal cases.

This contradiction supposedly had been cured by adding to the amended Pauper Act a proviso to Section 1, which read as follows:

> *Provided,* That in any criminal case the court may, upon the filing in said court of the affidavit herein before mentioned, direct that the expense of printing the record on appeal or writ of error be paid by the United States, and the same shall be paid when authorized by the Attorney-General.[8]

The original bill was introduced and passed in the Senate during the Second Session of the 66th Congress[9] but was not considered by the House. The bill was reintroduced as S. 426 in the First Session of the 67th Congress and became law in the Second Session. Senate Report No. 20 on the reintroduced measure was nothing more than the earlier report, and House Report 626 merely copied that of the Senate. Hence the basis for the bill was the original Senate Report No. 546 of the 66th Congress which stated the end in view as follows:[10]

> The object of the bill is to amend the act of 1892, as amended,[11] to cover a defect pointed out by the decision of the Comptroller of the Treasury, dated November 5, 1919,[12] in which he holds that notwithstanding the provisions of the above acts, a defendant in a criminal case who files an affidavit *in forma pauperis* is not entitled to have the record printed at the expense of the Government in cases in which an appeal is taken.

The Report then gave an excerpt from the Attorney-General's letter to the chairman of the Senate Committee on the Judiciary in which the chief law officer asked that the bill be passed. It was noted in the communication that due to pressure for cheaper costs in civil and criminal appeals Congress had enacted a Statute on February 18, 1911,[13] which required records on appeal to be in printed form and that this absolute requirement complicated matters for the indigent appellant. The Attorney-General quoted the closing paragraph of the above-mentioned Comptroller's decision:

> While running through all the statutes quoted[14] is evidence of a benevolent intention on the part of Congress that a poor defendant shall have the free and unrestricted right from a financial standpoint to make his full defense to final conclusion, yet the effect of the statutes seems to be to render this intention nugatory, since the final requirement of the legislation, a printed record, is expressly prohibited from being furnished at the cost of the United States.[15] It will be seen, therefore, that the situation in this case, though admittedly a hard one, can be relieved only by Congress; and you are advised therefore that you are not authorized to direct the printing of the record involved at the expense of the United States.

The Comptroller's Decision just referred to had denied the Attorney-General administrative authorization to pay, from United States funds, the cost of printing the record on appeal by a defendant in a criminal action. The trial court had granted a motion to have the printing thus taken care of. The Comptroller recalled two previous decisions made relative to the use of "Miscellaneous Appropriations" by the Attorney-General in the furtherance of judicial administration. The decision of October 16, 1892[16] denied authorization for paying for the record on appeal in a civil case, although the Comptroller indicated he would have approved the payment had Section 5 of the 1892 statute not forbidden it, since a printed record was for the benefit and convenience of the court. He also recalled his decision of October 27, 1894[17] in which he approved the use of the special appropriation for printing criminal appeals records for the indigent, because such records were in the interest of the poor man and for the convenience of the courts.

Criminal procedure did not come within the impoverished man's statute of 1892. When Congress specifically amended Section 1 of the 1892 Act,[18] Section 5 was not modified and the result was that no public money could be spent for records on appeal in criminal cases. The 1911 statute[19] was thrown into the picture. By that law appeal records had to be printed before the appellate courts could receive them. The Comptroller ended by giving the status quo of record printing as of 1919:[20]

> The act of 1892, as amended by the act of 1910, allows a defendant in a criminal case to take an appeal without furnishing security for costs or for printing the record, but it expressly prohibits the United States from incurring any costs on this account; and the act of February 18, 1911, imposes a further limitation to the effect that there shall be a printed record[21]— thus precluding the preparation of the final record by means of typewriting in the office of the clerk of the court under a court order. *Were the printing to be done by the United States the difficulty imposed in the act of 1911 might be overcome;* but, of course, no court order or statute can operate to compel a private printer to print a record for a poor defendant on credit or without security....(Emphasis supplied.)

Congress, after digesting the original Senate Report, recognized that the 1910 amendment of the 1892 Act had neither succeeded in bringing criminal cases within the full compass of the Act nor added to or imposed any liability whatever in the way of money upon the United States. Something had to be done for the impecunious man, especially in his prosecution of a criminal appeal. Therefore a very slight modification of Section 5 of the *in forma pauperis* Code was made in the form of a proviso at the conclusion of Section 1 of the Code, which reads as follows:

> In any criminal case the court may, upon the filing in the said court of the aforesaid affidavit, direct that the expense of printing the record on appeal be paid by the United States and the same shall be done when authorized by the Attorney-General.

The bill passed with little discussion in either House.[22]

NOTES TO CHAPTER IV

[1]Speech, Chicago, Aug. 6, 1912 (pamphlet).

[2]36 Stat. 866, 1910. See Appendix A-I. Seamen, regardless of nationality, may initiate and prosecute appeals in federal courts in their own name and for their own benefit for wages and salvages or the enforcement of laws for their health or safety without payment of fees and costs or putting up security. They have to meet the conditions relative to poverty that the indigent law requires, if they want to avoid payment for printing papers (39 Stat. 313, 1910; 40 Stat. 159, 1917). The privilege was separated from the Seamen Acts and placed within the poor person's code as 28 U.S.C.A. Sec. 1916. United States veterans, for certain purposes, were allowed to proceed under the Pauper Act, if they could take the oath, by the Veterans' Act of 1924, 28 U.S.C.A., Sections 445, 551.

[3]27 Stat. 252, 1892.

[4]Rep. No. 152, to accompany S. 5836, 61st Cong., 2nd Sess., 1910.

[5]Cong. Rec., pp. 1532-34, 61st Cong., 2nd Sess., 1910, gives discussion *supra*, pp. 43-44.

[6]H. Rep. No. 1591; Cong. Rec., pp. 8211, 8554, 8627-37, to accompany S. 5836, 61st Cong., 2nd Sess., 1910.

[7]See *supra*, Ch. III.

[8]42 Stat. 666, June 26, 1922. See Appendix A-I.

[9]S. 4273, S. Rep. No. 546.

[10]S. 4273, S. Rep. No. 546, 66th Cong., 2nd Sess., 1920; S. 426, S. Rep. No. 20, 67th Cong., 1st Sess., 1921; and H. Rep. No. 626, 67th Cong., 2nd Sess., 1922.

[11]27 Stat. 252, as amended by the act of 1910, 36 Stat. 866.

[12]26 Comp. Dec. 362, 1919.

[13]36 Stat. 901, 1911.

[14]1892 and 1910, 1911.

[15]Act of 1892, as amended in 1910, Sec. 5.

[16]1 Comp. Dec. 17, p. 14, *supra*.

[17]1 Comp. Dec. 26.

[18]36 Stat. 866, 1910.

[19]36 Stat. 901.

[20]26 Comp. Dec. 562, 1919.

[21]Not a typewritten record.

[22]42 Stat. 666, 1922. This amendment and that of 1910 were embodied in the original Act of 1892 as 29 U.S.C., sections 832-836, 1926. A restatement may be found in 28 U.S.C. Sec. 1915, a, b, c, d, e, 1948, plus certain other amendments. See Appendices A, I and II.

CHAPTER V

JUDICIAL INTERPRETATION OF THE INDIGENT CODE OF 1892, AS AMENDED, 1910-1956

The language of the Code remained very much the same for the entire period under consideration, although additional legislation supplementing it, as well as judicial interpretation of such legislation, affected the application of the Code. It is due to this circumstance that the author has extended the period some forty or fifty years.[1] It was shown in the preceding chapter that the lower Federal courts controlled the application of the original Code and seemed to think that the Code was made for them to interpret. In civil cases the same courts continued their interpretation in the important area of who were to participate in a damage suit for injury or death under the Code. The rule that everyone in an indigent case who had a financial interest in the possible returns of the suit was obliged to take the pauper's oath before the principal party, suer or sued, could take advantage of the free procedure. The alternative was the putting up of the cash or giving bond for surety.

Two cases following on the heels of the 1910 amendment proved the continued enforcement of the rule. One was a widow's suit to recover damages for her husband's death.[2] She could not put up cash or give security for costs and fees of the suit and was forced to hire a lawyer on a contingent fee basis to handle the case for her. The trial court, on motion of the defendant, ordered the lawyer either to put up bond for costs and fees or take the pauper's oath. The other case involved the suit for personal injury by a mining company.[3] The company forced the complainant into the federal court under the diversity rule. When the defendant brought out the fact that the plaintiff had made a contract to give his attorney 50% of whatever amount was recovered, if any, the plaintiff answered by saying that under state law no guardian could be forced to put up money for costs. The federal district court said that no state law could destroy the terms of the Pauper Act, more especially when the attorney was in a real sense guilty of *champetry*.

The Supreme Court took part in the interpretation of the amended 1892 Act for the first time in 1915.[4] The Chief Justice, speaking for the Court, said that while the Act of 1910 extended pauper process to both plaintiff and defendant, to relator and respondent, and enlarged the type of cases in which pauper procedure could be had, "the discretion of the trial court in permitting appeals, both as to poverty and merit, is its discretion in allowing poverty proceedings to be initiated in the trial courts." The Court was dealing with a long drawn-out case in which the plaintiff had repeatedly tried to appeal a "decision" which never had been made. Lack of merit, however, was the real basis for affirming the lower courts.

The 1915 Kinney decision seemed to approve the trial court's exercise of wide judicial discretion in allowing *in forma pauperis* procedure in initiating civil suits after 1892 and criminal suits after 1910. Discretion in civil cases took the form, among others, of determining the conditions precedent for free judicial service: a) the leveling-down of all parties interested in the results of a suit; b) the decision in each case of what did or did not constitute "poverty" as used in Section 1 of the Pauper Statute, whether amended or not. With one rather mild exception to be noted later, the Kinney case was the last statement of the Supreme Court on the a) and b) interpretations until 1948, although the Court was not making a judgment on the two points as such. In fact the lower courts continued to be free construers of the indigent code in non-criminal cases and it was not until 1923 that a small number (a minority) of decisions began to appear in opposition to a) and b) constructions which had begun after 1892.

In civil cases, the rule concerning suers and sued after 1910, including counsel, became more binding since the rule had been extended in a majority of cases to mean that no person could begin to sue (or defend) *in forma pauperis* after 1910 unless all who were interested as parties in the results of a case had signed poverty oaths.[5] At the same time the inclusion of attorneys who got their fees or rewards on contingent contracts, if at all, had hardened into written rules of the district courts, rules that were being enforced as though they were specific congressional directives.

The inclusion of attorneys among those who had to sign sworn statements of poverty, or provide all costs, appeared to be at least as essential as the inclusion of the parties known as plaintiffs or relators, defendants or respondents. Under the original statute this was the result of the demand on the part of the defendant that the attorney sign an affidavit of poverty or provide for costs. After 1910 the defendant, or his equivalent, continued to insist upon the inclusion of attorneys among those who had to pay costs or sign the oath of poverty, if he had any kind of contingent contract to serve as plaintiff's counsel. This of course was one of the most likely ways of getting the action dropped, especially if the attorney happened to be a good one and dangerous to the defendant.[6]

The most justifiable case that came under the rule was one which involved damages for personal injury. The plaintiff contracted with a lawyer to prosecute his case in return for 50% of the "win."[7] When the United States happened to be the defendant in a case, the United States District Attorney insisted that the plaintiff's attorney, or attorneys, provide for the costs lest he be successful, or sign the pauper oath. The trial court insisted and was affirmed by the appellate court. The Supreme Court denied certiorari without giving reasons.[8] This was the only one found and it was a rather weak approval of the rule. Apparently the trial court depended at first on the defendant to bring out the fact that the plaintiff's attorney had a contingent contract for fees.

A defection among the courts from the rule that the attorney who prosecuted on a contingent basis must provide security for costs or sign the oath of poverty appeared in 1923. The case[9] involved a mandamus petition to a three-judge appellate court to compel a district judge to allow the petitioner to proceed with an appeal *in forma pauperis*. The appellate court held that the petitioner was entitled to appeal as a poor person, since the papers showed beyond doubt that he qualified as an indigent and that the sole reason why the *in forma* appeal had been refused was that the relator's attorneys, who had a contract for contingent fees, had not shown that they were unable to pay costs or give security therefor. The district judge cited cases, already considered, as firmly backing the inclusion of attorneys as parties at interest. The appellate court granted that the judge had precedent in his favor, citing, *inter alia*, the Esquibel case,[10] but according to the court, if that decision held that it was against the "policy of the law" for an attorney to agree to pay costs, it ought not to be tolerated that he could be actually forced to pay them. Further, the Act of 1892, as amended, indicated no difference between costs of trial and appeal, and certainly did not contemplate making an attorney responsible for costs or fees or for their security, if a proper contract for fees was made.

Nine years later a federal district court in Missouri held that a pauper affidavit by an attorney, who represented an indigent on a contingent basis, was not a condition precedent for leave to prosecute an action *in forma pauperis*.[11] This was a War Risk Insurance case, in which the respondent, the United States Government, accepted the plaintiff as a pauper but objected to granting pauper procedure because the plaintiff's attorney had been engaged on a contingent basis and therefore should be responsible for costs or sign an affidavit of poverty. "We do not follow the existing rule of law," said the court, "for the statute itself, even as amended, does not make such a demand on an attorney." The theory of the law, according to the court was:[12]

> No man shall be denied the right to prosecute a meritorious cause of action by reason of his poverty. He is to be allowed to institute and prosecute his suit without the payment of fees or giving security of costs. Justice is for all, not for those only who may be able to pay the cost of litigation.

In 1942 a motion was made to dismiss an indigent case based upon the Fair Labor Standards Act of 1938. The chief ground for dismissal was that the plaintiff's attorneys had a contractual interest in the outcome and had not signed an affidavit of poverty or given security for costs.[13] The district judge quoted his court rule to the effect that all parties interested in recovery, including especially the counsel, had to sign affidavits of poverty if they wanted to proceed *in forma pauperis*. In the case at hand, however, the judge stated that the attorneys' fees were provided for by law and, in any event, the court rule only contemplated cases in which there was a beneficial interest, secured by contract between the plaintiff and his counsel. "To hold otherwise would hamper poor persons who might have meritorious claims, since this might be the only way for indigent persons to secure a lawyer." The decision amounted to a breakdown in one lower court of the old rule by a technical interpretation.

The last lower-court case[14] before 1948 that touched the meaning of who had to sign affidavits of poverty and what "poverty" meant in Section 1 of the Indigent Code,[15] had to do with the Federal Employers' Liability Act. The defendant moved to dismiss the case for several reasons, among which two were of interest. One was the plaintiff's allegation that he was too poor to bear any cost, present or future, of his suit for personal injury. The respondent replied that the allegation was insufficient for free judicial procedure and, if he personally was sufficiently poor, then his attorney, who had a contract for contingent fees, had not proved his poverty by a proper affidavit.

The district judge was aware of the old rule relative to attorneys who took indigent cases on contingency, and he had also kept up with the minority cases that had begun to spring up in the 1920's. The judge was of the opinion that any attempt to force an attorney to pay the costs of an action was unenforceable in the federal and in most state jurisdictions. He believed that contingent fees in indigent cases were legal and if they were not the *judiciary* should make them so. The ground for this view was in close harmony with the minority decisions: the poor man, even if his cause of action were meritorious, could get little aid from really first-rate attorneys if they had to sign oaths of poverty. His immediate purpose, then, was to eliminate the attorney from the group of "signers"—a gloss on the Indigent Code that Congress never intended to be there.

During the period 1910-1956, the lower federal courts were in general inclined to be more generous in their interpretation of the word "poverty" in the Code. The *Zeitgeist* of the first half of the 20th century showed a bit more humaneness, for the lower federal and state courts had begun to express this spirit in their decisions involving suits between employer and employee, and the state legislatures and Congress had begun to direct that that spirit should be followed. In criminal matters it has been indicated that the judiciary was really sympathetic on questions of antisocial actions, especially if the parties concerned were on the indigent level. Still, the national courts and Congress were apparently unable to convey the meaning of "poverty" except in a negative way.

In a land foreclosure case[16] a party begged to proceed as a pauper but was not allowed to for the reason that he had been receiving $75 a month for work done in a manufacturing plant. This amount was a partial substitute for the denial of the use of his farm property which had been tied up in litigation as a result of the Great Depression. In the Jacobs case[17] already noted, the other ground for supporting the motion to dismiss was that the plaintiff had not proved his poverty to the extent necessary for securing *in forma* procedure. The district judge stated that the plaintiff's averments to the effect that he was without means to prosecute his suit, that on account of his personal injuries received in the railroad accident he had been unable to work and was thus heavily in debt, appeared to be true. The railroad's attorneys tried to rebut by asserting that the plaintiff possessed an eighteen-acre farm worth at least $800. His own counsel, however, obtained affidavits from the officials in control of the county land records to the effect that he had unforgiven chattel mortgages of $1,600.

Attention has already been called to the fact that the discretion of the trial court in allowing persons to appeal in civil cases had been very broad and that the lower appellate courts had approved such discretion, even though there was no legal basis for the prosecution of an appeal *in forma pauperis* before 1910. In the Kinney case[18] the Court had said that the discretion of the trial court was as deep and broad in allowing appeals after 1910 as it was in allowing indigents to prosecute suits under the 1892 Act. Therefore the common element of discretion in permitting the initiation of a suit (or action) applied to appeals. This meant that the trial court adopted the familiar rules regarding who had to qualify as paupers and what the meaning of "poverty" in each case was — the old a) and b) questions.[19] The Supreme Court had done little toward helping the lower courts to solve them.

In 1947 the legal battle between the Dupont Company and its workers over the application of certain terms of the Federal Fair Standards Act, as amended,[20] had taken a turn that was to lead to a searching examination of a) and b), among other questions. A Mr. Adkins had initiated a suit in his own interest (and as leader for twelve other workers) for overtime pay, damages, and the like. He had died before the case really began and his wife took over as administratrix of his estate and as leader for the other claimants. She sued in the trial court but not as a poor person, and having lost her case, asked for a new trial. On being denied, she decided to appeal. Since she and her wards, on advice of her attorneys, wanted the whole record to be transcribed and printed for the appellate court, Mrs. Adkins and her wards felt that they could not pay the estimated cost of $4,000. She asked leave to appeal *in forma pauperis*. Her accompanying affidavit stated that she could not pay the estimated cost; that she was a widow; that her deceased husband had left her a home assessed at $3,450; that her only income was from the renting of rooms; and that without that source of income she would be unable to keep her seventy-four year old body from speedy disintegration. No objection to the contents of the lone affidavit was found in the records. The trial court denied the motion to appeal as a poor person without giving reason and without holding a hearing. However, from a note to the petitioner's attorneys and the arguments of the defendant, the apparent reasons were:

> 1) the petitioner could not proceed *in forma pauperis* on appeal, when there were twelve other claimants involved who had failed to file affidavits of poverty;

> 2) the petitioner's lawyers had been employed on
> a contingent fee basis and they must sign af-
> fidavits of poverty ... all members of the firm
> representing her.

The petitioner then filed a similar application for appeal *in forma pauperis* in the appellate court. The trial court was affirmed.

In December, 1947 Mrs. Adkins tried a second time for the privilege of appealing as a poor person. She filed, with the district court, her old affidavit to which were annexed the affidavits of 10 of the 12 claimants, in which this statement, among others, appeared: "... because of my poverty I am unable to pay or give security for the costs ($4,000) of such appeal and still be able to provide myself and my dependents with the necessities of life." One member of the firm of law-yers filed an identical affidavit with the additional statement that he alone would receive his percentage of whatever moneys were won. The law firm also filed an affidavit asserting that the claims, in its opinion, were meritorious and that its total liquid assets were not over $2,000, an amount much less than the estimated $4,000 of costs. A hearing was accorded the petitioner on this second application, but on December 22, 1947 the district court again denied on the grounds that the petitioner had offered no evidence in support of her applica-tion; that all the claimants had not filed affidavits; and that all the affidavits were insufficient in that they had not stated the financial condition of the plaintiffs in such a way as to tell whether the plaintiffs were really penurious.[21] The judge, however, was not sure precisely what the affiants would have to show in the way of property, but believed that each should prove complete inability to pay at least a portion of the costs. All interested in recovery, he thought, "have at least got to chip in to the extent of their pay; and whatever they have, they have got to put in the pot for the purpose of taking the appeal."[22] Further, the judge was inclined to believe, but was not certain, that before Mrs. Adkins could be permitted to appeal, she must mortgage her home and "chip in" what she received from the mortgage loan. Again, the judge construed all the affidavits as showing only *hardship*, a condition that did not meet the statutory requirements of inability to pay because of poverty. The judge thought that the petitioner should not include in the record unnecessary material because it added to the expense of Government and encouraged the ill-use of pauper procedure.

Mrs. Adkins appealed from the denial of appeal *in forma pauperis* by the trial court and was met with an affirmation of the trial court's decision. She then applied as a poor person to the Supreme Court for certiorari to review the negative decisions of the lower courts. Her allegations and other papers were about the same in content as those made to the appellate court below. After reading the papers sent up by the petitioner, the Court entered an order stating that it desired to hear argument on most of the questions considered below as to the interpretation of the Indigent Code. The Solicitor-General of the United States, who had intervened in the lower courts to protect the Labor Standards Act from the petitioner's charge that some of the parts of that Act were unconstitutional, went far beyond his "call of duty" in responding to the order: he argued both sides of the case, indicated the weaknesses of the Indigent Code, gave the Government's view of curing the weak points and boldly stated the legal conclusions growing out of the instant case. The main points were:[23]

1) Every one legally interested in the potential results of a case must sign affidavits of poverty in which there is sufficient details of his financial condition to show beyond a doubt that he is unable to pay all or some of the costs or give security therefor: all for one and one for all.

   a) An attorney engaged on a contingent basis, despite the ruling of a majority of lower court cases, does not have to pay the costs, give security therefor or sign affidavits of poverty.

2) The phrase "inability to pay" has mixed the lower courts up badly and the Supreme Court should work out some kind of standard for the trial courts to

follow in initiated cases and on appeal.

Other points of interest to the Government and to indigent petitioners were:

1) It is an abuse of discretion for a court to disallow an indigent to begin an action or appeal, in which the truth of the allegation of poverty has not been contested, and which, on its face, states a cause of action and which contains nothing on its face indicating frivolous and vexatious intent: the court alone is the challenger.

2) The court should not allow the petitioner, as was done in the instant case, to demand that the entire record of trial be transcribed and printed for the appellate court. Unnecessary material should have been eliminated by the court and the proper Rules of Civil Procedure applied. Thus the $4,000 costs would have been greatly reduced and the Government would either have to pay less or have been free of such costs, because the smaller amount might well have been paid by the petitioner and her wards.

After hearing the arguments and reading the briefs, especially those of the Government, the Supreme Court granted certiorari together with the privilege of *in forma pauperis* procedure. The final decision of the case,[24] Mr. Justice Black speaking, contained the following by way of introduction:

The questions chiefly involve the scope and application of the statute which authorizes a citizen to prosecute and defend actions in the federal courts "without being required to prepay fees or costs or for the printing of a record in the appellate court... upon filing in said court a statement under oath, in writing, that because of his poverty he is unable to pay costs of said suit or action or to put up security for the same..."[25]

The Supreme Court then spoke in effect as follows:

1) The trial court had discretionary power to prevent the "stuffing" of the record on appeal and should have applied Rule 75(m) of the Rules of Civil Procedure--a simple record.
2) The affidavit of poverty should follow the language of the indigent statute, preferably; the punishment for lying is in the code itself, that is, pains of perjury, dismissing the case, and taxing costs. If the costs remain unsatisfactory after reconsideration by the trial court, then the court might well have parties make more detailed statements of ability to pay portions of the costs.
3) The petitioner cannot be denied the right to appeal, because one or more of those jointly interested in the results of the decision would not pay or give security for costs and would not sign the required affidavit of poverty; each claimant stands for himself and the only ones who share in the results are those who file affidavits.
4) Attorneys on a contingent-fee basis are not required by the statute to sign affidavits of poverty or pay costs or give security therefor.
5) Mrs. Adkins, in the instant case, or any other person, does not have to be destitute to proceed *in forma pauperis*.

Number 5 was elaborated upon:

We think an affidavit sufficient which states that one cannot because of his poverty 'pay or give security for the costs ... and still be able to provide' for himself and dependents 'with the necessities of life.' To say that no persons are entitled to the statute's benefits until they have sworn to contribute to payment of costs to their last dollar they have or can get, would be to construe the statute in a way that would throw its beneficiaries into the category of public charges. The public would not be profited, if relieved of paying costs of a particular litigation only to have imposed on it the expense of supporting the person thereby made an object of public support. Nor does the result seem more desirable if the effect of this statutory interpretation is to force the litigant to

> abandon what may be a meritorious claim in order
> to spare himself complete destitution. We think a
> construction of the statute achieving such con-
> sequences is an inadmissible one.[26]

The order denying appeal was vacated and the cause remanded
to the District Court for proceedings consistent with the above
opinion.

In a similar case decided a month later,[27] the Court in a
per curiam opinion vacated the Circuit Court's order and remanded the case to it for further consideration in the light of
the Adkins case. Without going into the lower court cases
again or without threshing over the records and briefs in the
Adkins case, it was evident that the High Court followed the
minority decisions of the lower courts and the argument and
briefs of the Solicitor-General of the United States. The latter's view as to group liability for costs and the more detailed
affidavits to inform of their actual inability to pay all or some
of the costs, varied slightly from the Supreme Court's holding.
In fact the particular view of the Solicitor's Office had never
been brought up in any case read by the author. For the most
part the conclusions of the High Court were based upon one or
another of the lower court decisions. The resulting rules,
whether of service or disservice to the community, passed
from the particular to the general.

In non-criminal cases, then, the Court made fairly defini-
tive rules governing the inclusion and exclusion of persons
who were to take the oath of poverty in order to enjoy the
advantages of the Indigent Code. Its rule concerning the
meaning of "poverty" was more negative than positive, but
it was still valuable in that it compelled the lower courts to
be more liberal after 1948. In criminal cases of course, there
could be no doubt who had to take the oath of poverty in order
to proceed as a poor person and the measure of poverty went
along with the general rule set up for those cases that came
under the head of civil procedures.[28]

It took the Supreme Court a long time to do away with the
procedural gloss resulting from the almost unlimited discretion
the lower courts found in the terms of the statute which was
considered in the Adkins case. The High Court itself had

INDIGENT CODE OF 1892, AS AMENDED

paid little attention to the meaning of important terms of the Indigent Code until 1948, and there was confusion as to which of the lower-court hierarchy was to have authority to pass on the eligibility for proceeding *in forma pauperis*. Indeed the Supreme Court's own changing rules and those of civil and criminal procedures made by that agency on a delegated basis only hesitatingly and haltingly provided for the moneyless man. The Attorney-General's assistants were in fact regularly confessing error in procedure under the Indigent Code, and many of the private attorneys were showing their ignorance in the handling of the poor man's cases, a fact that did not exactly encourage the poor to look upon their counsel as their benefactors. Why should there not have been confusion?

The Supreme Court in 1948 definitely limited the lower courts' discretion concerning the meaning of "poverty" and determining who should sign the oath of poverty. The same authority, instead of limiting the federal courts' discretion in the interpretation of such terms in the law as "frivolous," "malicious," "in good faith," and their equivalents (such as "meritorious" or "lack of merit"), encouraged the interpretation by denying certiorari or approving the actions of the lower courts. It was not until the 1950's that the High Court began to put definite limits to the trial and appellate courts' discretion in such cases. To be sure the first section of the 1892 legislation gave some direction for judging frivolity of a poor man's suit: the oath of poverty was to include a statement that the affiant believed that his cause called for relief and that he was to give sufficient facts to prove the sincerity of his actions.[29] It was assumed by the author that the trial court had exercised wide discretion in interpreting the term "frivolous" and its variations in non-criminal procedure, as it had done in giving meaning to the term "poverty" before the amendment of 1910, since there was no general practice of appeal before and none after 1892.

Between 1910 and the 1940's the discretion exercised in allowing appeals in both criminal and civil cases fell either to the trial court or to the appellate court. The better practice called for the trial court, but the confused situation permitted an indigent to go directly to the appellate court — which then acted as the original court in determining whether the action was taken "in good faith."

Habeas corpus appeals were civil in nature and after 1938 were definitely placed in that category of cases.[30] During the first years of the 1940's the courts of appeals began to instruct *in forma* litigants that they, as appellants, must give the trial courts the opportunity to pass on the eligibility of of the appellant; that in case the trial court refused to act on the matter, the appellate courts had jurisdiction to act as if they were the trial courts.[31]

The Supreme Court in 1915 attempted to explain the meaning of the Indigent Act of 1892 and its 1910 amendment in a case where the grounds for appeal from the court of appeals were quite ridiculous.[32] Chief Justice White spoke first to the original act:

> That statute imposed no imperative duty to grant a request to proceed as a poor person but merely conferred authority to do so when the ... case was found not to be frivolous, that is, was considered to be sufficiently meritorious to justify allowance of the request.

Again, to the amendment of 1910:

> ... it is clear that as to the new subject, the allowance of the right in those cases (appellate) was made to depend upon the exercise of the same discretion as to the meritorious character of the cause to the same extent provided under the statute before amendment.

After the 1915 essay of the Chief Justice on the meaning of the Indigent Code as amended in 1910, in so far as frivolousness and meritlessness were concerned, the lower courts paid little attention to the merits of an action until near the end of the 1930's.[33] They did not, however, in a majority of cases give up their application of the merit principle; they were often fortified by the denial of certiorari and final decisions of the Supreme Court. The Court had clarified the poor man's situation as regards the gloss on the oaths of poverty in 1938, some ten years earlier than it had begun to restrict the wide discretion exercised in matters of merit. The more detailed history follows.

Before 1938 the power of the district judge to refuse appeals to indigents in both civil and criminal cases under the amended Indigent Code of 1892[34] did not seem to worry litigants or courts to any appreciable extent. In that year, in a New Deal land mortgage case, a court of appeals held that an application to appeal *in forma pauperis* from a district court's adverse decision could not be allowed because the trial judge had certified that the action was not taken in good faith and the judgment "was supported" by the Supreme Court.[35] For a time it seems that the Wragg case was cited as authority for the broad discretion of the trial judge in cutting off appeals by poor persons, whether in civil or criminal actions.[36] Indeed, there was little thought given to the distinction between civil and criminal procedures, even after the Supreme Court was empowered to promulgate rules governing such procedures especially with respect to the discretion of trial judges in withholding appeals to indigents.

Other cases decided before 1945 indicated some thought on the part of appellate courts that it would be wise to examine more closely the reasons for refusing *in forma* appeals.[37] Welles, convicted of bank robbery and several other crimes, had been given a life sentence which he later got reduced. He then asked for habeas corpus on the ground that he had pleaded guilty without the aid of counsel but the case was dismissed. Welles then decided to try *in forma* appellate procedure. The Wragg decision was cited and accepted to a certain extent on the plea of Government counsel that the trial court's certification of lack of merit was non-reviewable. But the decision against the defendant-appellant turned, not directly upon the Government's argument, but upon the fact that the would-be appellant failed to answer the averment of the district judge's certificate and of the argument of the prosecuting attorney. The Supreme Court might have acted differently had Welles offered a sound argument against frivolity.[38] The High Court in the Steffler case,[39] an "original proceeding,'' forced upon both the trial court and the appellate court the correct procedure under the Indigent Code, as of 1943. Steffler had tried various procedures to overcome the judgment during a six-year period. He had gone finally to the trial court to have the judgment vacated but failed. He then applied for permission to appeal, first to the district court which certified lack of merit, and then to the appellate court which turned down his request. The Supreme Court granted certiorari and free service. It found that the district court had improperly refused to entertain an application for appeal *in forma pauperis*, since there had been no hearing to get at the facts of the case (that is, the justification for the lower court's action) and that the appellate court had similarly erred. After the cases were sent back for reconsideration, the court was satisfied. However, there was a warning that something more than certification was necessary.

Then came the civil case, Waterman *v.* McMillan,[40] which endeavored to outline the true procedure (civil or criminal), apparently, for *in forma* appeals from certificate of denial issued by the trial court: the certificate of the trial judge must be given effect, at least to the extent of being accepted by the appellate court in the absence of some showing that the judge's certificate was made without warrant or was itself not made in good faith.

The Welles and Steffler cases, together with Waterman *v.* McMillan, indicated that lower courts, under the guidance of the High Court, had moved to the position that the trial court's certificate of lack of merit depriving the indigent person of appeal was not the final word. From 1945 to 1957 this view was in competition with the old view of "no merit, no appeal." This was true only in criminal procedure, although the Waterman decision did not apply the procedural rules that were laid out for appeals *in forma pauperis*. Some appellate courts[41] adopted the practice of appointing counsel to look more carefully into *in forma* cases after conviction, when the appeals court saw some merit in the appeal, even though the trial court had certified that there was none. A few appellate courts[42] allowed *in forma* appeals, regardless of the negation by the trial court, while others held that the certification was

without warrant or arbitrary.[43] Still other courts held that a substantial question had been presented by the defendant-appellant and, hence, the certification of no merit was erroneous. Such a decision caused some hard thinking on whether the appearance of a substantial question necessarily was equivalent to no merit, or frivolousness.[44] Before 1957 any procedures, such as the motion under 28 Stat., Sec. 2255 and habeas corpus, having to do with ascertaining whether a person was in detention legally were excepted from certain aspects of procedure that were a part of the criminal process directly.[45] In none of the cited *in forma* appeals (between 1945-1947) was there a full identification of the steps to be taken by the indigent applicant.

NOTES TO CHAPTER V

[1]Application of the Black rule of 1938 relative to court-appointed counsel in criminal cases is reserved for Chapter XII.

[2]Esquibel *v*. Atchison and Topeka Railway Co., 206 F. 863, 1913.

[3]Silvas *v*. Arizona Copper Company, 213 F. 504, 1914.

[4]Kinney *v*. Plymouth Rock Squab Co., 236 U.S. 43, 45-46. 1915.

[5]Boggan *v*. Provident Life & Accident Insurance Co., 79 F. 2nd 721, 1935; Carter *v*. Kurn, 120 F. 2nd 261, 1941; *In re* American Mounting and Dye Cutting Co., 126 F. 2nd 419, 1942.

[6]Bolt *v*. Reynolds Metal Co., 42 Fed. Supp. 58, 1941; De Hay *v*. Cline, 5 Fed. Supp. 630, 1933; U.S. *ex rel.* Randolph *v*. Ross, Dist. Judge, 298 F. 64, 1924; Esquibel *v*. A. T. and S. F. Ry. Co. 206 F. 863, 1913.

[7]Silvas *v*. Arizona Copper Co., 213 F. 504, 1914.

[8]Chekovitch *v*. United States, 47 F. 2nd 894, 1931, cert. denied.

[9]U.S. *ex rel.* Payne *v*. Call, Dist. Judge, 287 F. 520, 1923.

[10]206 F. 863, 1913.

[11]Clark *v*. United States, 57 F. 2nd 214, 1932. Quittner *v*. Motion Pictures Producers, 70 F. 2nd 331, 1934, was a similar decision, but added that the old rule was merely a local district court rule and was not found in the 1892 Act, as amended.

[12]Clark *v*. United States, 57 F. 2nd 214, 1932.

[13]Evans *v*. Stivers Lumber Co., 2 F.R.D. 548, 1942.

[14]Jacobs *v*. No. La. and Gulf. Ry. Co., 69 Fed. Supp. 5, 1946.

[15]28 U.S.C.A. Sec. 852, 1940.

[16]Ruby *et Ux*. *v*. Federal Land Bank, 19 F. 2nd 549, 1937.

[17]Jacobs *v.* No. La. and Gulf Ry. Co., 69 Fed. Supp. 5, 1946.

[18]Kinney *v.* Plymouth Rock Squab Co., 236, U.S. 43, 45-46, 1915.

[19]See *supra,* p. 68.

[20]52 Stat. 1060, 1069, ch. 676, 1938, as amended by 61 Stat., 84, ch. 52, 1947, plus certain Executive Orders, leading up to the Adkins *v.* Dupont Co., 335 U.S. 331, 1948, the final appeal.

[21]The material dealing with the history of the Adkins case was found in 335 Supreme Court Records and Briefs 331 ff., Library of Congress Law Division, hereafter cited as S. Ct. R. and B., L.D.

[22]*Ibid.;* Adkins *v.* The Dupont Company, 335 U.S. 331, 1948. The court got its material given above from the oral arguments resulting from its Order before granting certiorari and leave to appeal *in forma pauperis.*

[23]335 S. Ct. R. and B. 331, 1948; Government's Brief, pp. 31-33 esp.

[24]Adkins *v.* Dupont Co., 335 U.S. 331, 1948.

[25]Quote from law taken from Indigent Code, 28 U.S.C.A. 832, 1948.

[26]Dupont case, pp. 339-40.

[27]Roberts *v.* Memphis St. Ry. Co., 335 U.S. 889, 1948.

[28]Supreme Court Rule number 53 uses this case for governing the conditions of free service for both civil and criminal cases.

[29]Whelan *v.* Manhattan Ry. Co., 86 F. 219, 1898.

[30]Rules of Civil Procedure, Rule 81(a), (2) as of 1940.

[31]See Smith *v.* Johnston, Warden, 109 F. 2nd 152, 1940, for a habeas corpus case; for a civil case, Waterman *v.* McMillan, 135 F. 2nd 807, 1943, certiorari denied, 322 U.S. 749, 1944. The matter referred to here was historical.

[32]Kinney *v.* Plymouth Squab Co., 326 U.S. 43, 45, 1915

[33]It should be recalled that the appellate court in Clark *v.* United States, 57 F. 2nd 214, 1932, declared that a man should not by reason of poverty be denied the right to prosecute *in forma pauperis* in a meritorious case. See also *Ex parte* Rosier, 133 F. 2nd, 316, 1943, certiorari denied, 321 U.S. 754, 1944.

[34]28 U.S.C. ,Sec. 832 as of 1938.

[35]*In re* Wragg, 95 F. 2nd 252, 1938, certiorari denied, 305 U.S. 596, 1938.

[36]*E.g.*, Stanley *v.* Swope, 99 F. 2nd 308, 1938; Smith *v.* Johnston, 109 F. 2nd 152, 1940; Nix *v.* United States, 131 F. 2nd 857, 1942 (certiorari denied, 318 U.S. 771, 1943); two *in forma* mandamus cases, Stewart *v.* St. Sure, 109 F. 2nd 162, 1940 (certiorari denied, 309 U.S. 653, 1940), and Prince *v.* Klune, 148 F. 2nd 18, 1945.

[37]Welles *v.* United States, 318 U.S. 257, 1943 (citing Wragg case). Steffler *v.* United States, 319 U.S. 38, 1943 ("original"), Waterman *v.* McMillan, 135 F. 2nd 807, 1943 (certiorari denied, 322 U.S. 749, 1944).

[38]Chief Justice Stone in the *Stone Papers* (Box 42, 1943, L.C.), gives this version of the case: "We think that, whereas in this case, leave is necessary to perfect the appeal, the certification must be given effect to the extent of being accepted by the appellate court as controlling in the absence of some showing that the certificate is made without warrant or not in good faith.

"We have no occasion to decide now what effect should be given to a certificate of bad faith in a case where the jurisdiction of the Circuit Court of Appeals is attacked upon the mere filing of the notice of appeal, independently of any application for leave to appeal as a poor person."

This last paragraph suggests that the procedural failure on the part of the defendant-appellant might have weighed heavily in the result.

[39]Steffler *v.* United States, 319 U.S. 38, 1943.

[40]Waterman *v.* McMillan, 135 F. 2nd 807, 1943 (certiorari denied,

322 U.S. 749, 1944; rehearing denied, 323 U.S. 812, 1946).

[41]*E.g.*, Taylor *v.* Steele, 194 F. 2nd 864, 1952.

[42]*E.g.*, Bernstein *v.* United States, 195 F. 2nd 517, 1952 (certiorari denied, 343 U.S. 980, 1952).

[43]*E.g.*, Higgins *v.* Steele, 195 F. 2nd 366, 1952; Passell *v.* United States, 215 F. 2nd 232, 1955.

[44]Jordan *v.* United States, 232 F. 2nd 262, 1956.

[45]*E.g.*, Newman *v.* United States, 87 U.S. Appls. D. C. 419, 1950 (certiorari denied, 340 U.S. 921, 1950; habeas corpus dismissed and appeal denied); Minntole *v.* Johnston, 147 F. 2nd 944, 1945 (certiorari denied, 324 U.S., 831, 1945).

CHAPTER VI

SUPREME COURT REVIEW OF STATE DECISIONS ON CONSTITUTIONAL GROUNDS: INDIGENT PROCEDURE, CIVIL AND CRIMINAL, 1789-1922

1. GENERAL PROCEDURE: ERROR AND APPEAL

The meaning of Section 25 of the 1789 Judiciary Act[1] was much disputed after the Civil War. That section certainly gave the Supreme Court an appellate jurisdiction by writ of error and appeal over non-criminal cases from state courts of law and equity. Judgments and decrees of such courts the Supreme Court could examine, reverse or affirm by error in the following situations: 1) where the question arose concerning the validity of a statute or treaty of, or an authority exercised under, the United States and the decision was against their validity; 2) where there was a question regarding the validity of a statute of, or an authority exercised by, any state on the ground of their being repugnant to the Constitution, statutes, and treaties of the United States and the decision was in favor of such validity; and 3) where any clause of the Constitution, treaty, statute, or commission held under the United States was put in question, and the decision was against the title, right, privilege, or exemption specifically set up and *claimed by either party.* (The italicized words indicate non-criminal action.)

Under this statute important state civil cases were reviewed by the Supreme Court on writ of error or appeal, just as important federal civil cases were brought up for review. No record of a criminal case was found, however, where review was exercised by the High Court, at least before the Civil War and before the national government begrudged the states' criminal jurisdiction.[2] Even review of capital cases originating in the federal courts could not reach the Supreme

Court on direct review before 1889, with the exception of those involving the division-of-opinion rule. After the War the Chase and Waite Courts succeeded in protecting the states from complete civil and criminal vassalage to the rather victory-mad Unionists.

In 1867 Congress had reenacted Section 25 of the 1789 Judiciary Act, changing the third category of reviewable cases to read in part as follows:[3]

> ...or when any right, title, privilege or immunity is claimed under the Constitution, treaty, statute, or commission held or authority exercised under the United States and the decision is against such right,...the decision may be reviewed by writ of error.

Beyond this the Fourteenth Amendment, originally proposed as a partial support for the 1867 Act, was ratified in July, 1868.

A Pennsylvania death penalty case[4] came up for argument before the full Court concerning whether a writ of error in a criminal case could legally be sent to the final court of the state. The murder had taken place before any change in the federal law had been made. The petitioner grounded his petition for the writ of error solidly on Fifth Amendment due process and the Sixth Amendment right to be informed of the nature of the accusation. He claimed that both rights had been taken away by a state law. Mr. Chief Justice Chase, speaking for the Court, conceded that neither the Judiciary Act of 1789 nor the restatement in the 1867 Act had made any distinction between civil and criminal cases in respect to revision of judgments of state courts by the Supreme Court; that his Court was not aware that it had ever been contended that such distinction existed; and that, certainly, his Court had never recognized such distinction. After explaining the technicalities of the writ of error procedure, he remarked:

> We are by no means prepared to say that, if it were an open question, whether the 5th and 6th Amendments apply to State Governments it would not be our duty to allow the writ applied for and hear

argument on the question of repugnancy. We think,
indeed, that it would.

After this apparently political nod to the radicals in Congress,
the Chief Justice refused the writ on the ground that the
Court had decided again and again that the Bill of Rights
limited the Federal Government, not the states.[5]

From the standpoint of federal *in forma pauperis* procedure,
it mattered little whether the first Judiciary Act bestowed
appellate jurisdiction on the Supreme Court over final judgments of state courts in criminal cases. There was neither
statutory provision nor judicial rule of practice for helping
the indigent in any category of criminal cases not originating
in federal courts. Not until 1889 was the common law rule of
one-court consideration of felonious acts partially discarded
by statute in federal cases. After that time, review in some
form by a superior federal court became the rule and the impoverished person was given more or less aid in appellate
procedure.

Once this principle of aid to the poor was established in
the federal courts, the Supreme Court did *not* hesitate to
extend it to cases that had begun to flow from the final state
courts into its own appellate jurisdiction. Clauses of the
original Constitution, Reconstruction legislation, and the
Civil War amendments followed by enforcing statutes began to
produce results in the 1880's and 1890's, especially in the
latter decade. Negro capital cases came up by writ of error
to the state courts, after 1875, on the basis of the Revised
Statute (beginning at Section 641), which provided for removal
from a state court to a federal court when the discriminatory
clause of the Fourteenth Amendment was alleged to have been
violated. Procedure in choosing grand and petit juries caused
most of the trouble. The only public aid given the petitioners,
so far as the record indicated, was free counsel.[6]

Chief Justice Fuller's court (1888-1910) developed pauper
proceeding for capital and some less serious cases beginning
in 1890. While the Supreme Court was very technical in deciding state (and organized territory)[7] appeals, it commonly
gave petitioners every chance to prove their points, regardless

of the view of the Court in the final decisions. The procedure, as a rule, ran like this: petition for filing of writ of error; motion to proceed *in forma pauperis*, with accompanying affidavit of poverty; motion to have record printed at public expense. The Court would usually grant one or more of the requests. Nothing was noted as to appointment of counsel, but it should be assumed that this was done unless the defense was carried on *pro se* or by some person or organization that had shouldered the burden.[8]

The prosecution of a writ of error (already noted above) to the highest state court in a civil case under the *in forma pauperis* Statute of 1892 was definitely refused a man named Galloway in 1902.[9] In fact the attempt of a poor person to appeal by writ of error to the United States Supreme Court from the highest court of a state was met with refusal on the general ground of lack of specific legislative authority. This decision anticipated a similar denial of any appeal by poor persons from federal court decisions. Therefore there was no successful attempt to go to the Supreme Court from a civil state decision between 1892 and the year 1910, when appeals were allowed to be prosecuted *in forma pauperis*. Between 1910 and 1922, the end of the period under consideration, no examples of civil cases were unearthed in which appeals were prosecuted *in forma pauperis* to the Supreme Court from the state courts.

2. SPECIAL PROCEDURE FOR STATE PRISONERS;
HABEAS CORPUS

Freedom from arbitrary imprisonment or detention was early considered by English judges to be a precious part of personal liberty, whether such detention arose from criminal or civil actions. Common law judges and commentators often stated with pride that their law furnished a remedy for every legal wrong even though the wrong could not be prevented. The writ of habeas corpus was the great remedy for freeing a person illegally held in detention without good reason and a procedure was developed for ascertaining the reason, if one existed. Some legal historians have argued that this great writ, under the skillful direction of the judges, had developed from an earlier one by the same name that had been a means of getting persons into prison.[10] This legal mechanism followed the migration from England; it became a part of the states' procedure and appeared in the federal Constitution in a negative form: "The privilege of Habeas Corpus shall not be suspended, unless ... the public Safety may require it...."[11]

Presumably the constitutional provision foreshadowed the protection of those held in prison by any authority of the Federal Government without just cause. The constitutional provision however was too general. Specific legislation was necessary if full discretion was not to be left to the courts to apply the clause in specific cases. Congress took the initiative in providing for the issuing of the writ in the First Judiciary Act of 1789.[12] All courts of the United States, as well as the individual Justices of the Supreme Court and judges of the lower courts, were empowered to issue the writ of habeas corpus and all other writs not specifically provided for by statute that might be necessary "for the exercise of their respective jurisdictions and agreeable to the principles and usages of (common) law."[13] This provision, bent one way or another by the courts, served as the basic habeas corpus statute for federal purposes beyond 1922, and the laws passed since 1789 were definitely considered by Congress to be extensions of, not substitutes for, the original.

In 1833 Congress projected federal habeas corpus jurisdiction onto certain state court actions in order to anticipate the application of the South Carolina Nullification Resolution, although compromise made the narrow extension of no immediate importance.[14] Some years later Congress gave the Supreme Court appellate jurisdiction over habeas corpus actions of lower federal courts and all state courts where a specified category of aliens was involved.[15] Powers of the United States courts and the several justices and judges manning them were enlarged in 1867, by allowing the grant of writs of habeas corpus in all cases where persons were "restrained of their liberty in violation of the Constitution, treaties and laws of the United States."[16] The procedure, always formally civil, for granting the writs was laid down in the statute and was later interpreted to mean that decisions of the original issuing courts, federal or state, could finally reach the Supreme Court on appeal. Chief Justice Chase said of the law:[17]

> This legislation is of the most comprehensive character. It brings within the habeas corpus jurisdiction of every court and of every judge every possible case of prevention of liberty, contrary to the National Constitution, treaties or laws. It is impossible to widen this jurisdiction.

This extension of the 1789 provision is often referred to as the "Great Federal Habeas Corpus Act," for the reason that now the writ potentially could be issued in behalf of both federal and state petitioners imprisoned on accusation, indictment, trial, or conviction.

Emphasis upon the writ of habeas corpus, its procedure and the jurisdiction of the national judiciary over the writ, had its justification at this time in that the uses of the writ for the protection of those illegally detained were worked out by judicial rule and statute (and later in the twentieth century were to be of great help to the indigent). In fact it was of little use to the poor in federal criminal cases until the latter part of the nineteenth century. The greatest help to the impoverished federal prisoner did not begin until 1938, although there were cases where the ruling of the judiciary foreshadowed its wider use.

Two early cases of habeas corpus were decided by the Supreme Court during the first twenty years of that body's existence—a period when the Court had to explore the meaning of the great common law writ and, at the same time, interpret the jurisdiction bestowed upon itself and the inferior courts. Both cases involved charges of the capital crime of treason: United States *v.* Hamilton grew out of the Scotch-Irish Bourbon Whiskey Insurrection of 1791;[18] the Bollman-Swartwout case was a part of the Aaron Burr Treason Plot.[19] The Act of 1790[20] gave very definite advantages to persons who were tried for treason and other capital crimes. The two cases, however, had they involved indigent persons, would not have fitted into any then existing laws providing for free service for the impoverished. Both cases had to do with commitment to prison on charge of treason. Indictment and trial were in the future. Counsel for Hamilton claimed that he had been clapped into prison without a hearing and asked that the Court either discharge him or grant bail. The Supreme Court granted bail at its discretion, as the law provided in capital cases.[21] There was little, if any, evidence to justify detention by a district judge, argued defense counsel, and therefore the prisoners should have been discharged, and the Court so ordered. As a matter of fact not one of them had been confined under judgment of a court. Perhaps the freeing of persons thrown into prison by officers of the government was the first use of the writ to prevent unlawful restraint.[22] In the Bollman case, Chief Justice Marshall remarked that habeas corpus could not be used to pass on the guilt or innocence of those held in custody, but was a means of determining the lawfulness of their incarceration.

Other federal cases, obviously free from pauper procedure, held that habeas corpus could not be used in criminal cases to review a judgment of an inferior court. The rationale of this holding seemed to be that the Supreme Court could not do indirectly (attack collaterally) that which it could not do directly (attack by writ of error or certiorari), since the Court had no direct criminal appellate jurisdiction.[23] Defense counsel in the Watkins case insisted that the High Court had used habeas corpus, aided by certiorari, as early as 1806[24] to review and nullify a lower court judgment in a criminal case. The Court's reply was that the inferior court had given no judgment to revise or nullify.

After the passage of the Habeas Corpus Act of 1867,[25] the Supreme Court had habeas corpus appellate jurisdiction in connection with criminal cases coming up from federal and state courts. Even with this broad power of application of the writ, the Supreme Court still had the task of wresting the meaning of the writ from the old common law complex or adding a meaning of its own. Two original habeas corpus cases, both decided before the Court had been given direct criminal appellate jurisdiction in non-capital cases, uttered a rule for the use of habeas corpus that was to be of great utility to

prisoners, especially to the impoverished ones: the Supreme Court, even without criminal appellate jurisdiction, could discharge on habeas corpus a person imprisoned in a criminal case, under sentence of a circuit or district court of the United States, if the sentence exceeded the jurisdiction of that court or if there was no legal authority to hold such person under the sentence.

In the Wilson case,[26] non-indigent in procedure, the petitioner had been indicted *on information* of the United States district attorney for the commission of two infamous crimes and had been sentenced for a long term at hard labor in the penitentiary. The petitioner's counsel claimed a) that the district court had exceeded its statutory power by entertaining cases of infamous crimes and b) that even if the court had not exceeded its power in that respect, it had violated due process by disregarding the requirement of the Fifth Amendment that all persons accused of infamous crimes had to be indicted by grand jury. The court decided in favor of the prisoner and discharged him. Five years later the Mills case[27] came up for consideration and the Supreme Court decided that a federal district court in the Indian Territory had gone beyond its authority in the category of crime and punishment provided by law. The Wilson case was quoted at length as a basis for the decision, and the petitioner was released from custody.

These two decisions were alike in principle, but that of Mills involved the *in forma pauperis* procedure under court rule rather than legislative permission. The Fuller Court (1888-1910) was ready to step in where the Congress had not prohibited, as in vouching for the non-capital prisoners of federal origin and capital prisoners of state origin in direct appeals (error or appeal). Cases of state origin after 1892 could not be brought up by the direct method if criminal in nature, but could be saved under the poor man's procedure provided they came up by the habeas corpus route, because of peculiarities explained below.

In re Frederick[28] came up from the old type circuit court in the State of Washington. Frederick had been found guilty of murder and condemned to death. He had appealed to the State Supreme Court on error, alleging that the state constitution had been violated in that the evidence presented did not measure up to first degree murder, only the second. The State Supreme Court agreed and sent the case back with orders for the trial court to change the charge and reduce the penalty to 20 years in the penitentiary without a new jury trial, a power apparently found in many of the highest state courts. Instead of going on to the United States Supreme Court for writ of error to the State Court, he was advised to ask for federal habeas corpus. He did so and the ɪederal circuit court agreed with his allegation that the State Supreme Court had violated the Fourteenth Amendment due process clause because a question of fact and law had been decided without a new trial with jury. However, the circuit court did not release the prisoner on the technical ground that habeas corpus was not the proper remedy at that point in the history of the case: the remedy was to go to the United States Supreme Court for a writ of error to the Washington Supreme Court.

The judge of the federal circuit court in the State of Washington, upon receiving the affidavit of Frederick's lawyer that his client was without property, money, or friends, ordered "that the usual cost and fees for the appeal herein for the order and decree from this court refusing to issue a writ of habeas corpus herein be remitted and that the clerk of this court be ordered, and that he is hereby ordered to transmit record in this case as set forth in the notice of appeal herein to the Supreme Court of the United States."[29] On receiving the material along with the motion to appeal as a poor person, the High Court granted the motion and ordered that the record be printed "at public expense." Counsel was also appointed.

The Supreme Court, after approving the action of the lower court with respect to the decision of the State Supreme Court and after refusing to pass on the possible antagonism between the decision and the Fourteenth Amendment due process clause, affirmed the principal conclusion of the lower federal court that habeas corpus should be a last resort and that a request for a writ of error to the State Supreme Court should have been taken. Mr. Justice Jackson, speaking for the Court, said that the writ of habeas corpus had been and still was one of the remedies for the enforcement of the right of personal freedom and security of life, that it would not issue as a matter of course and should be used cautiously by federal courts in dealing with state prisoners. He warned once more, since habeas corpus was a civil process, it should not be converted into a remedy for the correction of errors of judgment or of procedure in the court having cognizance of the criminal offense; that the Supreme Court would exercise no appellate jurisdiction of state courts nor review their conclusions of law or fact. He backed up his statements by quoting Mr. Justice Bradley in *Ex parte* Siebold (1879), in which that learned Justice stated clearly, with citations, the difference between cases, state or federal, where the writ would be applied and where it would not:[30]

> The only ground on which this court, or any other court, without some special statute authorizing it, will give relief on habeas corpus to a prisoner under conviction and sentence of another court, is the want of jurisdiction in such court over the person or the cause, or some other matter rendering the proceeding void.... The reason for this lies in the fact that a habeas corpus proceeding is a collateral attack of a civil nature to impeach the validity of the judgment or sentence of another court in a criminal proceeding, and it should, therefore, be limited to cases in which judgment or sentences attacked is clearly void by reason of its having been rendered without jurisdiction or by reason of *the court's having exceeded its jurisdiction in the premises.*   (Emphasis supplied.)

Justice Bradley then took particular pains to inform all persons interested that the Court should keep in mind the above distinction because the only decision possible in a well-supported case was the discharge of the prisoner. According to him, this was a very serious matter: the petitioner was in prison pursuant to a judgment of a state court and the state would lose control over the case absolutely, thereby affecting the jurisdictional balance of the *federal* system. It was also suggested that the *cave canem* marked the beginning of the judicial rule and its later expression in statute of "exhaust your state remedies before coming to the federal courts for habeas corpus."[31]

The freedom of appeal to the Supreme Court by prisoners held pursuant to state court judgment for review of habeas corpus proceedings under claimed federal rights was giving the Court a bit of anxiety. Congress offered certain limitations on such appeals in 1908.[32] The heart of the statute was that the federal court that had made a final decision, or a Justice of the High Court, had to give a certificate of probable cause before the Court would or could accept jurisdiction. This provision was carried over into all the restatements of the Habeas Corpus Code and now rests in the 1948 Code as 28 U.S.C., Section 2254, a section to be noted later.

NOTES TO CHAPTER VI

[1]1 Stat. 73, 83, Sec. 25, 1789. See Appendix B-I for modes of appellate jurisdiction.

[2]Logan *v.* United States, 144 U.S. 263, 1892.

[3]14 Stat. 385, Ch. 28, Sec. 2, 1867.

[4]Twitchell *v.* The Commonwealth, 7 Wall. 321, 1868.

[5]Cases cited were civil ones: *e.g.*, Baron *v.* City of Baltimore, 7 Pet. 243, 1833, and Withers *v.* Buckley, 20 How. 84, 90, 1857.

[6]For instance: Tennessee *v.* Davis, 100 U.S. 257, 1879; Strauder *v.* W. Va., 100 U.S. 303, 1879; Va. *v.* Rives, 100 U.S. 313, 1879; Neal *v.* Delaware, 103 U.S. 370, 1880; Bush *v.* Ky., 107 U.S. 110, 1882. Outside aid was not excluded.

[7]Organized territories had trial and appellate courts, the final judgment of which could go to the Supreme Court of the United States, especially after 1893.

[8]See Davis *v.* Ter. of Utah, 151 U.S. 262, 1894; Duncan *v.* Mo., 152 U.S. 377, 1893; Miller *v.* Texas, 153 U.S. 535, 1894; Murray *v.* La., 163 U.S. 101, 1896; Nobles *v.* Ga., 168 U.S. 398, 1897; Thompson *v.* Mo., 171 U.S. 380, 1898; Brown *v.* N.J., 175 U.S. 172, 1899; Carter *v.* Texas, 177 U.S. 442, 1900; Queenan *v.* Ter. of Okla., 190 U.S. 548, 1903. All of these cases were capital.

[9]Galloway *v.* Bank of Ft. Worth, 186 U.S. 177, 1902, followed by Bradford *v.* So. Ry. Co., 195 U.S. 243, 1904.

[10]*E.g.*, William Seagle, *The Quest for Law* (New York, 1941), p. 219, n. 22.

[11]Constitution, Art. I, Sec. 9.

[12]1 Stat. 73, 81-82, Sec. 14, 1789.

[13]Among the unnamed common law writs were the writ of certiorari, writ of error *coram nobis*, and writ of mandamus. Certiorari accompanied habeas corpus in criminal accusations, indictments, and

convictions, since habeas corpus alone did not suffice. See *Ex parte* Burford, 3 Cr. 448, 1806; *Ex parte* Bollman 4 Cr. 74, 1807; *Ex parte* Vallandigham, 1 Wall. 243, 1864; *Ex parte* McCardle, 6 Wall. 319, 324, 1867.

[14] 4 Stat. 634, Sec. 7, 1833.

[15] 5 Stat. 539, 1842; *Ex parte* Darr, 44 U.S. 103, 105, 1845, held that no general law permitted a federal court to issue a writ of habeas corpus to a person committed to prison under a criminal judgment of a state court.

[16] 14 Stat. 385, Ch. 28, Sec. 1, 1867.

[17] *Ex parte* McCardle, 6 Wall. 318, 325, 1867.

[18] 3 Dallas 17, 1795. Even this case had overtones of the question of separation from the Union.

[19] *Ex parte* Bollman, 4 Cr. 73, 94, 101, 1807.

[20] 1 Stat. 118, 1790.

[21] 1 Stat. 73, 91, Sec. 33, 1789.

[22] The late Justice Jackson wrote in Brown *v.* Allen, 344 U.S. 443, 473, 1953: "The historic purpose of the writ has been to relieve the detention by executive authorities without judicial 'trial'."

[23] *Ex parte* Kearney, 3 Cr. 448, 1808, and *Ex parte* Watkins, 3 Pet. 193, 1830.

[24] *Ex parte* Burford, 3 Cr. 448, 1806.

[25] 14 Stat. 385, Ch. 28, 1867.

[26] *Ex parte* Wilson, 114 U.S. 417, 1885.

[27] *In re* Mills, 135 U.S. 263, 1890.

[28] 149 U.S. 70, 1893.

[29]District Ct. Docket No. 15, 275, with original records, 1892, N. D. Washington State, as found in Supreme Court Docket 1,305, 1893.

[30]*Ex parte* Frederick, 149 U.S. 70, 76, 1893. For the latest style, see Townsend *v.* Sain, 372 U.S. 293, 1963.

[31]*Ex parte* Frederick, 149 U.S. 77, 1893.

[32]35 Stat. 40, Ch. 76, March 10, 1908.

PART I I

SUPREME COURT'S CLOSE SUPERVISION
OF INDIGENT PROCEDURE

1922-1963

CHAPTER VII

POSITION AND POWER

1. GENERAL

The Indigent Act of 1892, as amended in 1910 and 1922, had provided the poor man with the civil and criminal procedures by which he could sue or defend without cost to himself. There were some serious "bugs" in the procedure, to be sure, but the Court would find them sooner or later and call them to the attention of Congress or use the "do-it-yourself" method. The man with scant resources could enter the trial court and could reach the top of the appellate ladder, provided he had a reasonably strong legal basis or resorted to sharp practice. He could reach the apex of the judicial pyramid on error or appeal, whether his case began in a United States district court or in a municipal or state trial court, if federal jurisdiction existed. The 1922 statutory procedure in behalf of the poor person had placed the Supreme Court in a position to refine and add to the law by rulings in specific cases and had offered to the Court opportunity to provide almost complete liberty on the basis of the constitutional and statutory provisions upon which persons appealing could rely for protection.

Under the leadership of Waite, Fuller, and to some extent White, the Court had developed a powerful protection for individual property rights based upon laissez-faire philosophy. The individual rights contained in the Constitution and Amendments I - VIII were not altogether neglected in strictly federal matters, but the Slaughter-House Cases of 1873[1] had apparently defeated one of the alleged purposes of the Fourteenth Amendment, namely, the nationalization of the personal rights of state citizens. Even the Negro from 1890 on had little protection from claimed discrimination in state trials.[2]

But the Court had considerable confidence by 1900, perhaps because it had consistently supported the self-nationalization of business and industry. The prestige of the Court made it possible for it to continue the application of its laissez-faire outlook. The resulting "Golden Decade" of the Twenties, however, soon gave way to government interference in the national economy, a phenomenon fostered by the New Deal. Running parallel with the Court's conservative policy was a rather liberal attitude toward the civil liberties of the individual. After the New Deal policy had in large part been accepted, the protection of the liberties of the poor individual became exaggerated for a while; self-restraint was lacking in permitting cases to be brought up and, at times, in reversing and sending cases back to the lower federal and state courts for further examination. The rapid rise in the degree of "constitutional sensitivity," where personal rights were involved, was remarkable.

The prestige of the Court was built up after the Civil War largely as a result of its interpretation and use of Amendments I-VIII and XIV. The Court succeeded in establishing, for the federal Government at least, three categories of rights: 1) the substantive category, which included the rights of the First Amendment—those that were held to be inviolable by the federal Government; 2) the procedural category, represented by Amendments III-VIII—rights of procedures connected with arrest, arraignment, trial, and sentence in criminal cases, and certain procedures thought valuable in civil cases, such as trial by jury, a right twice stated in the Constitution as amended; 3) the category built up by court rulings in specific cases on the meaning of "nor shall any person...be deprived of life, liberty, or property, without due process of law," and the due process and equal protection clauses of the Fourteenth Amendment. This last category has been set up because the Court has used it to suit its timely purposes and the rights defined could be either substantive or procedural. Congress had and has power to add procedural rights that fit into category 2) or 3) (such as the right to be taken at once to a magistrate after arrest), but Congress cannot legislate the substantive rights, for permanence need not hold in legislation unless the Court weaves such rights into its own category of the inviolable, that is, constitutional rights.

In 1947 Charles P. Curtis, Jr. reminded students of constitutional history that James Madison's original plan had been to make the Bill of Rights (or some of them) binding upon both national and state governments.[3] This conception the states would not accept, and it took a Supreme Court decision as early as 1833 to assure them that the amendments limited the federal Government only.[4]

The principal clause of the Fourteenth Amendment remained dormant until the last decade of the nineteenth century. The Supreme Court, however, has used two parts of the Amendment to overcome much of what the decision of 1873 "had settled." Since that decision, the equal protection clause, through the Court's interpretation, has added a "steamboat-full," a "restaurant-hotel-full," a "train-full," a "bus-full," a "theater-full," a "public-school-full," a "college-university-full"—of rights on the theory that the person discriminated against cannot otherwise develop into a full-fledged citizen. Presumably, state action through any of its governmental agencies involving discrimination, regardless of its many manifestations, falls within the category of the substantive rights. The due process clause, like the Fifth Amendment due process plus the recent interpretation of the anti-discrimination clause, has done more to nationalize the substantive and procedural rights of the individual than any of the various amendments. And this nationalization is still going on. The Court can declare, and likely will be prompted by public opinion into declaring, that the freedom to secure an education at the expense of tne state is an inviolable one, and that state police power can be only used affirmatively, not negatively, in this area. In fact, anything that can be connected with resistance to the due process clause and to the discrimination clause of the Fourteenth Amendment is likely to fall into the jurisdiction of the national Government.

The *bête noir* that threatens the national set of rights found in Amendments I-VIII is the national Government; that responsible for violating the Fourteenth Amendment rights is the state government. Under Articles III and VI of the Constitution, the Supreme Court is the guardian of the Constitution and treaties and laws made thereunder, for the reason that the logic of the Constitution so dictates. But the Court, after all, consists of nine men; and five men, whoever they are at a particular time, may block the nationalization of personal rights or may push the movement with ardor. The "pushers," if consistent, have been referred to as "incorporation judges" and, if discriminative, "incorporative judges by special circumstances."[5] One writer has referred to such judges as those who use the "fundamental rights rule,"[16] Christopher Morley made up a witty but expressive name for the underdog sympathizers — "infracaninophile judges."[7] Other terms variously used are "humanitarian activists" and "preferred positionists or absolutists." All these terms seem to express the same meaning, although with different degrees of intensity. One or two come nearer to indicating those judges who are disposed to give the indigent man the best chance of freedom from a judgment below, or an amelioration of the original judgment, or simply a "run-around-rosy" that serves to put off the execution of the judgment for a period ranging from one to ten or more years.

The build-up of the power of the Court by 1922 had produced an awesomeness among the laity, the bar, and some of the judges of the lower federal and state courts. But at least one member of the Court itself approached his seat in that body with humility.[8] However, when William H. Taft became Chief Justice in 1921, he seemed not too greatly impressed either with the actual power being exerted by the Court or by its awesomeness. He wanted both, and was ready and willing to fight for recognizable indicia that would clarify to every interested person the real power and majesty that should accompany such a great institution, give it much financial independence, enable it to supervise the activities of the lower courts, and give it self-manipulation of the fundamental functions assigned to it by constitutional or statutory law. *Independence* was what the Chief Justice desired, and such a status Congress could do much toward establishing.

2. PARTIAL FINANCIAL INDEPENDENCE

Through the inaction of Congress, administrative decisions of Treasury officers, and incidental judicial backing,
the Supreme Court had become more or less independent in
aiding the poor man to reach its own jurisdiction. The clerks
of all courts of the national Government received as remuner-
ation, after subtracting official expenses, all fees and costs
taken in through the clerk's office. Between 1883 and 1921
the Clerk of the Supreme Court had had a statutory salary of
$6,000, which was to come from "fees, costs, and other
emoluments" taken in by the Clerk; the remainder, if any, had
to be turned into the Treasury. It was soon discovered that
the Clerk kept for himself all fees for admission to the Bar
of the Court and also interest on bank deposits derived from
moneys left with the Clerk by litigants for paying for services
to be rendered. Congress by inaction, Treasury comptrollers
through decisions, and the Court itself through the Court
of Claims, sanctioned this free money. The result was that the
Clerk took his official salary from the fees, costs, and emoluments and added the $8,000-$10,000 of free money, some of
which had to go for office expenses.[9] When Mr. Taft became
leader of the Court in 1921, he found that the Clerk was
receiving for his services and for running the office $3,000
more than the Justices of the Court.

The Chief Justice could not allow such a situation to
exist and on an Order of the Court the total income of the
Clerk was his statutory salary, plus $3,000 from the admis-
sion fees and interest on bank deposits.[10] The remainder of
the "free income" was left to the Court to make up any deficit in the management of the Clerk's office. The Court, after
further study of the free funds, made two Orders in 1921.[11] The
first Order (October 6) provided that admission fees, over
and above the $3,000 added by the Court to the Clerk's lawful
salary, should be kept as a special fund to be expended on
order of the Court for (a) the reimbursement of the Clerk for
any costs or fees in litigated cases in which the parties, or
either of them, were authorized to proceed *in forma pauperis*;
(b) the reimbursement of the Clerk for any deficit in managing

his office—apparently an attempt to stabilize his statutory salary; (c) and for providing for any other purpose deemed proper by the Court, a provision that supported (a). The second Order (October 10) provided for the setting aside in a special fund of the interest on bank deposits to cover the cost of an additional bond the Court set up to protect all interested parties from illegal actions of the Clerk; to cover non-governmental annual or special audits of funds deposited with the Clerk and their disposition; and to pay any deficits in the running of the Clerk's office or salary.

The Budget and Accounting Act of 1921 was in effect about the time Mr. Taft came to the Court as Chief Justice. Mr. Lord, Director of the Budget, informed the Chief Justice that estimates for the Supreme Court could not be revised by the Bureau of the Budget. The Chief Justice replied that he had been cognizant of that fact but that his belief in the soundness of the budget system of the national Government would lead him to present, through the Marshal of the Court, estimates and reasons therefor.[12] A check by the author (in 1947) indicated that the Court's estimates sent to the President had never been discussed before they reached Congress. That body itself, or its proper committee, usually engaged in some debate while the estimates were under consideration, but there was little if any cutting down of the original requests for operating expenses. Expenditures of the Court from money appropriated, when approved by the Chief Justice, were not checked even for arithmetical errors, according to a high official in the Comptroller's Office.[13]

Salaries for the important officers of the Court had been named by Congress before 1948 and the General Accounting Office would not allow any reduction of a named salary. Unexpended funds from the "fees, costs, and other emoluments" gathered from litigants furnished funds for paying the salary of the Clerk and certain other expenses of the Office.[14] By 1948 the Court had so established itself in the confidence of Congress that it was given complete power over the hiring and firing of the Clerk of the Court and all his aides, over their salaries which came from the non-free collections by the Clerk, and over other important officers whose salaries were to come from appropriated funds. Non-free fees and costs collected by the Clerk were still required to be turned into the Treasury after legitimate expenses had been subtracted.[15]

3. A "CASTLE OF ITS OWN"

Logically, the agency that is at the apex of the national judicial system should be possessed of a home of its own, expressive of its power and dignity. It should not be forced to dwell in a sub-standard tenement house which the Senate had abandoned for better quarters and which could not be recognized by the public, was altogether inadequate as to space, and could not be completely controlled by the tenant whose landlord was the Senate. When Taft became Chief of the Court, he found most of its members were so accustomed to the "landlordism" of the Senate that it took him some four years to persuade them to join him in lobbying for a proper home of their own. By 1925 they were successful in obtaining authorization and funds for building a Greek temple on a trapezoidal area facing the Capitol.[16] The Court moved to the new home in 1935, some five years after the death of Taft. In this "manor house," the Court rules supreme over both physical property and the human beings that labor or visit there.

It was during the decade of the Thirties that the prestige of the Court began to rise in the estimation of the poor and the untouchable and to continue, with some occasional slip-backs, to the present time. Now individuals or groups under the two categories seem to populate the Supreme Court Building rather than the Capitol or the White House: the "Grecian Temple" is the symbol of the power of the Supreme Court, power no single word is sufficiently strong to describe.

4. JUDICIAL ADMINISTRATIVE AGENCY AND RULE-MAKING

Chief Justice Taft initiated two reforms that enabled the Court to supervise judicial administration of the courts below and to review at its sound discretion what it considered doubtful decisions having to do with both rich and poor.

Pauper proceedings in the year 1922 were of great assistance to poor men but it was impossible for the Supreme Court to supervise the lower or intermediate courts: the power to review in specific cases is not the power to administer.[17] The poor man was too often caught in a judicial system which lacked an effective administration of judicial matters. Two Harvard Law School professors argued in 1928 that Congress had created a hierarchy of courts but not of judges.[18] The judges seemed to form horizontal layers that spread throughout the land and to be immune from control from the top of the judicial pyramid. Their lack of responsibility for decisions made *as men* extended to every phase of the judicial business, and their current work could just as well have been that of the year before or even of a much earlier date. In some jurisdictions as late as the Thirties, according to President F. D. Roosevelt, the "delays in the administration of justice" were "so interminable that to institute suit" was "to embark on a life-long adventure."[19] It might well have been that the men who filled the judicial positions thought of the system as a kind of benevolent machine of several pieces that, if let alone, would produce valuable results to both individuals and the community. When judges remained on the bench until their dotage, this conviction so hardened that the President felt it necessary to exclaim that they were "men tenacious of the appearance of adequacy."[20]

Within this situation emerged the idea, from both foreign and commonwealth jurisdictions, that an integrated, self-directed organization with the power of effective administration of the laws was a "must" goal of reform. Former President Taft had managed to turn the reform into national channels, and on becoming Chief Justice he set about finding ways and means of reaching that goal. His variety of experience as an observer of judges had taught him that it was the unconscious point of view of at least some of them that, in the conduct of the business of the court, the people were made for the court. He himself believed that every man on the bench should keep in mind that the courts were to promote the happiness of all the people by speedy and careful administration of justice and that internal directions of the business of the judiciary should be with an eye to the service of the litigants and the community. In 1924 he stated that a rich man could stand delay in the courts, and what was more often profit by it, but the poor man always suffered.[21]

The Chief Justice's main idea was to energize the judiciary by placing judicial administrative power in a Judicial Conference to consist of a small group of men, among whom were his official self, the senior circuit judges, and a few other judges as conditions warranted. They were to give direction to that energy which would flow from the top to the bottom (and perhaps upwards again, if and when the intake below stirred the receivers to action). This conception was put into the form of a bill. With the bait of twenty-two additional judges provided for, and with pressure exerted by the Chief Justice in person,[22] the Attorney-General, and eminent friends, the bill became law in 1922 despite congressional fear of encroachment of the judiciary upon the legislative function of investigation.[23]

President Franklin D. Roosevelt's running comment in his *Public Papers and Addresses* on the judiciary fitted in neatly with his attempt to better the conditions of the poorer elements of the population. He was thoroughly in sympathy with former Chief Justice Taft's ideas of judicial administrative reform with its emphasis upon a resultant mass welfare. The President's basic point of attack in 1935 was that "we have not weeded out the privileged and we have not effectively lifted up the under-privileged. Both manifestations of injustice have retarded happiness."[24] His theory of government seemed to argue that the effective power in the three major departments of government, whether legislative, executive, or judicial, lay in the administrative branch. Consequently, he assumed that his position as President obligated him to see to it that the judicial administration should be used to the utmost in adjusting the courts to the needs of the people.

Indeed, President Roosevelt claimed to be a leader, along with the Attorney-General and the Judicial Conference, in the administrative reforms of the judiciary during his terms of office. If to sanction or support was to lead, he could justify this claim by reciting the part he played in pushing through or advancing various proposals of reform suggested by other

individuals or groups. He was happy to inform the public that
he had urged Congress to delegate "to the members of that
great tribunal [the Court] who are preeminently qualified,"
the power to make, with the aid of an advisory committee, "a
simplified, flexible, scientific, and correlated system" of
rules governing the federal court in civil actions at law.[25]

Four years later the President was celebrating the adop-
tion of a set of rules of law and equity. At a press conference, he argued that the delegation of rule-making to the
Supreme Court, assisted by legal technicians, was "essen-
tially (a judicial) administrative problem" and was one that
ran parallel with the well-established delegated executive-
administrative rule-making. The President insisted that the
democratic process was preserved when the rules had been
placed before Congress for an entire session without being
altered. Somewhat later the President pushed a bill through
Congress which gave the Supreme Court power to make pre-
and post-conviction rules of criminal procedure.[26] The indigent person was especially protected under both sets of rules.

President Roosevelt used his influence to secure a statute which set up a permanent auxiliary agency designed to
take over the research and business affairs of the United
States Courts (the lower federal courts) under the supervision
of the Judicial Conference of the United States.[27] The chief
officers were to be a director and an assistant director, appointed by and responsible to the Supreme Court, who were
to be able to hold office during good behavior.

This idea of a permanent administrative agency came directly from the controversial Court Reorganization Bill of
1937. Attorney-General Cummings had suggested such an
agency in terms of an officer called the Proctor, and it had
as such appealed to the Supreme Court and the American Bar.
The director took over the auxiliary function formerly exercised by the Attorney-General in connection with the lower
federal courts.[28] But the chief functions of the director were
to keep the court dockets up to date, to see to the observance
of the court methods of doing business and the weaknesses
in the procedural laws and rules that the courts were applying. All this was to be accomplished by means of statistical

reports and visitations. The work was supposed to be done under the supervision of the Judicial Conference, chaired by the Chief Justice of the Supreme Court. Reports of the director were bases for all changes in procedural law or rule recommended by the Conference.[29]

The act setting up the Administrative Office of the United States Courts, as amended, resulted in an almost complete separation of judicial administration from the executive. There is at present a serious doubt that the administrative machinery for supervising the lower courts has been a complete success, a point noted recently by a staff member of the Senate Appropriations Committee.[30] According to this document, the fact-collecting agency of the Judicial Conference (that is, the Administrative Office) had not kept that body properly informed as to the administrative machinery and personnel needed to keep the lower federal courts working efficiently. Statistical information furnished to the Judicial Council was obtained from formal reports to the Administrative Office made by the district judges, but the reporting officer insisted that such statistics concealed the weaknesses of the district judges, who still insisted on "paddling their own canoes." The result was the long delays between initiation and determination of cases, a practice that was especially hurtful to sincere indigents.

The Report made two important recommendations: (a) that the chairmen of circuit conferences should be chosen on the basis of efficiency rather than on that of seniority, and (b) that the facts concerning what transpired in the district courts should be ascertained on the spot by personnel sent out from Washington. The investigating officer indicated that some good things had been done by the Administrative Office. It had performed well such routine jobs as approving financial aid for indigents, making up the budget for the lower federal courts, and defending it before the proper committees. The Office had also secured sufficient facts to aid the Judicial Conference in initiating and pushing through bills and rules that called for better procedures for indigent cases.

An important amendment had already been made to the law setting up the Judicial Conference.[31] It provided for district judges to sit as an effective part of the Conference. The Chief Justice was to summon annually the chief judge of each circuit, the chief judge of the Court of Claims, and a district judge from each judicial circuit, each of whom was to serve for three years and to be selected by his fellows in the circuit conference. The purpose of the amendment was to bring, or make it possible to bring, the best of the district judges into the policy-making body, since they represented the area where the judicial congestion, whatever the reasons, first appeared. They would not only educate their fellows but in turn would be educated. It was hoped that the scheme would build up an able group of judges who would not only know what administration meant but would be able to give the rationale for their actions.

5. OPTIONAL APPELLATE JURISDICTION

The second reform under the leadership of Chief Justice Taft was the broad discretionary power of review bestowed upon the Supreme Court, a power which not only added to the independence of the Court but, in adding to or taking away from its labors, at the same time extended its authority to unify (through specific decisions of cases brought up for review).[32]

Writs of error and appeals had been the most common methods of reaching the Supreme Court before 1925.[33] These two methods of review, both of the "as-of-right" variety, were used in federal and state cases. After the passage of the Judges' Bill, the writ of certiorari was not merely one of those unspecified writs unnamed by statute that might be "necessary for the exercise of their [the courts'] respective jurisdictions and agreeable to the principles and usages of law," but was a named writ that would call up the record for review, whether the record was that of an ordinary civil or criminal case or that of a habeas corpus proceeding. To be sure, in purely legal questions appeal and certification were still possible. The writ became more important, as a means of relief to the Court, when the review work of that body became heavier. Perhaps, because of the Court's very uniqueness, it has somehow been able to reduce its compulsory jurisdiction during the last eighty years.[34] It was in connection with the 1925 Judges' Bill that its members at that time gave a detailed account of the mechanics of handling review work of every kind.

Justice Van Devanter, testifying before the House Committee on the Judiciary, gave the clearest statement of how the writ of certiorari was handled. By way of preface, he distinguished between what was known as writ of error (a mode of reviewing actions at law) or appeal (a mode of reviewing decrees in suits of equity) and writ of certiorari. He said:

> One [method] is by writ of error or appeal, and is commonly spoken of as an obligatory jurisdiction because it may be invoked as of right by a litigant whose case is within the class subject to that mode of review. The other is by writ of certiorari, and is commonly spoken of as a discretionary jurisdiction because the Court is invested with a discretion to deny a review unless it appears that the questions presented are of public importance or of wide general interest, or that in the interest of uniformity the Court should consider and decide them. [Even if certiorari is a discretionary writ] this does not mean that the Court is authorized to exercise a will in the matter but rather that the petition is to be granted or denied according to a sound judicial discretion.

He followed with the outline of the mechanics of the procedure in petitioning for the writ of certiorari:

> The party aggrieved by the decision of the circuit court of appeals (for example) and seeking a further review in the Supreme Court, is required to present to it a petition and accompanying brief, setting forth the nature of the case, what questions are involved, and how they were decided in the circuit court of appeals, and why the case should not rest on the decision of that court. The brief and petition are required to be served on the other party, and time is given for the presentation of an opposing brief. When this has been done, copies of

the printed record as it comes from the circuit court of appeals and of the petition and briefs are distributed among members of the Supreme Court, each judge examines them and prepares a memorandum or note indicating his view of what should be done.

In conference these cases are called, each in turn, and each judge states his views *in extenso* or briefly as he thinks proper; and when all have spoken any difference in opinion is discussed and then a vote is taken ... [I]t seems to be thought *outside* that the cases are referred to particular judges (to grant as a matter of whim). That impression is wholly at variance with what occurs.

We do not grant or deny these petitions merely according to majority. We always grant the petition when as many as four think it should be granted, and sometimes when as many as three think that way. We proceed upon the theory that, if that number out of nine are impressed with the thought that the case is one that ought to be heard and decided by us, the petition should be granted.[35]

Chief Justice Taft lent his "great weight" to pushing the bill through. He added that the brunt of the initial work lay with him in starting upon the round of considering all such petitions. He agreed with his colleagues that all cases must have had two court considerations before they could be brought to the Court and that two-thirds or more had been decided correctly. His mind seemed to be reaching out to the kind of justice that was meted out to rich and poor under the existing laws, when he remarked:[36]

Often in the legislature there is resounding eloquence on the subject that every poor man should have opportunity to carry his case to the last court. There is no statement that is so unfounded as that. The truth is that it is in the interest of the poor litigant that litigation should be ended, and, my dear friends, there is nothing that offers

such an opportunity for delay as a suggestion
that a profound constitutional question is involved
in sustaining a verdict in favor of a poor litigant
when the rich litigant has a long purse with which
to continue litigation.

The Judges' Law of 1925 gave the Supreme Court power
to bring up cases by writ of certiorari at its discretion according to the following: 1) certiorari to the federal circuit
courts of appeals on the petition of any party to a civil or
criminal case, before or after rendition of judgment or decree:[37] 2) certiorari, under similar conditions, to the highest
state court that can pass upon the particular matter a) where
is drawn in question the validity of a treaty or statute of the
United States,[38] and b) where the validity of a state statute
is drawn in question concerning the ground of its being repugnant to the Constitution, treaties or laws of the United
States or where "any title, right, privilege, or immunity is
especially set up or claimed under the Constitution, treaties,
or statutes of, or commissions held or authority exercised
under, the United States." Alternative writs of error or appeal
were offered but they called for a more limited consideration
of the questions involved. There were added, also, certified
questions of law from the circuit courts of appeal to the
Supreme Court, and in both civil and criminal cases the
questions could be considered as an appeal, at the will of the
Supreme Court.[39]

NOTES TO CHAPTER VII

[1]16 Wall. 36, 1873.

[2]Neal v. Delaware, 103 U.S. 370, 1880, reversed decision. Cf. Murray v. Louisiana, 163 U.S. 101, 1896, which took practice as the law.

[3]Charles P. Curtis, Jr., *Lions Under the Throne* (Boston, 1947), pp. 267-320. Thomas Jefferson, however, stole Madison's intention and made it his own.

[4]Baron v. Baltimore, 7 Peters 243, 1833, was the first pronouncement. W.W. Crosskey, in his *Politics and the Constitution in the History of the United States* (Chicago, 1953), goes back to Madison's intentions.

[5]Miles Chubb, 28 *Tex. L. Rev.* No. 236, 1949.

[6]L.G. Rockwell, "Justice Rutledge on Civil Liberties," 59 *Yale Law Journal* 27, 1949.

[7]*The Complete Sherlock Holmes* (New York, 1953), p. xv.

[8]Alpheus T. Mason, *Brandeis: A Free Man's Life* (New York, 1946), p. 628.

[9]For a more complete view of the Court's power over its own intake of moneys, see a) *Stone Papers*, L.C., Box 38, which contains Taft's Memo of 1928; b) Hearings before the House Committee on the Judiciary to accompany H.R. 10, 477, 67th Cong., 2nd Sess., 1922; c) Mr. Justice Roberts' testimony, Hearings of the House Sub-committee on Appropriations Bill, 78th Cong., 2nd Sess., p. 102, 1945, W.H. Taft Papers, L.C., I-28-E, 4, 1923, give additional detail.

[10]*Ibid.*, and Hearings on Judicial Appropriations Bill, House Sub-Committee, 78th Cong., 1st Sess., pp. 12-13. The Court soon withdrew the $3,000 added to the Clerk's legal salary but substituted other amounts.

[11]Official "Minutes of the Supreme Court" date the Orders as of October, 1921, though Taft records them as 1922.

[12]*Taft Papers*, Box 38, 1928; Box 71, 12-20-29.

[13]Personal conversation, in 1947, with a high-ranking member of the General Accounting Office. The Chief Justice, in 1921, reported that the Comptroller had refused to approve expenditure for stationery and Poland water for the Justices, a transaction which turned out to be more embarrassing to the G. A. O. than to the Court. See *Taft Papers*, Box 36, 1925.

[14]*Stone Papers*, Box 38, 1928, *E.g.*, the average service fees going to the Treasure, in 1921-28, were $10,000; take-in of free moneys, in 1928, around $60,000. *Taft Papers*, I-28-E, 4, 1923, gave these figures for 1922: Clerk's additional salary, $3,000; bond, $240; audit, $866.70; I.F.P., $11.54.

[15]28 U.S.C.A. Secs. 671-76, 1948.

[16]See Henry F. Pringle, *Life and Times of William Howard Taft* (New York, 1939), Vol. II, pp. 1075-76.

[17]It should be noted that in school integration and equal election districts, the Court undertook to administer in the manner of an executive department.

[18]F. Frankfurter and J.M. Landis, *The Business of the Supreme Court* (Boston, 1937), Chapter VI.

[19]*Public Papers and Addresses*, Vol. 6, 1937, p. 36.

[20]*Ibid.*, p. 42.

[21]Henry F. Pringle, *op. cit.*, Vol. II, p. 992.

[22]H. Rep. No. 482 to accompany H.R. 9103, 67th Cong., 1st Sess., Nov., 1921. As the House Committee on the Judiciary wrote, "This proposal has the hearty endorsement of the Chief Justice, who appeared before your Committee, and is likewise urged by the Attorney-General."

[23]42 Stat. 837, 1922; 28 U.S.C. Sec. 331, 1948. Lower organization was: Judicial Councils of Circuits, 28 U.S.C. 332, 1939, as amended, composed of all circuit judges of a Circuit, headed by the Chief Circuit Judge; Judicial Conferences of Circuits, composed of Chief Judge of the Circuit and all district judges in the Circuit.

[24]*Public Papers and Addresses, Vol. 4, 1935, p. 16.*

[25]*Ibid.*, Vol. 3, p. 304, 1934; 48 Stat. 1064, Secs. 1-2, 1934.

[26]*Ibid.*, Vol. 7, pp. 555-57, 1938. See 54 Stat. 688, 1940, for criminal law procedure..

[27]53 Stat. 1223-26, 1939.

[28]As Judge Stevens put it: "This bill has two purposes...the other to insure their (the Court's) independence from the executive branch of the Government." Hearing of H.R. Judicial Committee on H.R. .2973 and H.R. 5999, p. 48, 76th Cong., 1st Sess., 1939.

[29]S. Rep. No. 426, to accompany S. 188, 76th Cong., 1st Sess., 1939.

[30]Report to the Senate Appropriations Committee on "The Field Study of the Operations of the United States Courts," April, 1959.

[31]71 Stat. 476, 1957, amending 28 U.S.C.A. Sec. 331.

[32]The Judges' Bill, 43 Stat. 938, 1925.

[33]The Chief Justice later persuaded Congress to change writs of error and appeals to simple appeals in 1928.

[34]Frankfurter and Landis, *op. cit.*, Chapter V.

[35]Hearings in the House before the Committee on the Judiciary on H.R. 8206, 68th Cong., 2nd Sess., 1924, pp. 7-8.

[36]*Ibid.*, pp. 28-29.

[37]43 Stat. 938-39, sec. 240, 1925, if before rendition of deci-

sion, writ is "original," but not in the sense of original jurisdiction under the Constitution.

[38] 43 Stat..937, sec. 237 (b), 1925.

[39] 43 Stat.. 938, sec. 239, 1925.

CHAPTER VIII

THE SUPREME COURT'S
INTERNAL INDIGENT PROCEDURE:
RULE AND PRACTICE, 1922-1963

The period to be considered here embraces the regimes of Taft, Hughes, Stone, Vinson, and, in part, Warren; ends eleven years after the thirty-seven year delayed recodification of the United States Judicial Code. Although the Civil Indigent Act of 1892, as amended in 1910 to include criminal cases as a sort of poor man's code, had been applied to some extent before the amendment of 1922, it was not until the latter amendment that the judges, the lawyers, and the prison population began to take note of what special privileges had been provided for poor persons involved in suits, defenses, and judgments. The 1922 provision (which permitted, under certain circumstances, charges against the United States for printing the records in criminal cases) seemed to have left the way somewhat open for cases coming up from lower courts.

Under Chief Justice Taft the primary task involved the process of educating the poor man (and, perhaps his attorneys, if any) regarding the proper method or methods of bringing his case before the High Court. "The Supreme Court Series of the Taft Papers," Library of Congress, are full of material dealing with this subject. "The Chief" was constantly telling those who were applying for some form of appeal that they should distinguish between the work of an attorney and that of a member of the Court. To members of the Government or to appellants, he complained that each person who did not have a lawyer thought that the thing to do was "to write to the Chief Justice" on the assumption that he would act as his attorney.[1] Taft was a stickler for enforcing the rules of the Court and statutory provisions. An indigent could by Court rule submit papers in typewritten form, but other regulations had to be followed. At first failure to carry out the prescription often evoked the simple exhortation: secure a lawyer.[2] Applicants for the several kinds of writs, however, were often unable to understand the meaning or significance of such kindly advice, failed to heed it for lack of funds, or were misinformed by a prisoner-attorney or by an outside hyena-lawyer. One or the other of such conditions compelled the Chief Justice, or his agent, to supply the information that a first class attorney would have given [3] If a federal case (for example, habeas corpus) were dismissed in a federal district court, it usually could not be reviewed directly by the Supreme Court but had to go by appeal to a circuit court and then, if desired by one or both parties, to the High Court for writ of certiorari. From his own records it seems that the Chief Justice was willing to depart from what he considered to be the true function of a judge in order to see that justice was done in *in forma pauperis* cases: justice was available to the poor man on the condition that he knew how to take advantage of the procedure leading to such justice.

While Chief Justice Taft and his immediate successor had the administrative ability to organize the business of the Court, that ability either was exhibited in other specialized fields or absorbed largely in the personal activity of the Chief Justice himself.[4] Bookkeeping for the purpose of orderly processing of the various types of appeals had existed in some form since the early years of the Court. Until Taft became the Chief of the Court's business there was no great compulsion for reform; but beginning with the 1923 Term, the pressure for reorganization of "docketry" with a view to orderly handling of the types of appellate work began to build up. Before Stone became Chief Justice there had been only one definitely named docket, the Original Docket, which carried those matters adjudged by the Court to fall within its original jurisdiction as designated in the Constitution itself.[5] On this docket cases were consecutively numbered for each term. The second docket was a "common law" one, not named but used to designate in an orderly way the appellate actions within the Court's statutory jurisdiction. This came to be called the "Appellate Docket."

Over the years there began to appear miscellaneous applications for review. The earliest of such applications came directly to the Court under the "all-writs provision," found in the Judiciary Act of 1789, which authorized the Court to issue all writs not specifically provided for by law to aid in the exercise of its jurisdiction.[6] If the Court ordered such writs filed (and it did in some cases), they were given numbers and placed on the Original Docket. The theory seemed to be that since they came directly to the Court they were original in character under the Constitution. This could not have been the case, for the reason that the applications were for habeas corpus, certiorari, mandamus, and the like (common law writs sometimes referred to as "Thunderbolts of Zeus" when hurled by the Supreme Court), which existed for the purpose of indirectly voiding or modifying decisions below and therefore were by nature appellate.

Even if the granted writs of common law origin were placed safely on the Original Docket there were many applications therefor to which the Clerk gave no numbers and placed on no docket. They were merely a cluster of miscellaneous applications. After the Indigent Code of 1892 (as amended in 1910) was made effective there were writs of error and appeal prosecuted *in forma pauperis*, all of which were placed on the Appellate Docket whether they were granted or not. Under the Judges Law of 1925 certiorari and limited appeal soon practically monopolized the appellate procedure and were given a place on the Appellate Docket, regardless of how the Court disposed of them.

As more and more applications for review were being granted by the Court under the "all writs provision," it became apparent to the more perceptive members of that body that the Original Docket was being falsely expanded by adding purely appellate applications to it. For example, there were the Holiday v. Johnston,[7] and Steffler v. United States cases,[8] along with such "unless" threats of issuing "original" habeas corpus writs (as in Mooney v. Holohan[9]) all of which were so purely appellate that an illiterate indigent could recognize them as not being original. The Court, according to the Harvard Note,[10] abandoned the practice in the

1943 Term. Each common law writ which was granted was assigned a number on the Appellate Docket. Up until the 1943 Term each non-granted common law writ application had been given for identification the unnumbered designation as "No._____ Original." In 1943 "original" was dropped and the denied application was designated as "No._____." Obviously no shepherd in the Clerk's Office could know his sheep.

In 1945 the unnumbered applications for common law writs that had not been granted leave were placed in orderly fashion on a newly instituted docket known as the Miscellaneous Docket.[11] This was the beginning of the move to place all future applications for common law writs of certiorari, habeas corpus, and others,[12] for motions to vacate,[13] for notice of appeals, and ultimately for applications accompanied by motions to proceed *in forma pauperis* regardless of the method of reaching the High Court, or of the source of the original decision. In the 1952 *Report of the Director* the following statement appeared:[14]

> Beginning with the 1947 term, all cases accompanied by motion to proceed *in forma pauperis* have been carried on the miscellaneous docket of the Court. This includes pauper petitions for certiorari theretofore filed on the appellate docket. Petitions for certiorari docketed on the miscellaneous docket are transferred to the appellate docket if certiorari is granted. If, however, the motion to proceed *in forma pauperis* and the petition for certiorari are both granted and the case is then disposed of by the same order, no transfer is made.... Motions for leave to vacate (are included also).

The Director's Report (1957) contained this information:[15]

> Beginning with the 1954 term, all appeals accompanied by *in forma* motions have been carried on the miscellaneous docket and are transferred to the appellate docket, if the motion to proceed *in forma pauperis* is granted or jurisdiction is

> noted. If, however, the motion to proceed (as a
> pauper) is granted and the case is then disposed
> of on the merits by the same order, no transfer is
> made.

It will be noted from the above that the Original Docket
was cleared of its obscurities and the Appellate Docket
received some proper additions, and that a third docket was
established to take care of a special group of miscellaneous
actions. The immediate result was better administration but
there was still an imperfect distribution of the Court's actions. Under the leadership of Chief Justice Vinson most of
the applications for various forms of appeal, accompanied by
motions for *in forma pauperis* proceedings, were placed on the
Miscellaneous Docket; and Chief Justice Warren added appeals, accompanied by motion to proceed as a poor person,
to the Miscellaneous Docket. In addition the Chief Justice
had seen to it that separate recording books had been properly
maintained for each of the three dockets. It would seem then
that orderly bookkeeping was essential for the proper processing of the numerous cases of review by the Supreme Court.
This was especially true of *in forma* cases. If such cases
were "lost" in unnumbered, unassigned areas of paperdom,
it would be serious for the poor man who had little or no help
to push his appeal through the Court or have that body take
cognizance of the papers. On the other hand, if the books
were not properly kept it would be possible for the perceptive
indigent to abuse his privilege.

The procedure, from the standpoint of the outsider, has
not been perfected to date, in so far as the poor man is concerned. It is an interesting fact that while the legal fraternity
and similar groups consider it a major sin to cite a case in a
written article or treatise without adding the date and the
exact page, the Supreme Court and most of the lower courts
usually cite cases without adding dates and, less frequently
perhaps, without specifically locating the material involved.
Similar practice appears in indigent cases: it is indeed rare
for an opinion writer to inform a reader whether the case has
been handled in the Court in an *in forma* proceeding. One has

to look back one or two terms to find out whether the case was classified as miscellaneous. Even then such a designation does not indicate in advance whether it is a case of a poor person; further facts are necessary. The answer may be that such a case has no special significance.[16]

In forma cases began to reach the Court during the second half of the 1923 Term. Before the 1926 Term had got fully on its way there was evidence of a definite trend toward establishing the form of approaching the Court for review. Chief Justice Taft, with the consent of his colleagues, allowed indigents to file for review without requiring them to pay (or give surety for) the then legal filing fee of $35, and without demanding the printing of the arguments for coming to the Court and the supporting papers. One person, a Mr. Ackerson, had been convicted of using the mails to defraud and the appellate court had affirmed. He had moved for *in forma* petitions for certiorari and for stay of the penalty. Justice Stone had previously denied a stay. The Chief Justice then directed the Clerk to give the following information to the petitioner:[17]

> So far as the application to grant leave to proceed *in forma pauperis* in the application for certiorari, you may advise Ackerson that his application will come up for hearing...October 6, and that the question will then be whether, upon the examination, which the Court may be able to make in the case presented in a typewritten petition, it involves such questions that the Court is not at all likely to grant a certiorari. If the members of the Court feel differently advised from the written or typewritten petition and the opinion of the court below, that there is no probability that the application for certiorari will be granted, it will do what it has done many times upon such application for leave to proceed *in forma pauperis*, namely, direct the Clerk to pay the costs of filing the petition, denying the writ, and denying permission to proceed any further in preparation of the application for certiorari. You can advise Ackerson that no consideration will be given to his petition

to proceed *in forma pauperis*, further than to allow him to file his petition in typewriting and delay further consideration until the 4th of October when the Court meets.

Nearly a month later the Chief Justice, after the Court had denied certiorari to Ackerson, instructed the Clerk as follows relative to payment of costs:[18]

> I have your letter of October 27 in which you ask me with reference to the payment of the costs in the Ackerson case. These I expect to direct you to pay. You may prepare an order directing you to pay costs and any other costs that have been incurred under the statute as to *in forma pauperis* proceedings. The order should be to pay you or to authorize you to transfer from the special fund that we created, and in which we made special provision for the use of the fund to meet the cost of *in forma* ... proceedings. You will have to examine the orders made, and you should refer to them with the date and some general description of the order.

The above seems to have been an attempt to make it easier for the Clerk to utilize the free funds set aside by Orders of the Court in 1921 for paying the fees and costs of indigent cases.[19] On October 29, 1926 one Webb, after being convicted of a crime, petitioned for certiorari and moved to proceed *in forma pauperis* and to have the records of his case printed.[20] Two days later the Court ordered:[21]

> Proceedings further *in forma pauperis* denied for the reason that the Court upon inspection of the record of the proceedings below as submitted (by another party to the case) finds no ground for certiorari and certiorari denied. *Costs already incurred by direction of the Court shall be paid by the Clerk from the special fund in his custody as provided by the Order of October 29, 1926.* (Emphasis supplied.)

The Order in the Webb case was the first one found by the author, though the instructions to the Clerk in the Ackerson case were doubtless made by the Chief Justice in anticipation of the newer and more convenient Order of October 29, 1926, which supplanted parts of the Order of 1921.[22] Also, the same Order applied to cases in which certioraris, appeals, and certificates of circuit judges were granted or answered. In Meadows *v.* United States the following Order was made:[23]

> Motion to proceed *in forma pauperis* granted. Clerk directed to cause the record to be printed, and to cause the cost thereof and the Clerk's costs already incurred and such as may hereafter be incurred to be paid as provided for in the Order of October 29, 1926.

Chief Justice Stone (in 1942) sent a memorandum to his colleagues which was to result in a slight modification of the October 29, 1926 Order. It had been called to his attention, he wrote, that on docketing applications for certiorari and notices of appeal (the main avenues to the Court), the Clerk had been collecting $35 per indigent case, whether the requests for review were granted or denied; that as a result, the special fund set aside from "free moneys" was being depleted at the rate of $6,000 each term. He went on to note that according to the established internal procedure for free indigent access to the Court, the money taken from the special fund under control of the Clerk had been going into the United States Treasury, if any money had been left after the payment of the expenses of the Clerk's Office; and that the whole matter had been and was still merely a paper Office. He then stated that the Clerk had offered a solution, which the Court, after due consideration, adopted in the form of the following Order of October 5, 1942:[24]

> No Clerk's costs shall be taxed against a party presenting a case *in forma pauperis* unless otherwise ordered by the Court.

Chief Justice Taft, instigator and co-promoter of the Judges Law of 1925, felt obligated to initiate the formulation of new rules for putting the law into effect. In a letter to his son, Robert (in June, 1925), the Chief Justice stated that such rules contained some very important changes, due to the Court's new jurisdiction, and that the greatest innovation had to do with the reduction of "almost everything to certiorari."[25] What he meant was that the Court's power of review by writ or error and appeals had been greatly limited and that the hitherto restricted power of bringing cases up by certiorari had been greatly extended. Nearly two years later the aging and ailing Chief commented in writing to his son Charles: "The certioraris have become, under the new rule, a heavier burden than they ever were before, and I am not sure but that we shall have to make some different arrangement with respect to their disposition."[26] The main question had to do with the judicial administration of the discretionary mode of review, one that tended to relieve the Court from too much required work of such character.

The Chief Justice had taken upon himself the burden of processing all certioraris, whether they came from federal or state petitioners, whether they were civil or criminal in nature, or whether they were accompanied by motion for *in forma pauperis* procedure or not. Changes with regard to processing certioraris necessarily affected the indigent petitioner. In 1928 the Chief Justice informed a state judge: "I usually prepare a memo of each case, stating grounds for asking certiorari, and giving such examination of questions presented as is necessary to understand what the case is, why it should not be brought up."[27] This required an immense amount of work on the part of the Chief Justice, especially when the petitioners were indigent, since petitions were handled *pro se* in most cases, were poorly written, poorly organized, and were almost impossible to clarify. If the records of proceedings in lower courts were clear, and if an alert attorney had provided a brief, the task was made easier. Evidently Taft's clerk aided in this processing: copies of all the original materials, together with the Chief's opinion and motions for *in forma* procedure and for printing the record, if any, were sent to each member of the Court for his consideration.

Taft's successor, Charles Evans Hughes, took office at the age of 68 and did not relinquish it until he had reached 79. He continued the processing of all certiorari petitions under the rules of his predecessor; indeed he enforced them with the vigor and acumen of a man of 40. The new Chief Justice was an expert in administration, executive and judicial. The latter type was really unknown to the average run of attorneys and to the great mass of laymen who appeared before the courts. The new Chief believed in orderliness in all appellate procedures, and was rarely nonplussed by the sloppy arguments of the *pro se* indigent petitioner, his ill-chosen supporting materials, or their entire absence. If he failed to see the intent from the facts presented, he called on the Clerk to supplement the materials with the necessary documents.

On the basis of a statement by one of his clerks he placed the growing number of indigent petitioners for certiorari into three categories:[28] 1) pleas of those "teched in the head," all of which were thrown aside;[29] 2) those for reviewing denial of habeas corpus, which came up from the great federal prisons (most of which were usually denied); 3) those in which there was some content such as those that claimed denial of attorney or forced testimony — all of which were considered carefully and often granted. In statistical terms, the Chief Justice declared that 60% of indigent petitions for certiorari should never have been made; that 20% were short of a good basis; that the remaining 20% had good grounds and were on the average granted. He further asserted that the chief advantage to the 80% of such litigants was that litigation was quickly settled after reaching the Court; that the Court itself gained the end aimed at in the Judges Law when it did not have to carry the 80% to a conclusion.

Associate Justice Harlan F. Stone succeeded Mr. Hughes as Chief Justice in July, 1941. He had joined the Court in March, 1925, and at his death in April, 1946, had served most of the term of Mr. Taft's Chief-justiceship, all of that of Mr. Hughes and, of course, that of his own. He knew the procedure of the Court and left worthwhile material thereon in his *Papers*. He was interested in the administration of the Judges Law of 1925, especially in the extension of the writ of certiorari as the chief method of review by the Court. He endeavored to work out for himself a method of handling certioraris when they came to him as Associate Justice and when, as Chief, he processed all of them.[30] Since he had served as Dean of Columbia Law School, he became the source of information concerning the Court's internal procedure not only to his former colleagues but to many other law teachers and some lower court judges as well.

Professor Felix Frankfurter of the Harvard Law School tried to ascertain the internal procedure connected with granting or denying certiorari and used his fellow teacher of former years as an aid in doing so. The correspondence of 1928 indicated that Justice Stone felt that a study should be made of "the operation of certiorari" with particular reference to the type of questions selected for review. Stone's statistics were lacking on the subject, but he seemed to think that a tendency could be found by detailed examination of petitions denied outright and of those granted.[31] Professor Frankfurter wanted to know how the Justice made up his mind on petitions for certiorari. His reply was similar to that of Taft: ascertainment of the exact nature of the question the petitioner sought to present and a clear statement of the reasons for granting the writ.

Justice Stone, however, was a bit more forthright in explaining his operating methods than either Taft or Hughes. He had his clerical force prepare memoranda on the petitions and any briefs or documents accompanying them.[32] An undated memorandum of a former clerk of the Justice went even further.[33] He stated that as clerk he would examine the petitions and the records, prepare for each a brief memorandum setting forth the facts, a discussion, and a recommendation for the disposition of each petition, and send them together with the original papers to the Justice. A clerk usually mastered the viewpoint of his "boss."

As Chief Justice, Mr. Stone addressed the Fourth Circuit Judicial Conference on certiorari procedure in 1942:[34]

The Court has continued the practice, which has
been followed at least during my 17 years on the
Bench, of having an independent examination of
all applications made by each member of the Court,
and in case of applications for certiorari, granting
them if four of the nine judges favor the grant. As
has long been the practice, the Chief Justice examines, in the first instance, the typewritten records of all applications *in forma pauperis*. Those
which are found to present any question of substance are then circulated among all the members
of the Court and voted on at conference. The concern of the Court for the protection of civil rights
has resulted in a large increase in this class of
applications. During the term just closed [October
Term, 1941] I have examined personally the records in 178 cases, 58 more than were filed in the
previous term. But the merits of those applications have not kept pace with the increase in number. During the term we granted 16 of these applications as against 19 during the 1940 term.

The mechanics of processing indigent petitions for certiorari were, until 1944, somewhat different from those for
"cash-on-the-barrel-head" type. The Chief Justice cast aside
those which he considered for good reasons to be without merit
and presented only those that seemed to contain points of substance for consideration by each member of the Court.
Stone's statement (quoted above) then clarified the procedure worked out under Taft and Hughes. There were no published rules of the Court indicating this "casting-out" procedure, but there seemed to be some serious doubts among some
members of Congress, among poor petitioners, and among defense attorneys that the Indigent Code was being applied properly by the Court. Criticism appeared under the general head
of granting or refusing petitions for certiorari. Justice Clark
indicated the beliefs rampant outside the Court regarding who
controlled the disposition of petitions.[35] Senator Stennis, according to the *New York Times*,[36] insisted that the appointment of clerks by the Justices be approved by the Senate,

since they took too great a part in granting or refusing petitions.

The Chief Justice might well have sensed the feeling outside as well as inside the Court, as early as 1944. It was then that he issued the following memorandum to his colleagues:[37]

> Until further notice the following procedure will be regularly followed with respect to all unprinted *in forma pauperis* applications:
>
> The clerical assistants will prepare memoranda with respect to each case. I will distribute one copy of each memorandum to each Justice after I have examined the memorandum and the record. In appropriate cases I will circulate the records. On Saturday at conference, none of these cases will be taken up except such as appear upon a taking-up list appended to the regular special list. Any case will be added to the list at the request of a Justice.

Professor Frankfurter was also curious about the Court's failure to give reasons for its actions on petitions for certiorari. In a communication to Justice Stone he argued strongly that reasons should be given for denials.

When Vinson succeeded Stone as Chief Justice in 1946 the Court had not attempted to control its discretion in denying certiorari by establishing rules requiring the giving of reasons therefor.[38] This failure was understandable, to be sure, but there must have been some undisclosed basis for keeping "sound judicial discretion" from passing over into personal whims of individual judges. There were rules to guide the Court in granting certioraris but they were rules stated, for the most part, in the Judges Law itself, the latest edition of which was Rule 19, 1954.

Chief Justice Vinson took a broader view of the application of discretion in petitions for certioraris. His criticism of the Court was that at times it had violated the terms of the law in that it had transmuted its discretion given for certain great purposes into non-discretion, thereby acting as a court for

correcting errors. In a speech before the American Bar Association in 1949[39] he asserted that the Supreme Court had not
and had never been primarily concerned with correction of
error in the lower court decisions, because in almost all
cases within the Court's appellate jurisdiction the petitioner had already received one review in the federal hierarchy (and more in cases arising in state courts). He continued
to assert that the purpose of discretionary review, as envis-
aged by Congress, had been to secure national rights and
uniformity of judgments and to consider the review of questions that involved greater spread than the particular facts of
the case called for. Such broad purposes, to be sure, included
the overall supervision of the lower courts.

The Chief Justice was not content to summarize the intent of Congress with regard to certiorari review. Also, he
suggested to the lawyers, who made up the audience, that
they should aid the Court in reaching the objectives of the
law and the rule: they should spend less time discussing the
merits of their respective cases and more time in demonstrat-
ing why it was important that the Court should hear the particular case. Involved in a large number of certioraris in
direct and indirect reviews and in an appreciable number of
appeals "as of right," are the indigents as well as persons
with funds. And the desire of each category points to one
end, namely, the voiding or modification of the judgment
from the court below regardless of merit.

The academic lawyers have kept up with the Court's procedure in applying the terms of the Judges Law of 1925. Especially have they concentrated their attention on this phase
of the Court's action, beginning with the 1945 Term. To
illustrate this emphasis, material will be taken from the law
magazines of Pennsylvania and Harvard Law Schools.

Harper and Rosenthal[40] claim that during the 1949 Term
the Supreme Court failed to decide altogether too many cases
in that certiorari had been denied without reasons being given
and, where reasons had been given, the writ had been dismissed without argument of counsel, that is, in summary
fashion. The old criticism of failure to give reasons for denying certiorari reappeared,[41] but a new element had entered,

namely, summary decisions made by the Court on granted reviews.

The *Harvard Law Review* critics[42] have been directing their remarks chiefly toward the disposition of granted writs of certiorari rather than toward denial of such writs. Such criticisms have passed over the failure to state reasons for granting certiorari and have reached more deeply into the practice of the Court. First, the Court, in applying the Judges Law,[43] has been granting certiorari both in regular and indigent cases and summarily reversing the federal courts of appeal or the final state courts contrary to one or the other of the due process clauses of the Constitution. After 1954, appeals cases (which constituted 7% of all appeals) are handled the same way: one-half of total on the average.[44] This criticism is arrived at by assuming that due process on appeal requires a hearing, a step which the Court too often fails to take. Final action is based on papers from lower courts, which papers may or may not have even a reasoned brief for the petitioner, *pro se* or otherwise especially in indigent cases. The Court seems to insist that such cases have no sound basis and that a hearing would be a waste of time. The formula for indigent cases runs thus: motion for *in forma pauperis* granted, certiorari is granted and the case is disposed of on the papers. Stern and Gressman backed up this summary procedure in 1954 for the general reasons given by the Court and also for more specific ones.[45]

In the second place, Professor Brown claimed that though jurisdiction by writ of certiorari had been given by Congress for reviewing general and very important matters that touched the entire national community, the Court had become largely a court of error-correction devoting entirely too much time to cases that depended upon sundry circumstances that could never be woven into general rules such as Congress contemplated.[46]

In developing his argument he charged, as had others before him, that the Court had not followed its Rule of 1939 (Rule 38) nor that of 1954 (Rule 19), both based upon the Judges Law of 1925.[47] Former Chief Justices Hughes and Vinson were quoted as authority. The former was not on the

Court when it had begun to act as a court of error, the latter was "Chief" during the time when the pressure was on to have the Court hear every complaint on appeal and he was often condemned for refusing to make the Court one of error under the Judges Law.[48] Professor Brown modified his criticism somewhat by asserting that the Court could be following the law in choosing the cases it should bring up for review, and that the action as a court of error was merely in addition to the Judges Law by Supreme Court rulings.[49]

NOTES TO CHAPTER VIII

[1] *Taft Papers*, I-24-A2, Box 41, 1926; I-24-A3, Box 51, 1927; I-24-B1, Box 66, 1929.

[2] *Ibid.*, I-28-F1, Box 751, 1926.

[3] *Ibid.*, I-24-A1, Box 36, 1925; I-24-A2, Box 40, 1925; I-28-E4, Box 745, 1925; I-24-A1, Box 36, 1925.

[4] This ability of the "Chief" may lie in recognizing the contributions of able men on the Court. Chief Justice Hughes left little of value in his administration of the Court, with the exception of his complete domination of its business, though in a subtle way. See his forcing the Court to sit in conference several times a week to get ahead on certioraris (the *Hughes Papers* are replete with such orders).

[5] The history of dockets, from the earliest times of the Court to 1945 was for the most part taken from a note in 59 *Harvard Law Review*, 604-06, 1945-46 (copyright 1945, 1946, by *Harvard Law Review* Association, Cambridge, Massachusetts). The Note was written in cooperation with the late Charles Elmore Cropley, Clerk of the Court, 1922-1952. Until the complete "Minutes of the Supreme Court" are available (they are in the process of being microfilmed by Archives), no full check is possible. "The Supreme Court Journal" (excerpts from the "Minutes") was available from the late 1880's as well as the Rules of the Court. Also available were the *Papers* left by C. J. Taft and C. J. Stone, the latter touching on later developments; the Annual Reports of the Adm. Office of the U. S. Courts; Stern and Gressman, *Supreme Court Practice* (1954 edition); and other tips from law clerks.

[6] 1 Stat. 73. 81-82, Sec. 14, 1789; and 28 U.S.C., Sec. 1651, 1948. See also *supra*, Chapter V.

[7] 313 U.S. 342, 1941.

[8] 319 U.S. 38, 1943.

[9] 297 U.S. 103, 1935.

[10]The author could find no Order in the "Minutes of the Supreme Court" in the microfilm for Term, 1943, or the last of Term, 1942, changing the practice. This and other materials in microfilms appeared later.

[11]Likewise, the author could find no Order for this in the microfilm for Term, 1945.

[12]28 U.S.C., Sec. 1651 (a), 1948.

[13]*Ibid.*, Sec. 2255.

[14]Director's *Report* for 1951-1952, Note 1, p. 111, Table A1. This Table is furnished by the Clerk of the Supreme Court as a matter of courtesy. The statistics on indigent cases seem to be complete since 1954. The fact that motions to vacate, 28 U.S.C., Sec. 2255, 1948, have many of the characteristics of habeas corpus and are generally supposed to precede that writ in strictly federal cases, throws them into the miscellaneous class.

[15]*Ibid.*, 1956-1957, Note 1, p. 159, Table A1. Before 1954 all appeals to the Supreme Court, indigent or not, were carried on the appellate docket. Affirmation of this appeared in the Director's *Report* for 1959, Table A1, Note 2.

[16]Perhaps the American Society for Legal History will see to it that part of the funds derived from the Holmes Devise will be used to document cases falling under the Indigent Code, from 1892 until the date of the conclusion of its documentation. *Law Week* has begun to inform the researcher whether a case came up under IFP, but such a source is not always available.

[17]*Taft Papers*, I-24-A2, Box 44, 1926; 273 U.S. 702, 1926 (Ackerson *v.* United States).

[18]*Ibid.*, I-24-A2, Box 45, October 28, 1926.

[19]See Chapter VII, Sec. 2, *supra.*

[20]Webb *v.* United States, No. 703, was finally decided, Nov. 1, 1926, 273 U.S. 718.

[21]*Ibid.*, p. 79, Nov. 1, 1926; *Taft Papers*, I-24-A2, Box 45, October 29, 1926; Ferguson *v.* Florida, 273, U.S. 663, 1927. The Davids *v.* Holland, a civil case, combined Nos. 190-191, p. 39, October Term, 1929.

[22]Edwin McElwain, Esq., in a letter to the author, March 15, 1954, notes that the new Order gives Clerk C. Elmore Copley's statement that Justice Brandeis, as member of the Court's Accounting Committee, suggested the change in the Clerk's method of taking care of indigent expenses.

[23]280 U.S. 550, 1929; also found in *S. Ct. J.* as No. 269, October Term, 1929, p. 39 with comments. See also, Alston *v.* United States 274 U.S. 289, 1927, and *S. Ct. J.*, October, 1926, No. 898, 1926.

The author was able later to check the "Minutes of the Supreme Court" in the microfilm copies put out by the National Archives. The Order, after repeating the Orders of October 6 and 10, 1926, 1921, amended them to the following extent:

> . . . in litigated cases in which the parties or either of them, are authorized to proceed *in forma pauperis*. It is hereby ordered that, pursuant to the direction of the Court, the Clerk shall be, and is hereby, authorized to pay costs in proceedings *in forma pauperis* in cases which may be docketed upon the filing by petitioner of a proper affidavit in accordance with the law. Per Chief Justice Taft, October 29, 1926.

This Order, slightly modified in 1942, as has been noted, seems to be the present procedure.

[24]See *Stone Papers*, Box 40, November 3, 1942, for reasons for Order. This Order was incorporated in the manuscript after the appearance of the microfilm of the complete "Minutes of the Supreme Court" for October Term, 1942, read in the Archives in Washington. It will be noted that the word "costs" used by the Court in its Orders dealing with payment of cases, includes clerk's fees and costs of printing the record.

[25]*Taft Papers*, I-24-A1, Box 17, June 7, 1925.

[26]*Ibid.*, I-24-A3, Box 48, February 27, 1927. His much needed vacations were spent on "certs."

[27]*Ibid.*, I-24-A4, Box 59, February 28, 1928.

[28] Edwin McElwain, "The Business of the Supreme Court as Conducted by Chief Justice Hughes," 63 *Harvard Law Review*, 5-26, 1949-1950 , and letter to the author , March 15 ,1954.

[29] Excellent examples of these were found in the *Hughes Papers*.

[30] See also Bennett Boskey, "The Mechanism of the Supreme Court's Certiorari Jurisdiction," 46 *Columbia Law Review*, 255-265, 1946.

[31] *Stone Papers* , Box 8, 1928.

[32] *Ibid.*, Box 9, March, 1937.

[33] A memorandum made for the biographer of the Justice by a former clerk.

[34] 28 A.B.A.J. 519, 1942. Bennett Boskey, who served as clerk under Hughes and Stone, emphasized the part that the Chief played in *in forma pauperis* petitions and in withholding those applications that had no substance. See his article, "Mr. Chief Justice Stone," 59 *Harvard Law Review*, 1200-1202, 1946.

[35] "The Supreme Court Conference," 19 *F.R.D* 303-310, 1956 Chief Justice Taft took a shot in advance at the criticism of the discretionary clause in the proposed Judges Bill, H.R. 8206, 68 Cong., 2nd Sess., 1924, Hearings. He pointed out that "the Court does not distribute among the Justices a certain number of certs to give away as each sees fit, as a member of Congress thought about the distribution of pardons among his colleagues, two pardons per session."

[36] 27: 6, May 7, 1958. *Stone Papers* contain individual petitioner-complaints.

[37] *Stone Papers*, Box 40, November 1, 1944.

[38] See Rules of the Supreme Court, June, 1928 (275 U.S. Appendix); of February, 1939 (306 U.S. Appendix) and of July, 1954.

[39] Speech reproduced in Robert L. Stern and Eugene Gressman, *Supreme Court Practice, op. cit.*, pp. 107-108.

[40]"What the Supreme Court Did Not Decide in the 1949 Term...,"
University of Pennsylvania Law Review, 293ff., 1950. This criticism
was carried on in volumes 100-02, 1951-1953. There is no intention
of comparing the literature of the two schools except as to emphasis.

[41]Justice Frankfurter, in a formal note attached to Sheppard *v.*
Ohio, 352 U.S. 910, 1956, defended the denial of certiorari by the
Court, a note that could well have been in the *Harvard Law Review*.
The Sheppard case involved a vicious sex murder. Press, radio, and
legal speeches had aroused a kind of mob spirit, which, it was
claimed, resulted in injustice.

[42]Among whom is Ernest J. Brown, "The Supreme Court, 1957
(Term)," 72 *Harvard Law Review* 74, 77-82, 1958-1959 (copyright
1958, 1959 by *Harvard Law Review* Association, Cambridge, Massachusetts). Pages 82ff. furnish evidence of this thesis. Arthur E.
Sullivan reviewed the Court's work of the 1956 Term, giving interesting statistics which harmonized with certain parts of Brown's
argument, 71 *Harvard Law Review*, 85-93, 1957-1958.

[43]43 Stat. 936, 1925.

[44]Stern and Gressman, *op. cit.*, p. 225. Also included in the summary action were appeals from the denial of a motion to vacate under
28 U.S.C., Sec. 2255.

[45]*Supreme Court Practice, op. cit.*, p. 148.

[46]Brown, *op. cit.*, pp. 79-80.

[47]43 Stat. 936, 1925.

[48]Stern and Gressman, *op. cit.*, p. 107, gives the text of Vinson's
speech at St. Louis on September, 1949, in which he argues the
meaning of discretionary certiorari.

[49]Brown, *op. cit.*, p. 78.

CHAPTER IX

ACTIONS TAKEN OR PROPOSED BY CONGRESS
AFFECTING INDIGENT PROCEDURE: 1922-1948

For many years it had been the practice of both state and federal courts to use the transcript of the record of hearing in the trial as a basis for agreeing upon what should go to the appellate court. There were no official reporters paid by the Government in the federal courts. All transcripts of the trial record were made under contract with some outside firm and there were no free transcripts to hand out to indigents for perfecting appeals in criminal cases. Under the *in forma pauperis* as of 1916 a federal district court denied the motion of a convicted poor man for an order to direct the district court reporter to transcribe the testimony taken at the trial at the Government's expense. The basic reason for the motion was that a bill of exceptions simply could not be made without such transcript.[1] The Court, however, could not make an effective order, for two reasons: 1) the Indigent Statute, as it stood at the time, expressed clearly the congressional intention that no liability of the United States should be incurred under the law according to section 5; 2) section 3 of the statute as amended applied only to officers of the court and a contract reporter was not such an officer and his contract did not call for free transcripts for poor convicts.[2]

In 1927 after the amendment permitting defendants on appeal to have the records of their cases printed at the expense of the Government, if the Attorney-General should approve, the same question of securing a record to print was again up for consideration. It was in connection with a petition asking a court of appeals for a mandamus to compel a district judge to make an order requiring the court reporter to transcribe the testimony in a criminal case.[3] The appellate court held that it was not in error to deny the motion for transcription, since there was no way to force the reporter, who was not an official under section 3 of the law as amended, to do the work without prepayment or giving surety therefor. Accordingly, it seemed that the pauper statute, as amended in 1910 and 1922, did not provide free transcripts to the indigent in criminal appellate proceedings. The trouble really lay in the lack of organization in the federal system of courts for carrying on business.

The two decisions noted above indicated a persistent push by indigent convicts to ascertain whether the trial courts could ever legally order transcripts of the testimony for use in perfecting their appeals to the circuit courts of appeals. The Attorney - General asked the Comptroller - General in 1930[4] whether he could pay from the "Miscellaneous Funds," or any other funds under the control of the Department of Justice, a bill of $1,850 for transcribing the testimony of a five-day criminal trial for the legally required twenty-six original copies. The trial court had issued such an order, because the case was a capital one and the defendant was a pauper. The Court of Appeals approved of the pauper proceedings and gave leave to file the literal transcript of the trial proceedings as a part of the record, *when it was actually presented.* But the same court withdrew its order to accept the literal transcript of the trial, not reduced to narrative form, partly because it found the payment thereof would not be cared for by the Government. The answer to the Attorney-General was that a transcript in type form was not payable from any appropriation available to the Department. Reporters were employed by contract and could not be compelled to furnish the defendant with such typewritten transcripts at the cost of the Government or of the reporter.

The Comptroller's decision, however, failed to halt the furnishing of a transcript to an indigent person convicted of murder in at least one case. The petitioner had appealed to the Circuit Court of Appeals and had moved that he be furnished with a transcript of the record on appeal, that the time within which to file a transcript of the record on appeal be extended and that the case be remanded to the District Court for the purpose of permitting a new trial on the ground that new evidence had been discovered. On agreement between the Solicitor's Office and petitioner's counsel, the Supreme Court vacated the appellate court's order dismissing the request of the petitioner - defendant and remanded the case to it with directions to grant the petitioner a reasonable extension of time for perfecting his appeal and to reconsider the motion to remand, when it should have before it a transcript of the evidence. The reason for this change in the case lay in the discovery that the District Court had, legally or not, a part - time reporter who was receiving a salary of $500 for doing such work. A transcript was furnished and the record completed for the appellate court.[5]

Nevertheless, it was not until the notorious Miller kidnapping case[6] that the Supreme Court took a hand in the judicial settlement of the construction of the *in forma pauperis* statute as it was after its amendment in 1922 — a settlement that was the Court's approval of what had been the case since 1789. The Court granted Miller certiorari in order to ascertain whether he had had a fair trial. The point of interest here was that Miller claimed that he could not carry an appeal to a higher court without having a complete transcript of the testimony on one of the important defenses in the case. His appointed counsel told him that appeal was useless without the complete transcript of the trial proceedings. The difficulty of securing a typewritten transcript for completing the appeal at the expense of the Government was commented on fully by Mr. Justice Roberts, speaking for the majority of the Court:

> There is no law of the United States creating the position of official court stenographer and none requiring the stenographic report of any case, civil or criminal, and there is none providing for payment of services of a stenographer in reporting judicial proceedings. The practice has been for the parties to agree that a designated person shall so report. The one selected must be paid by private arrangement with one or more parties to the litigation. The amount paid to him is not costs in the cause nor taxable as such against any of the parties. . . . The Act of 1892, as amended, applies only to court costs, permits the taking of an appeal without prepayment of cost of printing the record in the appel-

late court and provides in certain cases for the
printing of the record at Government expense. It
does not authorize the procurement of a transcript
of the testimony nor the payment for the services
in reporting evidence taken at the trial nor for obtaining it by the Government in behalf of an indigent defendant.[7]

The Court called attention to the arguments on both sides.
Miller's counsel urged that the trial court had "inherent power,
in the interests of justice, to order the preparation of a transcript for the petitioner's use in making up a bill of exceptions
and to impose the expense of so doing upon the Government."
Counsel for the Government as respondent, limiting their ideal-
ism to what was possible, pointed out that the Comptroller-
General had ruled that there was no appropriation from which
such expense might be paid.[8] The Court then remarked that
whether that officer was or was not right, it remained that no
appropriation was available without authorization of the Attorney-General and that he appeared unwilling to test the matter by making such an authorization.[9] In other words, the Court,
probing toward a more fundamental problem than expense, approved the *status quo* until Congress should see fit to extend
its credit further to the impecunious, or until it should so
reorganize the business of the judicial system that it would
fit into the basic poor persons' statute.

Mr. Justice Roberts, in discussing the particular problem
of the Miller Case in 1942, found that there would have been
no difficulty in making up a first-class bill of exceptions had
there been what was known in the state systems as *official*
court reporters. He took occasion to inject into the opinion
of the Court the following:[10]

At the instance of the Conference of Senior Circuit
Judges, legislation has been introduced in Congress to provide an official reporter system of
reporting and to defray the cost of it. That legislation, as we understand it, will, if adopted,
obviate the difficulties presented in this case. As
the matter stands, however, it is clear that the

judge's secretary who stenographically reported
the trial is not an officer of the United States in
his capacity as reporter, is not entitled to fees from
the United States, and his compensation cannot be
treated as costs.

The above statement struck at the root of the weakness of the
pauper statute in so far as the privilege granted could not be
easily enjoyed in appealing from the trial court. As noted
earlier, the only indigents who could legally call upon the
"Miscellaneous Expense Appropriation," which could not be
disbursed until approved by the Attorney-General, were those
involved in criminal appeals. Even then, the payment could be
used only for printing of the record.

The phrase, "printing of the record," was used in the 1922
amendment to the pauper statute. Behind it was a process that
was perfectly valid historically, but of doubtful continuing
utility. The usual method of making a record for appeal in
earlier history was to put the longhand notes of the judge with
the notations of counsel, mix a little memory of the witnesses,
shake thoroughly, and make from the result the bill of exceptions for the record on appeal. After all, that was merely an
administrative process developed by the American judiciary
since its establishment. The majority of the states had given
up such out-of-date practice and had provided for an official
reporter for all cases. It was the weakness of the process
behind the "printing of the record" that made it practically
impossible to secure a record to print. Once that process was
provided for, the pauper criminal could appeal and get the advantage offered in the basic statute, if the approval of the
Attorney-General, or later the Director of the Administrative
Office of the United States Courts, could be secured.

Rules of Civil Procedure, Rule 80 (b), 1939, provided that
any district court might designate one or more "official"
stenographers and fix the charges for the service of transcribing the notes at trials. Such charges were to be paid by
the litigants. In outlying districts there was no reporting of
civil proceedings, unless the litigants furnished their own
private stenographers. Where "official" stenographers had
been appointed by the district court it was not unusual for the

Government, when in court itself, to make contracts with the stenographers to do the work of taking down the evidence and other pertinent proceedings, to furnish the Government with five or six transcriptions, and to pay, in addition, $500 into the Treasury. In order to make money, therefore, the stenographers made the litigants pay high for their transcriptions. A New York City firm doing shorthand reporting was said by Judge August N. Hand to have made a contract with the Department of Justice to do its reporting for the large sum of $1 a year. That, said the commentator, was the rich man's area and left the poor devil out in the cold.[11]

In criminal cases the fact was that most of them went unreported. In the well-known Holmes case,[12] for example, there was a nineteen-day trial and no record was kept other than a sketchy one made by a witness for the defense, a record found to be more or less biased. It was a difficult matter to make up a bill of exceptions for appeal. In numerous instances in which conviction was later challenged in habeas corpus proceedings, there was no reliable evidence of what actually occurred from the time of the defendant's arraignment to his sentence. The defendant often asserted that he was not properly advised of his right of counsel, or that his rights in other respects were not properly safeguarded. The only way to establish the facts satisfactorily was to have a verbatim record of what occurred at the trial and that was rarely possible. The poor man did not have a chance, for there was still the question of paying for a transcript of the proceedings, since a contract "official stenographer" was not an official of the court under the Act of 1892, as amended. He had to be paid by the litigants for transcribing all notes since the Government could not be charged with the outlay of funds for this purpose.[13]

The Judicial Conference made the following statement in its report of 1941:

> That the present system of reporting in the courts of the United States is inferior to that prevailing in most of the States and that the enactment of a comprehensive bill, for a system of official reporters to be compensated for their attendance and taking notes, and for transcripts by fees at rates fixed by

the district courts, subject to appeal to the Judicial
Conference, is essential to the proper administration of justice in the federal courts.

Therefore, identical bills were introduced in the two Houses.
In the hearings on the Bill in the Senate[14] and the House,[15]
the various organized interest groups gave testimony as to the
value of the proposal. All through the printed record one could
see bobbing up the interest of the poor man. The exorbitant
costs of the contract reporters, especially where the Government was a party, was contrasted with the inability of the
pauper to secure a record on appeal. The question which Mr.
Justice Roberts raised in the Miller case,[16] whether a transcript of the testimony and of other proceedings in the trial
court was necessary, was discussed, especially in the House.[17]
Mr. Hobbes asked Director Chandler whether the absence of
such a transcript of the evidence would in effect bar an appeal
(to a poor man). The reply was that it was possible to do so.
Mr. Chandler insisted, however, that in nearly all cases the
appeal without the ability to show what the record was could
only be an empty right. It was *almost* essential, he continued,
to have a record in order to predicate errors upon it. He concluded his testimony with the following statement:

> I would say to you gentlemen that I think the ob-
> taining of records in criminal cases involving the
> life and liberty of a man which will show definitely,
> accurately, and beyond peradventure what the court
> did in the original case, is alone a gain which
> would justify the cost of the bill many times over.

Chief Justice Groner, of the United States Court of Appeals
of the District of Columbia, stated that it was a scandal that
cases involving long terms of imprisonment, and at times
death, were brought without an adequate record because no record was accessible to the appellant. Therefore, there was no
doubt as to the need of the law proposed.[18] Both sets of hearings considered the expense and it was the consensus of the
groups represented that from the standpoint of administration

and the gain in human values, the extra cost would not be too great. In the House Hearings it was stated that the reporter system would cost more than the contract system cost at that time, but that the expense and time devoted to habeas corpus proceedings would fall very rapidly, because the court record ordinarily would be so clear that no person could secure such a writ!

The bill became law in January, 1944,[19] and had the President's enthusiastic approval. The pertinent provisions are easily summarized. Official court reporters could be appointed by the district courts, under the close supervision of the Judicial Conference and the Director of Administration as regards qualification, number, and fees charged for transcripts. One such reporter was to attend each session of the trial court and every other proceeding of the court as ordered by the judge. His duty consisted in recording verbatim by shorthand, or by some mechanical means, all proceedings in criminal cases had in open court in connection with plea, trial, or sentence; all proceedings in other cases had in open court, unless by agreement of the parties and the court certain matters were to be omitted. The reporter was to attach his official certificate thereto, and deliver it to the proper party upon payment of the fee for the transcribing. At the same time a copy of each transcription was to be given to the clerk to file with the record free from cost. All such transcripts were to be deemed as prima facie correct. Compensation for the reporter consisted of two parts; a salary paid for the time spent in court and the fees paid by the Government or private parties for transcripts. Fees for transcripts furnished in criminal or habeas corpus proceedings to persons allowed to sue, defend, or appeal *in forma pauperis* were to be paid by the Government out of appropriated funds. Fees for transcripts furnished paupers in other than criminal and habeas proceedings were to be paid by the United States, if approved by the trial judge. The court, in its discretion, could tax such fees as costs in the case but all such fees paid by the Government for indigents in civil cases had to be taxed in favor of the United States, in case of future enrichment.

The Hearings, the Report, and the discussions on the floor of the two Houses did not provoke any formidable disagreement. In fact, debate was useless when apparently all organized groups were at one on the value of the proposed bill that became the Court Reporters Act. The Second Deficiency Appropriation Act of 1944[20] for the Judiciary eliminated the budget estimate for court reporters in the new Act without prejudice. The House Committee handling the matter suggested that there should be something more definite as to what the total salaries of the reporters would likely be, because of the double source of income named in the law. Not until the 1946 Budget was under consideration did the proper subcommittee provide for the amount asked.[21]

The 1946 Report of the Judicial Conference, after a year's trial of the official reporter system, accounted for 183 reporters of the 200 needed[22] with a total tax expenditure of $757,622. It was asserted that the new system had proved better than the private party arrangement for the following reasons:

1. Parties could count on having a reporter at court at the proper time who was paid by the Government for his time while there;

2. All non-impecunious litigants, including the Government and humblest citizens, paid the same rate for transcripts. The old contract system gave the Government transcripts for its own trial needs free, at a low rate, or free with a cash bonus, while the difference was made up by high costs to individuals for transcripts;

3. Indigents were given free transcript service;

4. On the whole, transcript costs to litigants were lower.

After the Reporters Bill became law a companion measure, the Public Defender Bill, began to appear on the program of the Judicial Conference as a part of its judicial *must* legislation in the interest of the indigent person. For a number of years leading jurists, lawyers, and a few members of Congress had been interested in installing a public defender system for impecunious defendants charged with crimes in the federal courts.[23] The various bar associations and the Attorney-General had approved proposals of such nature, and Representatives Celler and Kefauver had been pouring public defender bills into the legislative hopper regularly for some time.

The Judicial Conference began to review the proposals with a view to making one of its own. The general plan was to its liking but a different system was proposed. In a letter to Chairman Sumners of the House Committee on the Judiciary, dated December 17, 1945, Director H. P. Chandler gave the story of the bill. Plans theretofore suggested had provided either for public defenders appointed by the district courts and paid a salary from public funds or the appointment of defenders by the court in particular instances who also were to be paid from federal appropriations. The Judicial Conference favored the first plan. After making an investigation the Conference found that many of the district judges preferred the appointment in particular cases and the payment for services and expenses from court appropriations. Judge August N. Hand was then made head of a Judicial Conference Committee for further investigation and writing of a bill.

The Committee, after conferring with the different classes of persons concerned with the defense of indigent criminal defendants — judges, prosecutors, representatives of legal aid societies, and a committee from the American Bar Association — presented a report and a proposed bill based on the findings to the Judicial Conference in September, 1944. Since the support of the numerous federal district judges was all-important, all material was submitted to that body of judges for comment and questions. The result of this consultation was a change in both the report and bill, and the Administrative Director got Representative Kefauver to introduce the measure in the House in January, 1946.[24]

The bill was a compromise of the two prevailing viewpoints, namely, permanently appointed public defenders and appointed counsel by the case. Each district court was empowered to appoint a public defender on salary, but the court of each district, except those containing a city of more than

500,000 inhabitants, had the power to appoint counsel by the case and pay for services and other expenses up to $3,000 per year. If additional services were required of appointees, the court had to appoint a full- or part-time public defender. In districts of over a half million inhabitants salaried public defenders had to be appointed. These obligations were to be fulfilled if salaries were to be paid from appropriated funds. The courts were free to appoint members from their respective bars to serve for nothing, but all sides agreed that counsel for indigent defendants must be paid well if their services were to be worthwhile. Too, proposers of the bill did not dare to include free public defenders in civil cases until it was proved that the system was a success in criminal cases.[25]

The Director did not bring out any theory as to why a minority of the district judges were insistent upon the appointment of counsel from their respective bars for each indigent case. Trial judges, of course, are human and are likely to respond to the needs of the unsuccessful attorneys, especially when the Government pays the fees. In large urban districts the bar generally is overcrowded by "poor" lawyers, even hungry ones. But trial judges of wide experience in city areas have become more articulate and have not hesitated to offer theories in their fight against the public defender system. One theory widely discussed is that the judge and public defender, due to the appointer-appointee relation, would work together with their respective interest in mind rather than that of justice: this is a theory of immorality. A second theory is that when the State has taken over both prosecution and defense of the accused criminal, communism or fascism is knocking at the door.[26] The relation between judge and public defender as to appointment would be similar to the present relationship, the difference being in the time each public defender serves: the moral weakness is not fed by permanence. If the appointment is accompanied by a schedule of fees paid from federal funds, it is the judge who determines who feeds at the public crib. Perhaps, as some have suggested, the federal Government is destined to take over the defense of the criminally accused, rich or poor, as the state has in the past taken over from private persons the prosecution of criminal cases.

The failure of Congress to agree on the Judicial Conference's method, or methods, for providing paid attorneys for service to indigents in criminal proceedings has been due to a variety of reasons, among which the following are suggested: tradition, political trafficking between judge and appointed attorneys leading to corruption, the building up of an unsuccessful class of attorneys living off the taxpayers' money, and for the theorist, the dread of the functions of prosecution and defense falling into the direct control of the national state. The tradition of non-payment has not been an important negative factor, however, for the general opinion of the legal fraternity, as well as the responsible outsiders, has favored payments by the Government. Free service given by professions, special skills and the like, is not a modern habit in either government or in private or semi-private affairs. Meanwhile, another proposal has appeared for consideration: the subsidization of existing legal aid bureaus, organized locally and nationally and closely related to bar associations. The bureaus would keep a list of qualified lawyers for serving indigents in lower federal court proceedings of a criminal nature; the number available and used would be determined by the congressional appropriations provided. From the attorneys listed, the judges would select specific ones for a case or for a period of time, if the law so read. Such a method *could* cut down political trafficking and keep the panel of attorneys in the hands of the legal fraternity, although the appointing judge would be the selector from the list and the decider of the time-period. In fact, the suggestion provided only for "by case appointment." Furthermore, it would be easy to add civil cases over and above habeas corpus proceedings, non-Article III court cases, and all administrative tribunals and other administrative procedures.

In 1960 a modified form of the legal aid type was actually enacted into law, though its application was limited to the District of Columbia.[27] As a kind of pilot scheme, especially for urban areas high in the number of indigents, its provisions cover all federal courts in the District of Columbia Circuit, non-Article III courts and tribunals of the federal Government, and courts and tribunals of the District itself. The law, entitled the District of Columbia Legal Aid Act, sets up a legal aid organization which furnishes a group of salaried attorneys, all of whom must be members of the District Bar and who may not carry on any other legal work than that of serving indigents in criminal cases before the courts and tribunals within the District in criminal proceedings. In felony cases the attorneys are obliged to serve the poor man from the beginning of the preliminary hearing to the close of the case and on appeal proceedings. A list of volunteer members of the District Bar is kept by the organization, but only out-of-pocket costs are paid from federal funds.

The Agency (organization) is headed by a Board of Trustees appointed for three year terms by a panel made up of the chiefs of the various courts in the District and the President of the Commissioners of the District of Columbia, any four of whom constitute a quorum. The Trustees appoint a Director, who has named powers and those delegated to him by the Trustees. He receives a named salary of $16,000 per year, serves during good behavior, and maintains a list of salaried attorneys from which the district judge or the chief of the circuit chooses one or more to aid the indigent and appoints his office force. He cannot expend the money budgeted, however, without the approval of the Director of the Administration of the United States Courts, who is the executive officer of the Judicial Conference, chaired by the Chief Justice of the Supreme Court. The defender system, or some closely related one, is still an important item of business before Congress. Pressure was exerted by the Judicial Conference, the President, the various organizations found among the lawyers, and by the Supreme Court, which was very busy during the spring of 1963 tightening and expanding its rulings on the required use of counsel in criminal cases.[28]

The President's faithful Attorney-General in 1961 had appointed the special Allen Committee to make a study of poverty and the administration of indigent criminal cases in the federal court system. Reported early in 1963, its substance seemed to please the legal profession if press reports can be trusted. One general comment was of interest: "For the rich there is no problem; for the poor, if the Committee's recommendations were accepted, there would be satisfactory legal service; for the in-between class there could be only the legal service its members could pay for — a very limited service." This comment was a special application of a universal truth.[29] But the Report and the proposed bill based thereon, plus earlier hearings, were widely circulated and the Congressional Houses received identical bills from the President with an accompanying note emphasizing the great need for their consideration.

The Eighty-eighth Congress, First Session, numbered the bills as H.R. 4816 and S. 1057. As events proved the bills were in competition with several that the Administration considered to be more important, and H.R. 4816 met its demise in Committee on July 16, 1963; S. 1057 got as far as a favorable report and the content of the measure is summarized from the Senate Report.[30]

The Criminal Justice Bill, according to S. 1057, had as its purpose the furnishing of first class legal services, including counsel and expert in getting at the facts, for those charged or convicted of federal crime and unable to furnish protection of their own in whole or in part. The services were to begin in serious criminal cases at the earliest effective moment and continue through to the end of the case and then on appeal, if necessary. Each judicial district was to furnish such free service and according to several options stated in the bill. Adequate compensation was to be provided for counsel and experts, when needed, and no plan could be implemented until approved by the Judicial Council of the circuit in which the district is located. Overall responsibility for the administration of the bill was to lie in the Judicial Conference of the United States for the plans, rules and organization for instituting each plan. Alternative plans or options named in the bill were meant to spell out to the judges, lawyers, and citizens of the area how counsel and expert would be provided to protect the interest of indigent persons in criminal proceedings. Such plans would also enable Congress to follow out the plan in its working in each district and enable the

Budget Director and Congress to assess the need for money.

The plans under the direction of the Conference may provide for different procedure for preliminary hearings and trials. Each plan must provide for screening applicants for pauper procedure, by hearing, by affidavit or by panel of private attorneys. The plans may establish standards for paying counsel and for expert fact finding, for guide lines at every stage of the trial or appeals and rosters of private attorneys capable of defending may be kept for service.

Specifically, the bill called for the following plans:

1. Appointment of attorneys from private practice for not more than $15 per hour—not a high standard of pay but, added to public duty, quite adequate.

2. This plan permits the establishment of the office of public defender, with the necessary number of assistants and experts to back them up in fact-finding. Private bar may furnish attorneys to work with the defenders. To guard the independence of the public defender from control of the judge or executive-administrative officer, appointment of the public defender by the Circuit Council for a four-year term, with pay equal to that of a federal attorney and that of assistant public defenders with pay equal to that of assistant federal attorneys. Part time public defenders may be appointed when necessary.

3. Where other local aid societies or clubs had shown that they were able to handle free service, a representative from such organization could appoint worthy attorneys to aid the poor, but the pay therefor would go to the organization to be distributed as it saw fit.

4. A possible combination of the above three plans.

This flexibility in plan indicates that there could be no general agreement on a single method; that no attorney could be built into any of the plans; that every one of the legal fraternity must have an opportunity to partake of a plan, either for whatever cash it produced or for the love of doing something for his fellow men. Another doubtful short-range good that the proposers thought might result was the development of one or more technical procedures that would result. A long view might result in such development and the States might seize onto the best forms thereof. The House Committee on the Judiciary, whose members had not recognized the cooperative spirit of the present age, did not, perhaps, see the good in departing from the existing method, plus pay.

Again, the matter has not been settled and the American Bar Foundation, in cooperation with state bars, has been busy prosecuting a nation-wide inquiry into the matter of providing aid for the indigent in criminal proceedings and the Ford Foundation has granted the National Legal Aid and Defense Association a third of a million dollars for research into the problem. Within another decade the judiciary will defend the poor man on the basis of pay.

NOTES TO CHAPTER IX

[1]United States *v.* Fair, 235 F. 1015, 1916.

[2]Rule 80 (b), Federal Rules of Criminal Procedure then current.

[3]Estabrook *v.* Otis, 18 F. 2d. 689, 1927.

[4]9 Comp. Gen. 503, 1930, A-31864.

[5]Evans *v.* United States, 312 U.S. 651, 1941.

[6]Miller *v.* United States, 317 U.S. 192, 1942.

[7]*Ibid.*, 197.

[8]*Ibid.*, brief filed by Counsel for petitioner, pp. 27-53; 9 Comp. Gen. 503, 1930; Cf, 21 Comp. Gen. 347, 1941.

[9]Miller *v.* United States, 317 U.S. 192, 197-98, 1942.

[10]*Ibid.*, 197.

[11]*Hearings* before Committee on Judiciary on H.R. 3142 (3611), 78th Cong., 1st Sess., November 2, 1943.

[12]United States *v.* Holmes, 115 F. 2d. 528, 1940; Holmes *v.* United States, 314 U.S. 583, 1941; 319 U.S. 776, 1943.

[13]*Report* of the Director, 1943, p. 12; House Report No. 868, to accompany H.R. 3611, 78th Cong., 2nd Sess., 1943.

[14]S. 620.

[15]H.R. 3142 (3611).

[16]317 U.S. 192, 1942.

[17]*Hearings*, p. 14, to accompany H.R. 3142 (3611) before Committee on the Judiciary, 78th Cong., 1st Sess., November 2, 1943.

[18]*Hearings* before the Senate Committee on the Judiciary on S. 620 (3611), 78th Cong., 1st Sess., 1943.

[19] 58 Stat. 5. "The new law has a very laudable purpose of doing away with the contract system which has prevailed in the federal courts and substituting a federally controlled and operated system of reporting the proceedings of the courts." House Report No. 1660, 2d Defic. Approp. Act, 78th Cong., 2d Sess., 1944.

[20] H. Rep. No. 1660, to accompany H.R. 5040, 78th Cong., 2d Sess., June 16, 1944, pp. 3-4.

[21] H.R. 2603, 79th Cong., 1st Sess., Apvd. May 21, 1945 by Depts. of State, Justice, Commerce, the Judiciary, and the Federal Loan Agency.

[22] The 1952 *Rep.* gave 199 reporters with 24 to be added later.

[23] *A.B.A.J.* second draft of Poor Litigants Statute opened up free service for all poor litigants, citizens or not, who, with funds not exceeding $500 or maximum of $25 wages or income per week. This potential statute was for States but was applicable to Federal Government also, 50 *A.B.A.R.* 456, 1925.

[24] As Bill H.R. 5188, 79th Cong., 2d Sess., 1946, recognized as the authentic Judicial Conference Bill.

[25] *Report* of the Director, p. 15, 1945, and the bill itself.

[26] *E.g,* Judge Edward J. Dimock, "The Public Defender: A Step Toward the Police State," 42 *A.B.A.J.* 219-20, March, 1956.

[27] Public Law 86-531, 74 Stat. 229, July 27, 1960.

[28] The Supreme Court had put pressure on Congress to provide, in addition to supplying counsel, in all cases in trial courts, but had reinforced its demand for counsel in appeals to the circuit courts (Coppedge v. United States, 369 U.S. 438, 1962); indirectly, it has forced the attention of the Federal Government to reconsider the whole matter of furnishing counsel for the poor by overturning Betts v. Brady, a 1942 state case excusing the appointment of counsel for indigent non-capital cases, thereby universalizing the service of free counsel in all types of criminal cases involving the poor (Gideon v. Wainwright, 373 U.S. 335, 1963).

[29] *E.g., Richmond Times-Dispatch*, March 8, 1963, p. 24, col. 1; *New York Times*, August 30, 1963, p. 39, cols. 1-3.

[30] Senate Report No. 346; Committee on the Judiciary Hearing on May 13, 20, 27, 1963. Other valuable documents are found in Appendices of the Report. The Allen Report had informed the Senate Committee that 10,000 cases of indigent criminal cases came to the federal courts — one-third of the total per year. A *Hearings* of the Senate Committee on the Public Defender Bills in 1958 found that 8 out of 10 cases of felony rank involved indigents and that in special urban areas the proportion was greater than the average. The figures for the federal prison on population in 1958 was 20,000 and for the States, 179,415. Both sets of figures should be much higher in 1963.

CHAPTER X

SUPREME COURT RULINGS ON
HABEAS CORPUS AFFECTING INDIGENT
PROCEDURE: 1922-1948

Collateral attacks by habeas corpus could kill a judgment or sentence of a trial court before 1922 under the following circumstances: first, when there was a total lack of jurisdiction over either the person or the cause; second, when the court had exercised its jurisdiction in the premises[1] — as when some other matter rendered the judgment or sentence void.[2] This second circumstance simply left room for some unexpected "something" that might call for the use of the writ. There had been a broad assertion by Chief Justice Chase to the effect that the new habeas corpus legislation of 1867 had given all United States courts the almost unlimited power to issue the writ in carrying out their respective jurisdictional duties.[3]

Pressure for using the writ to aid both those with and without funds began to find expression in a number of cases, especially those arising under state action.[4] A federal territorial case suggested that the denial of any constitutional right could be attacked by habeas corpus.[5] In the Frank case in Georgia[6] the majority held that the record was *"perfect"* and that review by habeas corpus was not possible. Justice Holmes, however, dissented on the ground that the whole story had not appeared and that the writ of habeas corpus would sooner or later come to be used to ferret out the suspected facts that did not appear in the record (facts *dehors* the record) in cases where the jury and counsel were suspected of being intimidated by imminent action of a mob.

After 1922 the development of the use of the writ of habeas corpus in collateral attack on judgments and sentences moved faster. The Supreme Court found cause to grant the writ in a

state murder case which appeared to have been wholly dominated by a mob.[7] Chief Justice Taft assigned Justice Holmes
to write the majority opinion. This gave the Associate Justice an opportunity to apply his basic thought uttered in the
Frank case of 1915: if in fact a trial was so dominated by a
mob that there was interference with the course of justice,
there was a departure from due process (14th Amendment);
and if the state, supplying no corrective process, should carry
into execution the judgment of death or imprisonment based
upon a verdict produced by mob domination, the state would
deprive the accused of his life or liberty without due process
of law and federal habeas corpus would issue, regardless of a
perfect formal record. In the present case, the Justice went to
the heart of the matter.[8]

> It is certainly true that mere mistakes of the law
> in the course of a trial are not to be corrected [by
> federal habeas corpus]. But if the case is that
> the whole proceeding is a mask — that counsel,
> jury and judge were swept to the fatal end by an
> irresistible wave of public passion, and the State
> Courts failed to correct the wrong, neither perfec-
> tion in the machinery for correction or the pos-
> sibility that the trial court and counsel saw no
> other way of avoiding an immediate outbreak of
> the mob can prevent this Court from securing to
> the petitioners their constitutional rights [by fed-
> eral habeas corpus].

The Arkansas Supreme Court had refused to allow habeas
corpus or any other corrective process at hand to inquire into
the facts of the case. On petition the five condemned men
men went to a United States district court for a federal writ of
habeas corpus, but the judge dismissed the petition without a
hearing. The convicts then reached the Supreme Court on
special certiorari where the majority rebuked the judge for not
attempting to ascertain whether the alleged reasons for issuing the writ were actually true, for if true, for granting it.
The order dismissing the petition was reversed and the district
court was directed to ascertain the facts *dehors* the record

and act according to directions.[9] Two Justices dissented.

The Supreme Court in a per curiam opinion of 1935,[10] presumably written by Chief Justice Hughes, seemed to push further the use of the writ of habeas corpus. Tom Mooney had been tried, convicted, and sentenced to death for murder in 1917 (although his sentence was later commuted to life imprisonment by the State Governor). Vigilant attorneys had noted the expanding use of federal habeas corpus and independently had been searching for evidence that might possibly secure Mooney's release from state custody. A petition to a federal district court was denied on the ground that state remedies had not been exhausted and the appellate court had affirmed. Mooney then petitioned the Supreme Court for an "original" habeas corpus, alleging, *inter alia*, that he had been convicted by the use of perjured testimony known to the prosecution. The state Attorney-General met the allegation not only with categorical denial, but with a general argument that due process could not possibly be expanded to include due process as used in California, even if the Court thought that due process of the 14th Amendment might be allowed in the case. The answer of the Court was a repudiation of the Attorney-General, but this opinion turned on the fact that state remedies had not been exhausted. The petition was dismissed without prejudice — that is, Mooney could come back for the writ after having exhausted state remedies without securing relief. Here the doctrine of exhausting state remedies was merely a judicial ruling. The Court placed squarely before the lower federal courts, as well as the state courts, the fact that the "original" writ of habeas corpus would be the chief means of forcing the states to provide corrective methods in post-conviction cases or suffer direct federal intervention.

Following the two state-origin cases, came that of the famous "Victory of the Marines."[11] Two of those fighters, vacationing in Charleston, S. C., "happened" to have in their possession a number of $20 counterfeit bills. In their "ignorance and inexperience" as long-time members of the Marines (one a corporal), they happened to pass a few of them as legal tender. The nature of the bills was quickly detected and the two men were arrested. They obtained a lawyer (for real money) at the preliminary hearing, but he vanished when such money was spent. They were tried, one acting as a rather bright attorney, and convicted. The sentence was a maximum of six years of confinement in Atlanta Prison. After due allowance for quarantine time, "they were made a part of the prison community." In talking over their case with a wise inmate, they learned that if there had been a material fault in the trial procedure, they could go to the circuit court on error. They found that review on error was untimely. Then this fellow prisoner suggested that habeas corpus might serve their purpose. Accordingly, one of them was told to petition the nearest federal district court for habeas corpus to attack the judgment and sentence of the original federal trial court. A well-conducted hearing was held and the district court admitted that the whole decalogue of procedural sins had been committed by the trial court, whose judge had gone "a-fishing" when he thought that he might be called to give evidence of what happened in his court at the trial. However, the district court dismissed the petition on the ground that the petitioners were trying to get a review of their case, a procedure that did not involve habeas corpus (collateral) attack. On appeal the same answer was given. Petition for review by certiorari was asked, along with pauper procedure, and was granted.

Justice Black, the first of the Roosevelt appointees, was assigned the task of writing the majority opinion. He began with the following statement:[12]

> Congress has expanded the rights of a petitioner for habeas corpus and the effect is to substitute for the bare legal review that was the limit of judicial authority at common law a more searching investigation in which the applicant is put on his oath to set forth the truth of the matter respecting the causes of detention, and the court, upon determining the actual fact, is to dispose of the party as law and justice require.

After making this statement of the use of the writ of habeas corpus, he ruled that a fundamental right had been denied Johnson (his partner in crime had already been released on parole) in that he had been denied counsel in a criminal case (6th Amendment); and that the trial court in denying this constitutional right had lost jurisdiction during the first trial over which it did have jurisdiction. The very doubtful utility of the saving clause uttered in connection with the denial of counsel — unless counsel had been intelligently waived — in most instances saved the immediate freedom of the convict. · This seemed to be a way of following the old rule that the writ of habeas corpus would issue in cases where the court had no jurisdiction.

Perhaps a majority of the Court thought that the decision would be more palatable to the legal profession if the old rule of lack of jurisdiction over the parties or the subject matter could be made to apply at any point in the proceedings. The Government's brief, and presumably its oral argument, called attention of the Court to the great jump made in moving from the conditions obtaining in the Moore and Mooney cases to those appearing in the instant federal case:

> The Court below held that habeas corpus could not be substituted for appeal except in extraordinary circumstances[14].... Even the cases of Moore v. Dempsey and Mooney v. Holohan, which were the outstanding exceptions to the rule, were marked by characteristics not found in the present case. Each of these cases involved such a departure from the ordinary course of an impartial judicial trial as to warrant the inference that there had been a break-down of justice. The instant case has no such characteristics.

The decision in this case was not unanimous; Justices McReynolds and Butler dissented and Justice Cardoza was absent on account of illness. The six remaining Justices agreed on the main objective, namely, that the procedure in the United States District Court of Eastern Georgia had to be remedied and that habeas corpus was the only remedy available under the circumstances. Justice Stone's reaction to Justice Black's tentative opinion was a technical one given in response to the latter's request for changes that might improve it.[15] His suggestion might have made it easier to expand the use of habeas corpus to correct denials of rights under the Constitution, without losing a jurisdiction which the trial court had at the beginning of the case. He wrote:[16]

> Your use of the word "jurisdictional." The word has come to have a technical significance, [that is] when the Court is without power to render any judgment, and the effect of your use of it, I think, is to narrow your opinion rather than to widen it, as seems desirable here.... Hence I should prefer, without applying a name to the Court's authority, to write the opinion in such a way that the petitioner in habeas corpus could always challenge a judgment where substantial constitutional rights were taken away from him in ways which make it difficult or impossible for him to raise the question in direct appeal. I do not suppose that in the Dempsey [Moore v. Dempsey] case there was any technical want of jurisdiction of the court, but because the court had proceeded in such a way as to deprive the man of his constitutional rights. The Court protected them on habeas corpus.

Justice Black agreed to make the change, if his fellow justices in conference should approve. They did not.

Since the conditions precedent for issuing a federal habeas corpus writ applied equally to persons detained pursuant to a court judgment in either state or federal courts, it seems proper to indicate that the basis for the issuing of the writ by courts of the United States as of 1938 was forecast for the future: initial lack of jurisdiction, special circumstances, and loss of jurisdiction during the proceedings in a case. In the following analysis, the decisions immediately following Johnson v. Zerbst will be selected from those originating in federal courts. Following this, additional important cases arising in state courts will be presented. All will deal with indigents since post-conviction cases are usually *in forma pauperis.*

The Bowen case[17] came on the heels of Johnson v. Zerbst and probably was connected with it in spirit and form. Bowen had been convicted and given a life sentence in Alcatraz Federal Prison for a murder committed in a park, the land of which Georgia had ceded to the United States for certain purposes. He petitioned a near-by federal district court in California for habeas corpus on the ground that he had been denied due process in that the federal court in Georgia had jurisdiction neither of his person nor of the subject matter, since Georgia had not ceded sovereignty to the United States over the area. He stated that he could not appeal because there was nothing available to him in the record and that the only way to attack the lack of jurisdiction was through habeas corpus. The district court dismissed the petition for the reason that the correction could not be brought about by habeas corpus and the appellate court agreed.

On certiorari, Chief Justice Hughes wrote the opinion. He made a note to the effect that the entire lack of jurisdiction from the beginning of a case, or the loss of jurisdiction during the proceedings, could be attacked by habeas corpus, as was done in Johnson *v.* Zerbst. He stated the rule requiring resort to appellate procedure rather than habeas corpus when the trial court had determined its own jurisdiction of an offense, had special application where there were essential questions of fact determinable by the trial court and was applicable also to determine, in ordinary cases, disputed matters of law relating to sufficiency of indictment or validity of statute. However, he continued, the rule might yield to *exceptional circumstances*, including a conflict on a question of law involving concerns of large importance, when need for remedy was apparent. Circumstances in the instant case permitted the use of habeas corpus in that the petitioner had to have the question whether the federal courts or those of Georgia had criminal jurisdiction over the parkland. The Chief Justice proceeded to get the information himself, pronounced that the United States did have jurisdiction, and affirmed the lower courts; but he did not remand the case because it would have been a waste of time!

Enlargement and refinement upon all but the first basis for granting the "freeing" writ followed very soon. Two men from the most select federal criminal population (bank robbers, kidnappers, murderers) resided at the Alcatraz Prison (soon to be abandoned for a more luxurious inland prison). Both were seasoned criminals and had learned what the two preceding cases had opened up to them in the way of habeas corpus. Each, at different times, had asked for habeas corpus to secure their liberty on the ground that material facts *dehors* the record showed that they had been denied rights under the Constitution and laws of the United States. Walker[18] made two specific claims: that he had been forced by the federal attorney to plead guilty "or else," and that the allegation, though *dehors* the record, should have been heard by the court in the presence of the petitioner. Justice Roberts did not free him, but had an opportunity to use his legal knife in cutting out a so-called "show cause" procedure that had been grafted onto the legal form of habeas corpus procedure in the western circuits. He reversed the decision and ordered the district court to hear the case with the prisoner present, take live testimony, and ascertain whether the allegation was true.

The second case was Waley *v.* Johnston,[19] one that dealt with allegations *dehors* the record. By 1942 the Court had hardened the rule into a "must," and the federal prison population had learned to play variations on the main theme. The rule read definitively as follows: "where facts *dehors* the record, which were not open to consideration upon appeal, are alleged to show a denial of constitutional rights, a judicial hearing must be granted to ascertain the truth or falsity of the allegations."[20]

It has already been shown that the Supreme Court, quite early in its history, had insisted that habeas corpus jurisdiction must arise from federal statutes. The Court, however, had been probing the meaning of common law practice in issuing the writ and also the meaning of the jurisdiction bestowed by law both in England and in the United States. Either the Court majority had not read the history of the bases for the issuing of the writ or had wanted to come out in the open with its expansion of the writ by its own action when the case of Price *v.* Johnston[21] came up for review. Justice Murphy spoke for the majority:

> However, we do not conceive that a circuit court
> of appeals, in issuing a writ of habeas corpus

under Section 262 of the Judicial Code, is necessarily confined to the precise form of the writ in
vogue at the common law or in the English judicial system. Section 262 says that the writ must
be agreeable to the usages and principles of law,
a term which is unlimited by common law or
English law. And since "law" is not a static
concept, but expands and develops as new problems arise, we do not believe that the forms of
the habeas corpus writ authorized by Section 262
are only those recognized in this country in 1789,
when the original Judiciary Act containing the
substance of this section came into existence.

This interpretation served as the theoretical justification
for the use of the writ in bringing a person into court to argue
his own appeal and for any further extension of its use. The
Supreme Court, ten years after the original judgment, reversed
and remanded the case on two counts: (1) the denial by the
circuit court of its power to use habeas corpus to bring the
petitioner before that court for arguing his own case; (2)
failure to investigate the allegation that the prosecution had
used perjured testimony knowingly to convict the petitioner.
The chief judge of the circuit court had ordered the case on
appeal to be heard *in banc* and the decision against the petitioner was made by a 5-2 vote. The majority of the circuit
court had not looked into the perjured-evidence allegation
and had conceded that if the court did have the power to bring
the prisoner from Alcatraz by issuing habeas corpus in aid of
its jurisdiction, it had sound judicial discretion to issue or
not to issue the writ. In other words, in its discretion it could
deny the petitioner's application on the basis of pure nuisance
and harassment (in that the petition was the fourth one and
that whatever was claimed as new among the allegations had
been known when the first petition was made). Statistics
were cited by the circuit court but Judges Denman and Stevens
pushed them aside, saying that administrative inconvenience
was of little moment when a poor creature was fighting for his
freedom from what was for him a life sentence.[22]
Price was a dangerous criminal proficient in the ways of

physical escape, but the treacherous ocean currents surrounding Alcatraz had blocked any such attempts. He thus had to rely upon his mental ability to secure his liberty. His extensive experience as a defendant in the federal courts had made him a real expert in criminal procedure and had given him a knowledge of the ways in which he could use civil procedure of the writ of habeas corpus to secure his freedom or to grind down the energy of the judges and administrative officers until they were almost ready to cease fighting. His effectiveness as a practical lawyer, of course, was greater before the recodification of federal procedure of 1948 took effect. He knew that it was not too fortunate for a convict to have his prison home in a circuit where the only available district court to petition for a writ of habeas corpus was the court that convicted him. He knew that his best chances for freedom through the writ and opportunity to abuse procedures lay in having his prison home in a "foreign" circuit, in which there were several district courts in which he could, in lieu of freedom, make the courts go full circle for each of the allegations based upon the facts not found in the record.[23] The Chief Justice and Justice Reed concurred in this dissent. Justice Jackson dissented for similar reasons, but in his own words: "...if one allegation is not successful, concoct another and in this case the tenth-year concoction was successful, though there was evidence that the first and all the other concoctions could have been given in 1940."[24]

It was indicated in the first part of this section that the Supreme Court had already begun to apply limitations on the states under the due process clause of the 14th Amendment. The Court had not utilized this due process clause to supervise state criminal procedure, whereas the states had been allowed great freedom in providing for their judicial organization and procedure, especially in criminal matters. However, in civil procedure, through the development from this clause of both a substantive and procedural due process, the free and broad concept of the police power (as in Munn v. Ill.)[25] had been very much narrowed by the substantive concept as in the railroad rate cases. In criminal procedure the Supreme Court hesitated to enforce upon the states the rights guaranteed by the Constitution and granted by the laws of the United

States, either because it believed sincerely in the states' autonomy in this field or because it desired to maintain a real balance of power among the federal units. Mr. Justice Holmes' dissent heralded a change in the easy-going view of the Court in Frank v. Mangum.[27] Moore v. Dempsey[27] "marked the abandonment of the Supreme Court's deference to decisions of state appellate tribunals on issues of constitutionality and the proclamation of its intention no longer to treat as virtually conclusive pronouncements of the latter that proceedings in a trial court were fair."

Collateral attack by habeas corpus, then, had already been approved by the Court as a means of voiding a state judgment under the due process clause of the 14th Amendment. Thereafter, every time the Court approved an extension of the habeas corpus attack on violations of what it considered to be an unjust denial of liberty, or more broadly of the principle of fairness in federal decisions, the greater the number of petitions from federal prisoners. Persons incarcerated pursuant to state court judgments would commonly attempt with some success to use collateral attack in the same manner and to incorporate the rights denied as being a part of the due process clause of the 14th Amendment.[28] Also, that Amendment killed many decisions of state courts because of discrimination — a substantive right.

As indicated in the first part of this section, the new use of the writ of habeas corpus had really begun, in a 1923 case of state origin, when the Supreme Court extended the writ of habeas corpus to reach a situation in the midst of which fairness could not exist.[29] Johnston v. Zerbst[30] universalized the extension of the writ for testing indirectly each and every claim that constitutional (or God-given) rights had been nullified. Just what rights could be claimed under the Constitution had to be spelled out by the Supreme Court, for the most part when the claimant was being detained as a result of a state court judgment.

It was after 1938 that the prison population of the states began to join that of the federal in attempts to secure freedom from incarceration by federal habeas corpus or some other collateral means. Most of the state, as well as federal, prisoners, were and are "poor persons" and, consequently, the extension of the writ by court action has involved factors that tended, in turn, to emphasize emotion often at the expense of reason. When procedural due process rights under the 14th Amendment were violated and were caught as error or exceptions in the record, the cure was by appeal or certiorari for review. But when claims by state prisoners were made on denial of federal procedural rights which never appeared on the record but were merely alleged on oath by the prisoner, the solution was more difficult; the rights of state prisoners that could be protected were for the most part those found in the due process and equal protection clauses of the 14th Amendment. Due process, as interpreted by the Court, has served as the basis for supervising and controlling the states in criminal matters; substantive due process, as interpreted by the Court, has extended the control by that body over the states.[31] The equal protection clause, on the other hand, has served to protect valuable substantive rights of the less fortunate man and has, in fact, tended to set up a new legal era for large minorities.[32]

The extension of the use of the writ of habeas corpus for protecting individual rights in federal cases of imprisonment had secured excellent results soon after 1938. This statement is made without taking into consideration the possible motive or motives of the several Justices in making the extension: for example, sympathy for the underdog, the unalterable belief in a wider area of individual rights (spheres of anarchy), belief in an absolute standard for procedural and substantive rights obtained directly from natural law, or taken from the Bill of Rights, or other provisions of the Constitution. Emphasis upon the protection of the individual at the expense of the state or society is understandable, for big government, big corporations, and big organizations of various kinds have tended to "lose" the individual. This extreme regard for the deserving, however, has frequently played into the hands of the undeserving; uses became abuses in federal detentions.[33] When state prisoners realized the uses of the writ of habeas corpus, abuses became no less flagrant.

Until 1948 much of habeas corpus procedural law came

out of court rules and decisions, in which it was claimed that federal rights in cases decided by state courts were involved. The usual means for protecting state citizens in original cases have served to protect their claimed federal rights: writs of error based upon the court record, and writs of habeas corpus or writs of error *coram nobis*, common law or legislative in origin. Procedures other than the writ of error have been termed collateral procedures for attacking the judgment of a court below and may be appealed to the highest court of the state or to some lower courts in the state's hierarchy.

Mr. Justice Frankfurter, who usually made an effort to protect the delicate balance between state and federal jurisdictions, frequently noted in his decisions on claimed federal rights that state court records were often of the common law variety. Such records usually included the indictment properly endorsed, the arraignment of the accused, the plea, impaneling of the jury, its judgment, the minute entry of the sentence, and the sentence. For the appellate record, there was required a bill of exceptions, together with appropriate excerpts from the testimony to clarify them.[34] Such a record satisfied the state courts, but the Supreme Court refused to accept as final such general statements of what happened during the course of the trial unless there was additional evidence concerning what had taken place at the trial. The Court had had difficulty in getting any reports at all of many federal criminal cases because the proceedings were not recorded or, if recorded by "private" reporters, there were no funds for transcription. After the Federal Court Reporters Bill became law in 1944,[35] the Court began to press for full court records in criminal cases in the states where federal claims of denial of rights appeared. When the Supreme Court granted certiorari it usually sent the cases back for further ascertainment of the facts.[36] If the Court made a final decision for or against the petitioner on the point raised, the judgment was affirmed and only a timely request for a rehearing, if wanted, could prolong the case.

The state prisoner could also attempt, in a post-conviction application, the nullification of the sentencing court by means of a writ of habeas corpus if state law permitted. If the application were denied "on its face" or dismissed after hearing, the applicant could appeal finally to the highest state court allowed by local law. If his appeal were denied he usually would petition the Supreme Court for certiorari to the highest state court, which denied his appeal, alleging the denial of the same federal rights that had taken place below. Before 1948 repetition of this procedure was all too common. Further, the state prisoner could attack his sentence by applying to his trial court for a writ of error *coram nobis*, a common law writ or legislative variation thereof, if the state permitted. This was a procedure by which the prisoner could ask the trial court to reconsider its verdict for the reason that facts later discovered, and which he could not have known at the trial, might show that he should be released or the judgment modified. If the *coram nobis* procedure failed him, he could appeal as in habeas corpus.

From the above discussion the following statements of importance in the state criminal procedure in which a state convict claims a state denial of federal rights are listed up to 1948: 1) a state must furnish effective procedures by which a state prisoner can have his "day in court" on claimed violation of federal rights (that is, if the federal courts are not to take over);[37] 2) the exhaustion of all state remedies by state prisoners (including denial of petitions for certiorari to the Supreme Court or denials with "no prejudice");[38] 3) the allegations made in a state prisoner's petition for habeas corpus to a federal court must not contain allegations that have not been presented to the state courts, lest the same be sent back for state action.[39]

NOTES TO CHAPTER X

[1]*Supra*, pp. 60-61, Part I.

[2]*Supra*, p. 64, Part I; *Ex parte* Frederick, 149 U.S. 701, 707, 1893.

[3]Note 1; Chief Justice Chase asserted the full competency of the Habeas Corpus Act of 1867 to reach any case involving actions in *Ex parte* McCardle, 6 Wall. 318, 325, 1867.

[4]*E.g.*, Talton *v.* Mays, 163 U.S. 376, 1896 (IFP); Creamer *v.* Washington State Board, 168 U.S. 124, 1897; Storti *v.* Massachusetts 183 U.S. 138, 1901; Ross *v.* Aguerre, 191 U. S.60, 1903 (IFP); Valentina *v.* Mercer, 201 U.S. 131, 1906.

[5]*Ex parte* Nielson, 131 U.S. 176, 182, 1889.

[6]Frank *v.* Mangum, 237 U.S. 309, 1915.

[7]Moore *v.* Dempsey, 261 U.S. 86, 1923, arising in Arkansas courts.

[8]*Ibid.*, p. 91. This might well have been one of the circumstances, other than absence of jurisdiction referred to earlier.

[9]The remedy did not lie in the discharging of the prisoner, or in the lack of jurisdiction, but in a forcing of the lower court to ascertain facts, before anything else was done.

[10]Mooney *v.* Holohan, 294 U.S. 103, 1935.

[11]Johnson *v.* Zerbst, 304 U.S. 458, 1938.

[12]*Ibid.*, 406; law cited as 28 U.S.C.A., Secs. 451 ff. for 1938.

[13]S. Ct. R. and B., L.C., Vol 504.

[14]The second set of circumstances noted above, p. 141.

[15]Exchange of notes, Stone to Black, May 19, 1938; *Stone Papers*, L.C.

[16]*Ibid.*

[17]Bowen *v.* Johnston, 306 U.S. 19, 1939.

[18]Walker *v* Johnston, 312 U.S. 275, 1941. Compare Holiday *v.* Johnston, 313 U.S. 342, 1941.

[19]Waley *v.* Johnston, 316 U.S. 101, 1942.

[20]*Constitution of the United States of America,* 1942 Ed., Sen. Doc. No. 170, 82nd Cong., 2nd Sess., 1953.

[21]Price *v.* Johnston, 334 U.S. 266, 1948.

[22]S. Ct. R. and B., Vol. 334.

[23]*Ibid.,* Price *v.* Johnston, 334 U.S. 266. 1948.

[24]Price *v.* Johnston, 334 U.S. 266, 296-97, 1948. Justice Frankfurter had stated in a non-indigent case (Sunal *v.* Large, 332 U.S. 174, 175, 1947): "I think it is fair to say that the scope of habeas corpus in the federal courts is an untidy area of the law."

[25]Munn *v.* Ill., 91 U.S. 115, 1877.

[26]237 U.S. 309, 1915.

[27]261 U.S. 86, 1923. Quote from U.S. Senate Document, *The Constitution of the United States of America,* 1952 Ed., p. 1139.

[28]Johnson *v.* Zerbst, 304 U.S. 458, 1938, loss of jurisdiction in trial, no counsel.

[29]Moore *v.* Dempsey, 261 U.S. 861, 1923.

[30]Johnson *v.* Zerbst, 304 U.S. 458, 1938.

[31]Near *v.* Minnesota, 283 U.S. 697, 1931, though it was not an *in forma* case.

[32]*E.g.,* Hill *v.* Texas, 316 U.S. 400, 1942; Patton *v.* Mississippi, 332 U.S. 463, 1947.

[33]Price *v.* Johnston, 334 U.S. 266, 1948, already cited.

[34]Carter *v.* Illinois, 329 U.S. 173, 176-77, 1946, for example. The content of the common law record in Illinois, 1892; see United States *v.* Taylor, 147 U.S. 695, 698-99, 1893.

[35]58 Stat. 5, 1944.

[36]It has been this practice of making the trial courts dig out the unrecorded facts that gave rise in part to the charge that the Court had violated the Judge's Law of 1925 by becoming a trial court, assigning the work of ascertaining the facts to the district courts.

[37]Mooney *v.* Holohan, 294 U.S. 103, 115, 1935.

[38]This topic is thoroughly discussed in the Hawk cases: Hawk *v.* O'Grady, 307 U.S. 645, 1940; *Ex parte* Hawk, 321 U.S. 114, 1944, where several remedies were said to exist. Wade *v.* Mayo, 334 U.S. 672, 1948, softened the *Ex parte* Hawk requirement of *all* remedies by reducing to *one* the remedies carried to the Supreme Court before federal habeas corpus could be legally applied for. The Wade case also broke the rule of requiring any or all state remedies to go to the Supreme Court by not requiring any such action outside the state jurisdiction. The Court, however, came back to the original rule through Darr *v.* Burford, 339 U.S. 200, 1950. See 94 Law Ed. 785-795, for Annotation of State Remedies. Congress accepted the "exhaust state remedies" rule, but allowed the Supreme Court to determine certiorari.

[39]*Ibid.*

CHAPTER XI

INDIGENTS UNDER THE
NEW HABEAS CORPUS CODE WITH PROPOSED
AMENDMENTS AND INTERPRETATION THEREOF:
1948-1963

1. PERTINENT LEGISLATIVE PROVISIONS OF THE NEW CODE WITH PROPOSED AMENDMENTS

The Judicial Conference of the United States, with the aid of the Director, endeavored to reinforce judicial administration by securing legislation to bolster any weaknesses that might appear.[1] The Supreme Court had expanded the use of habeas corpus beyond the mere questioning of jurisdiction by the beginning of the 1940's[2] and had done so with some very salutary results for the indigent prisoner held pursuant to both federal and state judgments. There had been some evidence before 1940, even as early as 1908,[3] that the use of the writ might reach the use-abuse stage in the not too distant future.

The actual abuse of the famous writ, however, became so noticeable by 1942 that the Judicial Conference appointed a Committee on Habeas Corpus which, with the assistance of the Director, had collected sufficient evidence to make a report to its parent. Two tentative pieces of legislation were prepared in 1943, one dealing with jurisdiction, the other with procedure. The two proposals had been prepared as bills by 1945 and presented to the proper committees of Congress as H.R. 4232 and H.R. 4233, and S. 1452.[4] The House did not hesitate to substitute its own resolution (H.R. 6723) for the jurisdictional bill (H.R. 4232). In 1947 the Conference offered the same bills with amendments and indicated that that substitute bill was not at all acceptable.[5] Copies of the three bills were sent out for further comment among the judges and legal fraternity, but by the time comments began to be received, the Chairman of the Conference Committee, Judge John J. Parker, had found that the Congressional Committee on the Revision of Law had, in revising the Judicial Code, adopted the essentials of the 1947 proposals for the Habeas Corpus Code. The task of the Judicial Conference was to advise Congress on the details and to see that nothing adverse to its best judgment went into the revision during congressional action.[6]

According to the Committee's Report there was no interest in changing the process in well-established habeas corpus proceedings. The Committee, however, thought that legislation was necessary to secure orderly procedure to avoid unnecessary and repeated applications for the writ to different federal judges and Justices, and to minimize the evils of unseemly conflicts between judges of the same rank (those who judged and sentenced and those who held habeas corpus hearings thereon) and between state and federal tribunals. Judge Parker was amazed at the development of the practice of using the writ to attack the judgment by which the petitioner had been imprisoned from a year and a day to life, or was being held awaiting execution. The result was actual abuses which as such opened the door to review by way of federal habeas corpus of every state and federal criminal proceeding in which a person was willing to make oath that he had been denied a fair trial.[7] Oath could be taken without fear of perjury, which was a long step from the earlier use of habeas corpus: the checking on jurisdiction from the record. The loss of jurisdiction in a particular criminal proceeding was added, because of the denial of a constitutional right that never was listed on the record (*dehors* the record).[8] Potentially, no judgment could be depended upon to close a case; and there was no rule to prevent repeated applications being made.[9]

One section of the Revised Code[10] established a modified principle of *res judicata* in habeas corpus. The judge had discretionary power to entertain a petition of the prisoner convicted of a crime when it appeared that the legality of his detention had been determined on a prior application for habeas corpus and the judge was satisfied by further inquiry.[11] Section 2245 of the Revised Code clarified and simplified the procedure in cases where hearings were to be held: the trial judge, in case the proceedings were attacked, might file a certificate setting forth the facts concerning the trial and such certificate might be used as evidence. Therefore, the trial judge could go fishing, remain quietly at home, or agree to testify before a hearing court as to the trial.[12] Sections 2246-2248 permitted affidavits, with counter affidavits or questions, at a hearing. Section 2249 provided for the filing of prior applications for habeas corpus to be used as evidence and Section 2250 required that free copies of all records should be supplied by court clerks to indigent petitioners. Section 2253 gave a restatement of the check on state prisoners who appealed to the Supreme Court on habeas corpus proceedings by the "probable cause" provision.

Section 2255, an added procedure, provided in the case of federal prisoners, the substitution of a "motion" (to vacate or set aside a judgment complained of in the first instance on grounds unknown at the time) for habeas corpus, as the first step in securing the relief sought, unless it should appear to the court that the remedy by "motion" would be inadequate. This additional remedy might be moved at any time without any formal petition. One of the outstanding differences between the "motion" and the writ of habeas corpus procedure lay in the requirement that in the former the movant must go to the original trial judge, while the latter had to go to a district court in a circuit where the applicant was imprisoned, as in habeas corpus proceedings. The court seemingly could hold a hearing without the presence of the prisoner (a procedure absolutely forbidden in habeas corpus actions), while the courts' decisions were to be *res judicata* normally, unlike those in habeas corpus proceedings. The motion, then, was an attempt to do away with the unseemly practice of a *hearing* district court passing on the judgment of a coordinate *sentencing* court, at least until the petitioner had failed to get his release from detention by the motion route, or unless the hearing court held that the motion was inadequate to secure justice for the petitioner. Too, the motion, as in habeas corpus, must involve facts not available and known to the defendant or the court at the time of the trial and the court, attacking collaterally, might free the petitioner, modify the penalty, or resentence him.

Section 2254 dealt with the resort to lower federal courts by *state* prisoners. A person detained pursuant to the judgment of a state court could not petition for habeas corpus in federal courts, unless it appeared (1) that he had exhausted the remedies available in his state and (2) that there was an absence of state remedies to correct the denial of petitioner's rights, or that the remedies available were incapable of protecting his rights. The phrase, "exhaustion of remedies," meant the use of state remedies to correct the claimed rights which assumed that there were such remedies. The section did not prevent the application for federal habeas corpus, if the remedies were inadequate. Such applications would likely be few, guessed Judge Parker,[13] since most States had adequate remedies (habeas corpus, common law, or legislative writs of error *coram nobis*, along with new trials and appeals to correct errors caught in the record).

When a state prisoner has carried one or all such methods of relief through the state judicial hierarchy, he may then go to the Supreme Court for certiorari. On failure there, he may then go to a federal district court for habeas corpus. If there are no state remedies, he may call on the High Court for an "original" habeas corpus (common law). Going to the High Court, according to the Judge,[14] was of great importance in maintaining the relationship between the state and federal judicial systems: such action brought the review of state judicial judgments and sentences before the Supreme Court for some kind of consideration and did away with, or blunted, the feeling that always accompanied the reversal of the final state courts by one-man federal district courts, an action often resulting in turning a convict loose to continue preying off society.[15]

Anyone who has studied the work of district judges knows how weak many of them are, when compared with their brothers above or with the state higher judges. In bringing the uses of federal habeas corpus up to 1948, exhaustion of state remedies had been developed as a rule before going to the federal courts, but it was fairly easy for the Court to change the rule,

as it did in Wade *v.* Mayo.[16] Section 2254 was thought to have
it pinned down.

2. JUDICIAL CONSTRUCTION

(1) 28 U.S.C., Section 2255

As soon as the Judicial Code became effective (June,
1948), there were a number of questions that could be answered
only by the rulings of the Supreme Court, despite the simplic-
ity and clarity of what has been referred to as the Habeas
Corpus Code within the larger revised Judicial Code. The
most contested, if not the most important, one that involved
the federal judiciary alone, was the requirement that the
"motion to vacate" was, in ordinary situations, to have pri-
ority in time over the writ of habeas corpus as the protector
of the constitutional personal rights of convicted persons.
The "motion" was not a wholly new procedure; it had been
adapted to the needs of federal prisoners from the legislative
writ of *coram nobis* existing in many of the states (a writ
which, in turn, had been a modification of the common law
writ of *coram nobis* which originated in England). Articles
expressing fear that the writ of habeas corpus was being neglected or weakened began to appear in the law journals,[17] and
at least one federal appellate court challenged the "motion"
as being unconstitutional, chiefly because it did not have the
Great Freer Writ which had been a part of the (unamended)
Constitution.[18]

The provision in Section 2255, Paragraph 4 (which gave
the district courts power to hold hearings on "motion" without
requiring the presence of the prisoner) meant exactly what a
similar provision dealing with habeas corpus had meant;
namely, that where the question in dispute was one of law
and not of fact the court was not obliged to have the prisoner
present. Both processes required the presence of the prisoner
when there were questions of fact, or mixed law and fact, to
be presented on the ground that the complainant could possibly aid in establishing the facts. In the Hayman case[19] a
majority of the appellate court, led by Judge Denman, was not

satisfied with the prosecutor's willingness to have the case reversed and remanded for rehearing solely on the ground that the prisoner was not brought from his place of detainment to give his version of the facts to prove that his attorney, without his knowledge, had served another defendant who had conflicting interests. The circuit court, holding the "motion" a nullity, ordered the motion dismissed to clear the way for the constitutional writ because the "motion" was unconstitutional.

The Supreme Court granted certiorari and vacated the decision, remanding the case with instructions to have the trial court hold a rehearing with the prisoner present to testify as to conflicting interests of his attorney. Section 2255 was not unconstitutional, for the following reasons: 1) Congress had the power to interpose the "motion" as a condition precedent to the granting of habeas corpus on the ground that judicial administration demanded its use to make possible the proper control of the abuse of the habeas corpus writ by prisoners of the federal Government. 2) The Judicial Conference, made up of lower court judges and chaired by the Chief Justice (who always consulted his colleagues), originated the "motion" as a substitute for habeas corpus in most cases and would not likely destroy it because of its being inconsistent with the Constitution. 3) The "motion" covered a wide variety of grounds, perhaps more than habeas corpus and, therefore, was of greater use than habeas corpus. 4) It was understood to demand, like habeas corpus, the presence of the prisoner when matters of fact were to be considered at the hearing. 5) Finally, the power to issue a writ of habeas corpus in aid of its jurisdiction, had existed since the foundation of the Constitution.[20] The decision was unanimous (8-0), Justice Minton not participating.

Another case involving Section 2255 was decided in 1954.[21] The "turning" of the decision was of great interest to the author, in that he learned that the Supreme Court not only had the absolutely new Section 2255 at its disposal, but could delve deeply into the old common-law mass of writs and extend a hand of friendship to a state prisoner who had already served his term. A man named Morgan had been convicted in

1939 of stealing government checks from the mail and forging the names of the payees. He was sentenced to four years of confinement. After serving his term, he committed a state crime, was convicted, and due to his previous federal conviction was given a second-offense penalty. While in prison he learned about the famous Johnson *v.* Zerbst decision of 1938, which demanded the service of counsel or an intelligent waiver of such service under conditions that he could simulate. His attorney advised him to move his sentencing court in the post office case for a "motion" in the nature of a writ of error *coram nobis* to set aside the conviction, in order to secure a reduction of the term of his sentence in the state court. The federal district court, considering the "motion" to be that of Section 2255, refused to grant it in 1952 on the ground of lack of jurisdiction, inasmuch as the "motion," like the writ of habeas corpus, demanded that the person be held in custody before it could issue from the court. As a poor person, aided by court-appointed counsel and attorneys furnished by a local legal aid bureau, he appealed to a New York circuit court of the United States manned by Judges A. N. Hand, Chase, and Frank — a rather formidable bench. His counsel took pains to set the circuit court straight on the meaning of the "motion" in the nature of a writ of error *coram nobis* which the district court had erroneously interpreted: on appeal the "motion" had been changed into a pure, unadulterated writ of error *coram nobis* of the common law variety and one, too, that could be applied for at any time.[22] The circuit reversed and remanded the case, ordering the trial court to hold a hearing on the common law writ.[23]

The Government petitioned for certiorari in the fall of 1953. Acting Solicitor Robert L. Stern desired the Court to consider 1) whether the United States district courts had jurisdiction to grant relief in the nature of a writ of error *coram nobis* to vacate a judgment of conviction and sentence after the expiration of the full term of the sentence; 2) whether, without any allegations as to his innocence or as to the reasons for delay, if such jurisdiction existed sufficiently to require the court to hold a hearing. The Government argued that the "motion to vacate" (Section 2255) was the only alternative writ to that of habeas corpus and the purpose of Congress was to supply such alternative in 1948. The circuit court had remarked that it was nonsense to say that the Section had killed the older common law writ which had existed since the 1789 Judicial Code as a writ within the jurisdiction of the district courts or the lowest trial court for such cases.[24] The Government contended in its brief that there had to be some limitation to the attacks on conviction and sentences and that it had taken fifteen years to arrive at the point where even a pretense could be made of ascertaining whether the allegations outside the record could be found true.

The Supreme Court in the Morgan case affirmed the appellate court, thereby giving the district court its sanction for using not only habeas corpus and "motion to vacate" to overturn decisions collaterally while the movant was in prison, but the use of the common law *coram nobis* to vacate a decision after the prisoner had served his sentence.[25] One of the difficulties that lower courts and attorneys must learn to endure is that Supreme Court legislation (rulings) is rarely bound by time, retroactively or prospectively. The Chief Justice was a dissenter in this case.

Other decisions of some import involving Section 2255 can be briefly summarized as follows:

(1) errors in the admission of evidence cannot be attacked collaterally;[26]

(2) the phrase, "otherwise open to collateral attack," is not limited to the correction of sentence;[27]

(3) motion procedure, like that of habeas corpus, to construe a statute;[28]

(4) certification of lack of merit by trial judge does not necessarily end the movant's chance for release; the circuit court, as in habeas corpus, has the responsibility of seeing to it that the movant has his chance to prove his allegation and with the aid of counsel, if he wants such aid;[29]

(5) motion to vacate cannot be used, any more than can habeas corpus, to change a sentence that the movant is not actually serving; applicable to so-called pyramiding of sentences, as in bank robbery;[30]

(6) prisoner may secure as a pauper a free transcript of his trial records on an appeal from a decision on a motion to vacate, but he cannot move to secure a recording of the trial court for the purpose of instituting a collateral proceeding. It is clear that the motion made in Section 2255 is the beginning of a new proceeding.[31]

The revised Habeas Corpus Code, Section 2255, had not been applied by the federal courts during the first five years of its life to the extent desired by its chief proponent, the Judicial Conference of the United States. Federal prisoners for the period (1949-1953) averaged 408 habeas corpus petitions to 100 motions to vacate, although the intention of the proponents of the Section was to apply the motion on collateral attack, if at all possible, leaving the habeas corpus as the last resort to secure justice. After 1953 the motion made a better showing but never reached the status of a rule as the ratio from 1954-1958 was 386-268, and for 1959-1961 (the latest statistics), 730-564.[32] The failure to make the motion the rule rather than the exception was due, perhaps, to the inability of the lower court judges, the federal prosecutors, and the petitioners themselves (including their counsel, if any) to accept the new provision in lieu of the ancient and highly revered old common-law writ that had had such a great record in protecting persons from unjust punishment.

(2) U.S.C., Section 2254

This portion of the Habeas Corpus Code reads as follows:

An application for a writ of habeas corpus in behalf of a person in custody pursuant to a judg-

> ment of a State Court shall not be granted unless
> it appears that the applicant has exhausted the
> remedies available in the courts of the State, or
> that there is either an absence of State corrective
> process or the existence of circumstances rendering
> such process ineffective to protect the rights of
> the prisoner.
>
> The applicant will not be deemed to have exhausted
> the remedies available in the Courts of the State,
> within the meaning of this section, if he had the
> right under the law of the State to raise, by any
> available procedure, the question presented.

This section clearly reflects, for the most part, a procedure
already worked out by the United States Supreme Court. For
indigent persons in prison pursuant to state court judgments,
this section is of great importance and is the basic method
of limiting the abuse of the use of federal habeas corpus by
state prisoners.

It will be noted that the wording of the section does not
contain the full meaning of "exhaust State remedies" that
had been given by the rule in the Hawk case of 1944,[33] but
came nearer to the Wade case[34] which was short of a rather
essential part of the Hawk rule: if the state remedies failed
to give relief, the prisoner must apply to the Supreme Court
for certiorari; failing there to secure relief, he could then go
to a federal district court for habeas corpus. Darr *v.* Burford,[35]
however, held in 1950 that in the absence of special circumstances, as to which the petitioner had the burden of
proof, the petitioner failed to apply to the Supreme Court for
certiorari.

The lower courts had guessed correctly. Justice Reed,
speaking for the Court, specifically overruled the Wade *v.*
Mayo case and the law in 1950 was Section 2254, plus the
application for certiorari.[36] Further, the Court stated, as a
consequence of the holding, a federal court, in passing on
an application of a state prisoner for collateral relief, should
distinguish between two situations: 1) where a state prisoner
had not applied for certiorari to the Supreme Court, the district

court might inquire only into the existence of special circumstances which would except the case from the rule requiring him to apply to the Supreme Court;[37] 2) where the prisoner had applied for but the Supreme Court had denied certiorari, the district court, although it had the power to entertain the application, might decline to examine further into the merits because they had already been decided on that basis against the petitioner.[38]

It is assumed that the ruling meant that the Court, in denying, had passed on the merits against the petitioner. The 5-3 opinion did not state clearly what effect was to be given by the district courts to a denial of certiorari by the Supreme Court. Justice Frankfurter, joined by Justices Black and Jackson, held to his often-repeated view that a simple denial of certiorari had no legal significance in habeas corpus proceedings or in any other proceeding. Justices Burton and Clark of the majority, while they concurred in the majority opinion, at the same time made it clear that the district courts should pay no attention to the Court's denial of certiorari, unless the Court gave its reasons therefor.[39] The opinion, under such circumstances, did not seem to state clearly just what effect was to be given by the district courts to a denial of certiorari by the Supreme Court in a succeeding habeas corpus case.

In Brown *v.* Allen,[40] which combined three separate cases for convenience, the Supreme Court accepted the Darr *v.* Burford opinion concerning Section 2254: that the pre-1948 ruling required that a state prisoner, in order to be able to make an effective application for habeas corpus in a federal court (in event of being denied a claimed federal right), must secure a denial of certiorari by the Supreme Court as a part of the exhaustion of state remedies. Additional statements were: 1) it was not necessary for the prisoner in such circumstances to pursue in state courts a collateral remedy based upon the same evidence and issues;[41] 2) Section 2254 was not to be construed as requiring repetitious applications to state courts for relief.[42]

The Court also clarified its ruling in the Darr case regarding the weight a federal district court should give to a denial of certiorari by the Supreme Court in a following application for habeas corpus: the answer "none" should be given.[43] Further, on a state prisoner's application for habeas corpus on constitutional grounds, the federal court must take into consideration the proceedings and adjudications in the state trial and appellate courts, even to determining from such records whether or not to grant the application for habeas corpus.[44] In the exhaustion of state remedies only one exhaustion should be considered necessary.[45] Finally, the Court ruled that where the district courts erroneously gave consideration to the Court's prior denial of certiorari, if it affirmatively appeared from the record that the error could not have affected the results, the decision was good and the error harmless.[46]

After Brown v. Allen, several capital cases involving habeas corpus came up to the Supreme Court before 1963, and two were of special interest. Irvin v. Dowd,[47] an Indiana case, was a peculiar as well as an important one. Irvin was convicted of a murder in a small geographical area in which several murders had recently been committed. The trial took place in the midst of hysteria superinduced by the modern means of communication and was further inflamed by county officers who announced that Irvin had confessed to committing at least six of the murders. Change of venue was granted but defendant's counsel found conditions the same and asked for a second change which was forbidden by state law. The jury convicted Irvin and assigned the death penalty. On the grounds that the court had made many errors in state law and that the 14th Amendment had been breached, appeal was made by counsel to the trial court for a new trial. This move was made while Irvin was an escapee from prison and the court, neglecting the merits of the case, held that a new trial could not be allowed under such circumstances.

An appeal was made to the State Supreme Court and the holding was affirmed, although the record seemed to indicate that the state appellate court had passed upon or considered the case on its merits, but not formally so. Petition for certiorari was denied "without prejudice to filing for federal habeas corpus after exhausting state remedies." The petitioner hastened to seek federal habeas corpus under 28 U.S.C.A., Section 2241, claiming that the conviction had been secured in violation of the 14th Amendment due process in that he had not received a fair trial. The federal court dismissed the application for the writ for the reason that the petitioner had not exhausted state remedies. The appellate court affirmed. On certiorari, the Court remanded the case to the circuit court for its decision on the merits or for remand to the district court for reconsideration. The appellate court retained jurisdiction and decided against the petitioner. Instead of freeing the prisoner, the Court declared that a fair trial had not been given him and sent the case back to the federal district court with instructions to order the state trial court to give the petitioner a new trial within a reasonable time.[48] Apparently the Court had decided to have the case settled on constitutional grounds rather than on state law. Under this rule when a state supreme court considered or even was suspected of doing so, the petitioner had exhausted one set of remedies for asking for habeas corpus from a federal district court.

The state trial court had not obeyed the Court's order to give the petitioner a new trial after a reasonable time. On the plea of the prisoner it made a similar order in 1961, adding the statement that unless a new trial was held within a reasonable time the prisoner would be released.[49] The Court controverted the claim that state law prevented more than one change of venue, saying that the State Supreme Court had allowed additional changes where justice demanded it. Of course, the burden was on the defendant to prove the existence of overpowering prejudice on a charge which inevitably brought the verdict of guilt and the penalty of death.

Justice Brennan, speaking for the majority, remarked that the result of deciding the case on constitutional grounds had to be governed by the principle that the doctrine of exhaustion of state remedies embodied in Section 2254 did not bar resort to federal habeas corpus, if the prisoner had obtained a decision on his constitutional claim from the highest court of his state, even though that court would have based the decision on other grounds. Was this a variation of the exhaustion rule? Justice Stewart concurred with majority on the understanding that Brown *v.* Allen[50] should stand and that Wade *v.* Mayo[51] should not be restored.

Justice Brennan did not seem to believe that his majority really knew that the State Supreme Court had passed on the merits of the petitioner's allegation that the 14th Amendment had been violated—a condition precedent for a negative response to certiorari which was, in turn, a condition precedent for securing a federal habeas corpus under the Brown *v.* Allen rule. Had the State Supreme Court merely passed on the state technical rule that the defendant could not be granted a new trial while he was an escapee? The Supreme Court was only making a determined guess on the basis of the record below that the final state court had in effect passed on the federal claim under the 14th Amendment.[52] Justice Frankfurter dissented on the ground that the decision should have been made on state law and rule in preference to the national principle. The Court reversed and remanded the case to the Federal Court of Appeals for ascertaining just what the State Supreme Court did pass on.[53] This was a maneuver to determine what the Court's majority had guessed to be the case.

The Chessman case[54] is a good example of what a smart convict can do under the 1948 restatement of the Habeas Corpus Code, especially when he is furnished with all the necessary law books (provided in his death cell), when he has free communication with friends on the outside (forbidden or not), and freedom to compose books and get them published. To be sure, Chessman's case could be used to illustrate almost all the problems of indigents' civil rights. His case was initially decided in a California trial court in 1948, and reached the pinnacle of the federal judicial hierarchy for the first time in 1950. His conviction resulted from a multi-count charge, two of which (kidnaping and attempted rape) called for capital punishment. Soon after the conviction and the denial of a new trial, the case, under state law, was to go automatically to the State Supreme Court for review upon the record. In the meantime, the official court reporter had died before completing even a third of the transcription of his notes on the case. The trial judge appointed a former partner of the deceased reporter to finish the transcription. It was brought to light during the struggle for the discharge of the doomed convict that the state prosecutor was related by marriage to the substitute reporter and that the completed transcription had been made in collaboration with the prosecutor and with the aid of two policemen who were witnesses for the state at the trial. The record had been settled in a proceeding in which the convict had been represented neither in person nor by counsel, although he had requested the court to allow him to be present in person. However, a copy was sent to the prisoner, who made 200 corrections, of which 80 were accepted. The State Supreme Court reviewed the case on the "settled record" and affirmed the action of the trial court, one that resulted in a stubborn fight that lasted into May, 1960, and served as a forum for national and international propaganda for abolishing capital punishment in both state and federal courts.[55]

In June, 1950 the State Supreme Court denied the convict a petition for habeas corpus and a month later he filed his first petition for certiorari in the federal Supreme Court, alleging that he had been denied procedural due process (14th Amendment) because he was not present when the trial judge considered objections to the transcript.[56] This action took place before the State High Court's decision on review and certiorari was denied. He had thus exhausted his state remedies and was free to go to the federal courts for an unlimited number of writs of habeas corpus under 28 U.S.C.A., Section 2254. When the state final court approved his conviction he turned to federal habeas corpus. Of the number of habeas corpus petitions in which the petitioner charged violation of procedural due process, four had alleged his non-participation in the settlement of the record, and the last such petition, the seventh, resulted in the instant case.[57] Until 1957 at least four had appeared in habeas corpus allegations and all had been denied without objection by any of the Justices. Three had alleged fraud and conspiracy of the prosecutor, trial judge, and the substitute transcriber. One had alleged forced confession.[58]

With the above background, it would seem that the 5–3 majority of the Court was meant "to negative" the peti-

tioner into the gas chamber. Pressure had been building
up before 1957 to such a degree that something had to be
done which would relieve the Court without necessarily re-
leasing the prisoner from his death cell. The majority did not
seem to relish the making of a rule that would require all
states to give all persons charged with crime a new trial if
the transcription of the court record had not been completed
before the official court reporter's death or in the event of his
serious injury. A clear and true transcription of one person's
shorthand by another could rarely be correct in every respect.
The majority (the Chief Justice not participating because of
earlier legal relations with the prisoner) concluded that the
decision should be reversed and the case remanded to the
state courts to prove, or else an order for the release of the
prisoner would be given.[59] By May, 1960, proof had been
given and the execution had taken place. Between 1948 and
1960, Chessman had gone to the Supreme Court fourteen times
on state and federal habeas corpus and there had been eleven
hearings by the state and lower federal courts.

Justice Harlan, speaking for the majority, came near
daring ordinary mortals to criticize the time-wasting delays
in this case:[60]

> Without blinking the fact that the history of this
> case presents a sorry chapter in the annals of
> delays in the administration of criminal justice,
> we cannot allow that circumstance to deter us
> from withholding the relief so clearly called for.
> On many occasions this Court has found it neces-
> sary that the requirements of the Due Process of
> the Fourteenth Amendment must be respected, no
> matter how heinous the crime in question and how
> an accused may ultimately be found to be after
> guilt has been established in accordance with the
> procedure demanded by the Constitution. Evidently
> it must be repeated that the overriding responsi-
> bility of this Court is to the Constitution of the
> United States, no matter how late it may be that
> a violation of that Constitution is found to ex-
> ist.... We must be deaf to all suggestions that a

valid appeal to the Constitution, even by a guilty
man, comes too late.... *The proponent before the
Court is not the petitioner but the Constitution of
the United States.*   (Emphasis supplied.)

Justice Douglas agreed with the ideals of the majority but
refused (*for once*) to be caught in such rare atmosphere. He
could not believe that Chessman had not been allowed to have
his say in the settlement of the record in the instant case; he
refused to agree that substantial procedural due process had
not been followed all too often during the preceding nine years
of legal skirmishing: "My dissent is based on the conviction
that in substance the requirements of due process have been
fully satisfied, that to require more is to exalt a technical-
ity."[61] The Justice stated further that Chessman was playing
a game with the courts, stalling for time while the facts of the
case grew cold.[62] To send the case back to the state courts
could not bring back the maker of the original record, and to
expect witnesses to remember facts that took place nine years
before seemed to the Justice futile and a miscarriage of justice. But it was the use of the Great Writ as a plaything in the
hands of a proved criminal that was the ultimate danger. Habeas corpus as the means of ascertaining jurisdiction or of
digging out unrecorded facts in a criminal trial was the great
protector of those who had been denied their constitutional
rights. The abuse of the writ, however, had brought its jurisdiction under fire during the preceding fifteen years. In fact,
habeas corpus jurisdiction might be taken from the lower
courts, much to the detriment of federal justice.[63]

(3) Congressional Consideration of Code Amendments

Pressures for legislative amendments to Section 2254,
along with others, began to increase as early as 1952 and
became almost insuperable by the end of the 86th Congress—
that is, within nine years. Chief Judge Denman of the Ninth
Circuit in 1952 sent to the Judicial Conference a resolution
adopted by his circuit conference[64] to this effect: since the
chief provisions of the Habeas Corpus Code of 1948 had been
passed to keep down the number of repetitious applications for

habeas corpus by state prisoners claiming denial of constitutional rights, Section 2254 should be amended in such a way as to prohibit any court or judge thereof to entertain a second or successive application, if it appeared that such application had been refused on the ground stated. The Conference threw it aside.[65]

But the members were exhibiting a more sympathetic attitude toward state prisoners (as well as toward federal prisoners). The Court seemed to realize that the constitutional rights were all that the state prisoners had and such rights were being increased yearly. On the other hand, the state prisoners had discovered during their trials and their associations with other prisoners that they could allege on oath, without fear of being punished for perjury, most any basis for taking away constitutional rights and possibly get entirely free from state detention or have their sentences reduced. The attention of the Judicial Conference was called to the objections to the granting of federal habeas corpus to state prisoners before 1954. The most insistent groups, however, were the Conference of State Chief Justices, the National Association of State Attorneys-General, and other organizations affected by the mounting number of federal habeas corpus writs applied for and secured. The result was a reactivation (in 1953) of the Habeas Corpus Committee by the Judicial Conference, with Judge Parker as chairman. The Committee made an elaborate report on the claimed abuses by state prisoners applying for federal habeas corpus, asserting violation of constitutional rights. A report was filed and approved by the Conference and a proposal was given to the 84th Congress, House of Representatives, 1st Session, and became H.R. 5649, and Subcommittee No. 3 of the Committee on the Judiciary held hearings.[66]

The bill endeavored to meet the criticisms formulated by the Conference of State Chief Justices in Chicago in 1954.[67] They were: 1) the final judgments of the State Supreme Courts were being reviewed by lower federal courts, often by a single judge in habeas corpus proceedings, notwithstanding "orderly federal procedure under our dual system of government should require that the final judgment of a State's highest

court should be subject to review or reversal only by the
United States Supreme Court''; 2) improper interference
with state court procedures and processes by proceedings in
habeas corpus in lower federal courts; 3) long delay in the execution of state judgments, especially in capital cases, brought
about by repeated habeas corpus proceedings in lower federal
courts and stays issued by such courts. The bill was favorably
reported by the House Committee on the Judiciary and approved
by the House. It was also favorably reported by the corre-
sponding Senate Committee but it never got off the calendar.
A bill similar to H.R. 5649 was in the 85th Congress and
passed by that body, but got no further in the Senate than the
calendar. Another bill of similar character was introduced in
the House in the 86th Congress, First Session, but made
little progress.[68]

H.R. 3216, the last bill mentioned above, had it been
passed by both Houses, would have made the conditions
governing the entertainment by a Supreme Court Justice, a
circuit court judge, or a district court so strict that a state
prisoner, claiming that he had been denied a constitutional
right, could rarely have succeeded in securing a federal
habeas corpus proceeding in a lower federal court. Such a
prisoner would have had to seek review of his grounds for
discharge from custody by certiorari, appeal in the Supreme
Court, or by an original application for a writ of habeas corpus in that court.

Members of the special committee appointed by the Judicial Conference in 1953 sought to excise the weaknesses
of Section 2254 of the Code by having the Supreme Court pass
on the judgments of the highest state courts. The idea was
not altogether a bad one in theory, since the committee was
rather confident that state procedure would sooner or later
be so well organized that the state prisoner would secure
as great protection of his fundamental rights therein as he
could in the lower federal courts.[69] To be sure, there were to
be no restrictions on applications for ''original'' petitions
for habeas corpus to the Supreme Court, in case the states
had no means of protecting federal rights of a state prisoner.

The Chief Justice and his associates had been giving

serious thought to the proposed amendment of Section 2254—
as noted in H.R. 5649, H.R. 8361, and H.R. 3216, identical
bills introduced respectively into the 84th, 85th, and 86th
Congresses. They concluded that if the amendment were
enacted, the advantages of the Judges Bill of 1925 would be
lost and the burden on the Court would be doubled by original
applications for habeas corpus and certioraris from state
prisoners. Furthermore, the Supreme Court knew that it could
not itself conduct a contested hearing on an application for a
writ of habeas corpus. It would have to refer the hearing to a
district judge nearest the prison or appoint a master. In either
case the result would likely be accepted and then the procedure would conflict with the first criticism of the Conference
of State Chief Justices. The Chief Justice, with the approval
of the Judicial Conference, appointed another special committee in the fall of 1958 to re-examine the solution offered
by that of 1953 [70]

The new committee was to draft a bill which would meet
the objections to federal habeas corpus in behalf of state
prisoners (chiefly indigent), which would answer the state
criticisms of the 1954 Parker bill, and which would protect
the Supreme Court from too onerous burdens. The committee,
taking the average yearly number of state-prisoner applications for federal habeas corpus for the period 1954-1958 as
705, estimated that only about 4% of such cases reached a
hearing stage. The remaining 96% were disposed of on the
applications which were accompanied by state court records
and other pertinent matters indicating their lack of meritorious
grounds. About 30 cases reached the hearing stage each year,
of which two-thirds consumed one hour per case and one-third
about four hours. Very few prisoners, however, were released
at any level of the judicial hierarchy. The above figures thus
tended to show that a lower court could handle the applications
without delaying justice in the state courts too long.[71]

H.R. 6742 (Phillips Bill) of the 86th Congress, First Session, was the draft accepted by the Judicial Conference in
lieu of the (1954) Parker Bill. Section 2254 was amended in
terms of the latter bill with respect to the grounds for an
application for a writ of habeas corpus by a state prisoner by

providing that it might be predicated only on a ground which presented a substantial federal question. The new bill, however, made this requirement applicable not only to applications to a Justice of the Supreme Court, a circuit judge, a district court or judge, but to an original application to the Supreme Court.[72]

The chief difference between the two, however, was the main locus of responsibility for the disposal of the applications. The Phillips Bill required that if an application for federal habeas corpus was made to a Justice of the Supreme Court or a circuit judge, or if the application was made to a district court, or transferred to such district court, the judge of such district court was to make a preliminary examination thereof to determine whether the writ should be granted (and he might, in his discretion, issue an order to show cause why the writ should not be granted). The later bill further provided that the examination might be made on pertinent named matters. If a writ should be issued, it was to be made returnable for hearing and determination in the district court having jurisdiction. Additionally, in the case of an application entertained by a Justice of the Supreme Court or a circuit judge, the proceeding was thereupon to be transferred by his order to such district court. The Justice or judge issuing the writ was immediately to notify the chief judge of the circuit involved, who was then to designate a district court of three judges to hear and determine the issue of whether the prisoner should be released from custody and determine all other issues remaining in the proceeding and enter final judgment therein. The circuit or district judge granting the writ was to be one of the three-judge court, which must have one circuit judge. A state prisoner was to be discharged from custody only by such district court, while the final order of the three-man court could be reviewed only by the Supreme Court on certiorari within thirty days after the decision. If the writ should be denied by a single judge on the preliminary examination, then an appeal to the circuit court could be made and finally disposed of under the law as it existed before amendment, but a certificate of probable cause would have been necessary.[73]

It will be seen that the main control of applications for

federal habeas corpus would have been switched from the Supreme Court to the district court of three judges. If such an act were passed, one of the main criticisms of the Conference of State Chief Justices would be greatly softened, if not entirely met, by a three-judge court (which would contain one circuit judge, thus avoiding the disgrace of having the judgment of the highest court of a state reversed by one district judge). This disposition of the cause would meet the objections raised by the states of the long delay in final disposition of habeas corpus cases brought by state prisoners claiming denial of constitutional rights.[74] Judge Phillips, chairman of the Judicial Conference's special committee to report on the modification of the Parker Bill, noted that H.R. 6742 modified Section 2244 of the 1948 Habeas Corpus Code to aid the control of state-prisoner writs of habeas corpus: the decisions of federal courts in connection with such habeas corpus proceedings were given expressly, though limited, *res judicata* standing. Repetitious applications would be cut potentially to zero — almost; even the action of the Supreme Court on appeals and review by certiorari from state court decisions entered into the prohibition on matters decided there, for the reason that state prisoners had often been known to have offered as grounds for habeas corpus those which had been definitely decided by the Supreme Court against the applicant. Such a provision would certainly reduce the time for final settlement of a habeas corpus proceeding brought by a state prisoner.[75]

The Senate, since 1948, has consistently blocked all bills proposed by the Judicial Council for the correction of the abuse of the procedure without reducing the legislative intent of that writ in protecting the rights of the poor man who has found himself in prison without just cause. The Senate was still the blocker as of January, 1961. This viewpoint of the Upper House seemed to indicate an approval of the centralization of control over all states-rights claims of constitutional rights ,especially by means of habeas corpus proceedings. The state revolt against the second Roosevelt Court and its successors appeared, in items of the press of the time, to have been supported by a majority of the House of Delegates of the

American Bar Association and its recent creation, the Conference of State Chief Justices.[76]

House Hearings on the Judicial Conference's promised legislation, amending Section 2254 of the Habeas Corpus Code of 1948, revealed that the executives and teachers of the leading law schools of the nation were exerting their influence successfully in backing the Habeas Corpus Code as a means of centralizing control over state prisoners' rights. The Chief Justice, as Chairman of the Judicial Conference, did not weaken in his determination to see that federal habeas corpus procedure had to reach down into the states, although he did do something toward soothing the feeling of the state judicial officers by a provision in the defeated bill for a three-man district court, one of whom was a circuit court judge, to consider indirectly the decision of the final state court. The popular, and possibly the correct, explanation of the view of the majority of the local lawyers and judges has been that the frozen ideas of the law have not been thawed out by changes in conditions in the rural areas of the states. By contrast the more sophisticated urban areas have become more sensitive to such changes and have responded quickly, if not too wisely, to the use of old tools without thinking through the future results.

(4) State Prisoners and Federal Habeas Corpus: March, 1963

The Supreme Court was not entirely satisfied with the application of the Habeas Corpus Code of 1948 or with some of its own decisions thereon. Two new judges per administration can upset the latest decisions! The failure of Congress to amend the Code, along with unsatisfactory judicial interpretations, caused the Supreme Court "to reassess" the policy of procedure by which state prisoners might reach any of the courts of the national hierarchy in their search for the protection of constitutional rights. As a vehicle for modifying law and former rulings, the Court seized upon Townsend v. Sain, a Cook County, Illinois case.[77] The official record of the trial of Townsend stated that he was 19 years of age;

that he was arrested in the early morning of January 1, 1954 for a murder committed the previous December; that he made an out-of-court confession to the police on January 2, 1954, another at the preliminary hearing before a magistrate; that he was held in custody until January 12, 1955, when he was arraigned for trial. The record also affirmed that he was assigned an attorney for the first time since his arrest; that when the prosecutor offered his signed confession of January 2, 1954 as testimony, Townsend, through his attorney (the public defender), vigorously objected on tne ground that such testimony was involuntary—upon which claim the court held a hearing without the jury, but later submitted the confession for what it was worth to the jury and the verdict was guilty and punishment death.

An appeal to the State Supreme Court failed and certiorari was denied by the United States High Court. Townsend next tried state collateral procedure but was turned down by the state higher court, and on petition for certiorari by the Supreme Court. He was then doubly prepared for federal habeas corpus. His request was turned down by a federal district court, and affirmed by a circuit court, on the ground that his record did not support his claims in any degree whatever. On certiorari, the Supreme Court vacated the judgment, remanded the case for a decision on whether, in the light of the state court record, a plenary hearing was required. The district and appellate courts were satisfied with the state record and vowed that the 14th Amendment due process clause had not been breached. The High Court again granted certiorari and heard argument twice. The judgment was reversed and the basic facts brought out. Some of them were: petitioner was 19 years old when the crime was committed, had been a drug addict for three years and fully drugged when the crime was committed, had a mind hardly distinguished from that of the moron; he had been questioned from early one morning until noon of the next day, with little rest, by the police; he had been given a truth serum by the police doctor (one a narcotic which produced a signed confession) and later made an open confession at the preliminary hearing; he had been kept in jail or in police quarters from arrest January 1, 1954 to January 12,

1955, without the aid of counsel; and, he was assigned public defender on arraignment on that date. Most of the above facts were *dehors* the record.

The Court then turned to a discussion of federal habeas corpus and a description of the meaning of a plenary hearing. A federal evidentiary hearing was required, unless the state-court trier of fact had, after a full hearing, reliably found the relevant facts. This meant that the federal district court must try the facts *de novo*, if the state court did not do so. This was the situation in the instant case and in all habeas corpus proceedings where the petitioner was in detention as a result of a state court judgment. The Court then briefly considered the special character of federal habeas corpus.

A habeas corpus proceeding is not an appellate review, it is a test by way of an original civil proceeding independent of the normal channels of review of criminal judgments. Its importance lies in the fact that it is the constitutional method of protecting individual rights (included in the Bill of Rights) which are embedded in a series of facts and the judgment made thereon. Only the Supreme Court of the United States sees through the series of facts and judgments to the specific rights of the individual. The minds of only five Justices at any one time are apparently considered as perceptive of human rights above all others! Perhaps it is that this number of the Supreme Court is assumed to have the final say under the Constitution.

The basic standard or test of a proper evidentiary hearing in habeas corpus proceedings is given above. This standard amended and corrected some foolish ideas expressed in Brown *v.* Allen,[78] which was decided a decade ago—a rather long period for even a procedural rule to stand unchanged. Some elucidation, by way of dicta, was given as advance notice of what the Court expects of the federal district court when

1. The merits of factual disputes are not resolved;
2. the state factual hearing is not fairly supported by the record as a whole;
3. the fact finding procedure employed by the state court was not adequate to afford a full and fair hearing;

4. there is a substantial allegation of newly discovered evidence;
5. the material facts were not adequately developed
at the state hearing;
6. for any reason it appears that the state trier of
facts did not afford the habeas corpus applicant
a full and fair factual hearing.

All the above are mandatory and include the warning that the
federal lower courts should not be deprived of all independent
judgment in evidentiary hearings, since they are better ac-
quainted with state procedure than members of the Court!

The dissenters, led by Justice Stewart, agreed with the
majority that the judgment in the instant case should be
reversed but objected to the elaborate directions for testing
the state procedure used in arriving at the essential facts in
handling claims of state convicts that their constitutional
rights have been violated. The charge of the minority, led
by Justice Stewart, seems to be that the establishment of
of federal standard in evidential hearings to bring out the
essential facts in federal habeas corpus proceedings must
be met by state courts, if their findings in such cases are
not to be superseded by *de novo* evidential hearings held
before federal district courts under federal standards of
habeas corpus. Irrelevant to the decision of the instant
case or not, advisory elements on the opinion or not, the
Court seems to be demanding that the state courts in such
cases use the federal standard; otherwise, there will be a
new trial of the facts in the federal courts according to the
standards set up, perhaps as an alternative to the Court's
frequent "or else"—meaning release of the prisoner.

The time may come when the state procedure will so
harmonize with the standards of the federal procedure that a
device such as habeas corpus, designed in a unitary state in
which the legislature was and is supreme, will serve a state
of federal design, with division and separation of powers,
dominated by one of the federal separate divisions.[79]

NOTES TO CHAPTER XI

[1]*E.g.*, permanent court reporter system and proposed public defender for indigents.

[2]Waley *v.* Johnston, 316 U.S. 101, 104-05, 1942.

[3]35 Stat. 40, 1908. This act limited appeals from state courts to the Supreme Court on habeas corpus proceedings by requiring the federal judge making the final decision below or a Justice of the Supreme Court to certify probable federal cause before the case could reach the Supreme Court.

[4]77th Congress, 1st Sess., 1941.

[5]80th Congress, 1st Sess., 1947.

[6]The above summary and much of what follows on the Revised Code may be found in the following: *S. Ct. R. and B.*, vol. 342, 197-224, L.C., to accompany United States *v.* Hayman, 342 U.S. 205, 1952; Reports of Jud. Conf. of 1943, 22-24; 1944, 22; 1945, 25; 1947, 17; and Report of the Special Session of the Jud. Conf., April, 1947, p. 46.

[7]Jud. Conf. Committee's Report on Habeas Corpus, to accompany the first bills introduced in Congress, H.R. 4232 and H.R. 4233, 79th Cong., 1st Sess., 1945, and as amended, 1947; Judge Parker's "Limiting the Abuse of the Habeas Corpus," 8 *F.R.D.*, 171-177, 1949; Ch. 153 of the Judicial Code, 28 U.S.C.A., Secs. 2244-2255 especially, 1948.

[8]These uses were cited in the treatment of the expansion of habeas corpus for the period 1922-1947 and also noted in particular cases in protection of specific rights, such as right to counsel, in other subtitles above. See also Judge Parker, "Limiting the Abuse of Habeas Corpus," 8 *F.R.D.*, 171, 1948.

[9]Price *v.* Johnston, 334 U.S. 266, 1948, represents an extreme federal case; Gene McCann *v.* Clark, 331 U.S. 813, 1947, at least 100 applications for habeas corpus, New York State case; a federal case, Casebeer *v.* Hunter, some dozen habeas corpus writs 1937-1947, mixed with wild charges, should have presented the fact that

the Government was paying out money for the actions of an insane prisoner.

[10]28 U.S.C.A., Sec. 2244.

[11]Smith *v.* Baldi, 343 U.S. 903, 1952. See also Mitchell *v.* Youell, 130 F. 2d 880, 1942.

[12]Mitchell *v.* Youell, cited above.

[13]Judge Parker, already cited, 171, 175-176.

[14]*Ibid.*, 176-177.

[15]*Ibid.*, 177-178; See Stonebreaker *v.* Smyth, 163 F. 2d 498, 501, 1944; 323 U.S. 754 (memo.).

[16]Wade *v.* Mayo, 334 U.S. 672, 1948.

[17]*E.g.*, "Notes" on Section 2255, 59 *Yale Law Journal*, pp. 1183-1190, 1949-1950.

[18]United States *v.* Hayman, 342 U.S. 205, 1952.

[19]Hayman *v.* United States, 187 F. 2d 456, 1950; ground for unconstitutionality, suspension of writ by Congress only in great emergency, Art. I, Sec. 9, Cl. 2 of Constitution. *S. Ct. R. and B.*, v. 342, 197-221, 1952, L.C., gives complete history of Sec. 2255 and briefs of the government and respondent.

[20]United States *v.* Hayman, 342 U.S. 205, 210, 214, 219-223, 1952/28 U.S.C.A. Sec. 1651 (a). See also G. F. Longsdorf, 13 F.R.D. 407, 421-424, 1953.

[21]United States *v.* Morgan, 346 U.S. 502, 1954.

[22]The all-writs grant was made in 1789 and appears in 28 U.S.C.A. Sec. 1651.

[23]Morgan *v.* United States, 202 F. 2d 67, 1952.

[24]Cited as near proof for the government's view were United States

v. Smith, 331 U.S. 469, 475, 1947, United States *v.* Alabama, 335 U.S. 252, 1948, which also approved its use in states to protect convicted state prisoners.

[25]A case made moot by administrative action had a motive beyond mere release from prison, though all action took place in the federal system: Fiswick *v.* United States, 329 U.S. 211, 220-223, 1946. It turned out to be moot because the departmental court reversed itself and allowed an alien to become a citizen, charged with felony, though not proved!

[26]Story *v.* United States, 337 U.S. 947, 1949.

[27]Robinson *v.* Swope, 197 F. 2d 633, 1952 (cert. denied, 344 U.S. 867, 1952).

[28]Tinder *v.* United States, 345 U.S. 565, 1952; Prince *v.* United States, 352 U.S. 322, 1957; Ladner *v.* United States, 358 U.S. 169, 1958.

[29]C.M. Johnson *v.* United States, 239 F. 2d 698, 1956 (cert. denied, 354 U.S. 940, 1957).

[30]Heflin *v.* United States, 358 U.S. 415, 416-420, 421-422, 1959. Federal Bank Robbery Act, as amended, 1940, 18 U.S.C., Sec. 2113 (C).

[31]United States *v.* Stevens, 244 F. 2d 866, 1955, citing United States *v.* Hayman, 342 U.S. 205, 222, 1952

[32]*Report of the Judicial Conference of the United States,* 1958, and the *Report of the Director of the Administration of the United States Courts,* 1959 and 1961.

[33]*Ex parte* Hawk, 321 U.S. 114, 1944.

[34]Wade *v.* Mayo, 334 U.S. 672, 1948.

[35]Darr *v.* Burford, 339 U.S. 200, 1950.

[36]*Ibid.,* 210. This requirement was based upon practice of comity.

[37]Section 2254 was merely declarative of Supreme Court rulings; the cases before 1948 were exceptions to the requirement of asking for certiorari, e.g., Ex parte Clio Hull, 312 U.S. 546, 1941; Cochran v. Kansas, 316 U.S. 255, 1942; United States ex rel. Bongiorno v. Ragen, 54 Fed. Supp. 973, 1944; White v. Ragen 324 U.S. 760, 1945. (Appeals prohibited by penitentiary rules.) After 1948, for the same obstruction, see Dowd v. United States ex rel. Cook, 340 U.S. 206, 1951.

[38]Darr v. Burford, 339 U.S. 200, 1950.

[39]Ibid.

[40]Brown (Speller and Daniels) v. Allen, 344 U.S. 443, 1953.

[41]Ibid., 447-450.

[42]Ibid., 448, note 3.

[43]Ibid., 489-497.

[44]Ibid., 457-458.

[45]Ibid., 488.

[46]Ibid., 458-460; Federal Rules of Criminal Practice, 1954, Rule 52.

[47]Irvin v. Dowd, 359, U.S. 394, 1959.

[48]Ibid.

[49]Irvin v. Dowd, 361 U.S. 717, 1961.

[50]344 U.S. 443, 1953.

[51]334 U.S. 672, 1948. In Fay v. Noia, 372 U.S. 391, 434-35, 1963, a delayed request for appeal did not prevent petition for federal habeas corpus because of this: federal habeas corpus will issue when there is no legal appeal because of timely failure to exhaust under 28 U.S.C.A., Sec. 2254.

[52]Irvin *v.* Dowd , 359 U.S. 394, 408-412, 1959.

[53]See Curtiss R. Rietz, "Federal Habeas Corpus: Impact on Abortive State Proceeding," 74 *Harvard Law Review* 1315, 1960-61.

[54]Chessman *v.* Teets, 354 U.S. 156, 1957.

[55]*Ibid.*, 166-173 and Appendix.

[56]No. 98, Misc., 1950 Term. Denied, 340 U.S. 840, 1950.

[57]Chessman *v.* California, 340 U.S. 840, 1950. See also Appendix.

[58]Chessman *v.* Teets, 354 U.S. 156, 172-173, 1957.

[59]*Ibid.*, 166. Had Chessman been released, another Court crisis would most likely have occurred.

[60]*Ibid.*, 165-166. The last sentence of this quotation was from Davita *v.* McCorkle, 248 F. 2d 211, 1947.

[61]*Ibid.*, 166-167.

[62]*Ibid.*, 168.

[63]*Ibid.*, 171-172. By May, 1960, the Court was satisfied with the true findings of the lower courts as to a fair hearing and released the petitioner for execution.

[64]*Report of the Judicial Conference*, 1952, pp. 223-24.

[65]Judge Denman's record for protecting federal courts from harassment resulting from repeated filings of habeas corpus petitions by both federal and state prisoners had not been too perfect.

[66]*Hearings* before Subcommittee No. 3 of the Committee on the Judiciary of the House on H.R. 6723, H.R. 3216 and others, 86th Congress, 1st Sess., May, 1959, p. 10.

[67]Conference of State Chief Justices, organized by A.B.A., 1949, was an anti-naturalization body that met at the same time as the A.B.A. and was supposedly composed of grass-root judges. It

issued statements and reports of significance.

[68]*Hearings*, pp. 10-11.

[69]*Ibid.*, p. 11. The Judicial Conference dropped hints that sooner or later the rural-minded judge would give way to the liberal-minded urbanite. This change seems to be the hope of executives, legislative leaders, as well as judges.

[70]*Ibid.*

[71]*Ibid.*, pp. 11-12.

[72]*Ibid.*, p. 13.

[73]*Ibid.*

[74]*Ibid.*, indigent state prisoners, especially.

[75]*Ibid.*, p. 14.

[76]In 1958 this new body put out a "Report of the Committee on State-Federal Relationships Affected by Judicial Decisions," in which hostility accompanied every criticism.

[77]Townsend *v.* Sain, 372 U.S. 293-334, March 18, 1963.

[78]334 U.S. 443, 1953.

[79]See Justice William J. Brennan, "Federal Habeas Corpus and State Prisoners: An Exercise in Federalism," 7 *Utah Law Review* 423-441, 1960-61, for the Supreme Court's view of its duty.

CHAPTER XII

SOME DECISIONS AFFECTING
THE MEANING OF THE INDIGENT
CODE: 1956-1963

1. THE RIGHT TO COUNSEL:
SIXTH AND FOURTEENTH AMENDMENTS

(1) Federal Prisoners

Of all the procedural rights named in the Constitution, that of appointed counsel in criminal cases seems to have tempted governmental authorities since 1789. It was indicated in Chapter II that neither Congress nor the Supreme Court viewed the Sixth Amendment's promise of appointed counsel to the man without funds as a *must* provision; it was merely a "fielder's choice" of the individual concerned. In Chapter III it was shown that the same two important bodies did not change their respective attitudes after the consolidation of civil and criminal procedure for the indigent in criminal cases until the beginning of the 1930's, the Supreme Court taking the lead in federal cases in Johnson *v.* Zerbst.[1]

But of all the procedural rights named in the Constitution of interest to the poor man charged with crime, that of appointed counsel presumably was the most important for it was the potential means of giving some assurance of the other rights. Between 1789 and 1938, the right of appointed counsel developed from a doubtful equal of other named procedural rights to the position first among equals and then to one of first importance. The Johnson case was mentioned in connection with habeas corpus and was declared to apply to all federal criminal litigation in indigent cases, unless the accused or convicted was able to make an intelligent waiver, preferably in written form. This definitely affected Section 4 of the Indigent Code, as amended.

To clinch the new rule Justice Black took occasion to block efforts of the Government and lower federal courts to defeat the purpose of the rule by enlarging the unwritten ways of expressing waiver. He chose the case of (Mrs.) Von Moltke *v.* Gillies ten years later to end the bickering. She was a German citizen who was charged with violation of the Espionage Act of 1917, pleaded guilty before a judge, and was convicted. Later she alleged, in her petition for certiorari, the absence of counsel on making the plea of guilty. Her case was reversed and Justice Black had this to say:[2]

> The fact that the accused may tell him [the judge] that he is informed of his right to counsel and desires to waive this right does not automatically end the judge's responsibility. To be valid such a waiver must be made with an apprehension of the nature of the charges, the statutory offenses included within them, the range of allowable punishment thereunder, the possible defenses to the charges and circumstances in mitigation thereof, and other facts essential to a broad understanding of the whole matter. A judge can make certain that an accused's waiver of counsel is understandingly and wisely made only from a penetrating and comprehensive examination of all the circumstances under which a plea is tendered.

The ideal attorney and the experienced judge are rarely found— in combination at least. A layman could seldom meet the Black ideal.

(2) State Prisoners

Chief Justice Hughes called on Justice Sutherland to try his hand at an opinion in the reversal of the Powell case from Alabama in 1932.[3] This was the first occasion the Court had been called on to incorporate in the Fourteenth Amendment the indigent legal service of the Sixth in a criminal case where a defendant had been tried and convicted of a state crime calling for the death penalty under circumstances indicating an absence of effective counsel along with other unsatisfactory area conditions. In the absence of precedent, the Justice proceeded to depend upon logical deduction: since historically a person charged with a crime had had a right to a hearing, and since counsel was necessary to bring out the facts and take care of the accused's interests, the due process clause included the Sixth Amendment legal aid clause. The case was reversed apparently on the ground of the allegation: a capital crime tried without counsel and a hostile environment.

Nine years later a non-capital case from a state court was reversed, although it was loaded with trickery by the prosecuting attorney.[4] In 1942 a Maryland non-capital case was tried without a lawyer on the ground that the State did not furnish free service in such cases.[5] The Powell and Betts cases, with some influence of Smith v. O'Grady, divided the members of the Supreme Court in state criminal cases into two blocs—the "absolutists" and the "circumstantialists." They became occasionally confused, but usually straightened themselves out. The "absolutists" insisted that the Constitution demanded the same protection for the accused, whether federal or state; the "circumstantialists" bloc based its action on *circumstances*, which seemed to be equivalent to fair play, a philosophy supported by Justice Cardozo.[6] The Court could not reach unanimity between 1942 and 1960 on whether the Fourteenth Amendment incorporated the legal aid provision of the Sixth. The Court usually compromised serious decisions by quoting from Uveges v. Pennsylvania:[7]

> When the gravity of the crime and other factors —
> such as the age and education of the defendant,
> the conduct of the courts or the prosecuting offi-
> cials, and the complicated nature of the offense
> charged and the possible defense thereto — render
> the proceedings without counsel so apt to result
> in injustices as to be fundamentally unfair, the
> Constitution requires that the accused must have
> legal assistance at his trial.

The first real break in favor of the "absolutists" came in November, 1961, when they won Hamilton v. Alabama,[8] a rape case calling for the death penalty. Particularly important was the fact that the State had provided by statute for certain steps, from arraignment to sentence, in which a lawyer was actually necessary for protecting the accused. Johnson v. Zerbst and the 1932 Powell case served as precedents. The rule was definitely stated that in all capital cases, counsel must be appointed by the court, if the defendant could not provide such service. Walton v. Arkansas[9] and White v. Maryland[10] were capital cases decided on the basis of Hamilton v. Alabama. A tinge of "circumstance" seemed to accompany even the capital cases and the "circumstantialists" bloc did not fail to use it in argument.

Fortified by new appointments favoring the "absolutist" attitude, the Court first reversed and remanded a state non-capital case,[11] using the term "total circumstances" and throwing the case into the category of the Powell v. Alabama case. The erosion of Betts v. Brady was almost completed and when Gideon v. Wainwright[12] came up from Florida as a non-capital case, Justice Black applied the rule of Johnson v. Zerbst directly to it, but through the due process clause of the Fourteenth Amendment.

The fundamentals of state criminal procedure had become nationalized. Then followed a plethora of automatic reversals of state in forma appeals without briefs or arguments, beginning with Pickelsimer v. Wainwright.[13] In overturning the Betts case, it must be said, however, that the Court had never turned down the possibility of applying the Fourteenth Amendment to such cases.

2. STATE DISCRIMINATION

Whatever may be the content of the "due process" and "equal protection of the laws" clauses of the Fourteenth Amendment, they are formally applicable only to judgments on state prisoners.[14] Both clauses have frequently been cited where the simple claim of denial of the equal protection of the laws is asserted. Evidently there must be, at least in the mind of counsel or defendant, some close relation between the two clauses. According to one view both clauses move to the same end, equality: the due process clause "tends to secure the equality of the law in the sense that it makes a required minimum of protection for everyone's right of life, liberty, and property which state agencies may not wit' hold ... guaranty of [equal protection] was aimed at undue favor and individual or class privilege, on the one hand, and at hostile discrimination or the oppression of inequality, on the other.''[15] The author suggests that these might well work together at all times, since the due process clause could be taken to mean due process or the accepted, and no other, way by which absolute equality of the laws may be modified without legal discrimination.

For a time before 1956 there were few cases of note. Negroes convicted of a capital crime in New York failed to secure relief from the Court on the allegation that the Southern rule of exclusion had been applied.[16] Chief Justice Warren extended the equal protection clause to persons of Mexican nationality,[17] thereby re-emphasizing Yick Wo v. Hopkins;[18] and, the importance of legal appeal as of right was held to have a limit in time and was protected by the same clause of the Constitution.[19] In 1956 the Court seemed to discover or rediscover a potentially universal protection of all rights guaranteed in the Constitution against the states.

One of the most interesting decisions dealing with ''equal protection of the laws'' clause of the Fourteenth Amendment was that of Griffin v. Illinois.[20] Two men, Griffin and Crenshaw, had been convicted of armed-robbery and sentenced to prison for ''scaled terms.'' Pending appeal, they immediately filed a motion in the trial court, asking that a certified copy of the entire record, including a transcript of the proceedings, be furnished them without cost inasmuch as they had no means of paying for it. Illinois law provided that writs of error in all criminal cases were writs of right and that, on appeal on error to the Supreme Court of Illinois, they were forced to furnish the court a bill of exceptions or a report of the proceedings at the trial certified by the trial judge. The allegations were not denied; indeed, the State admitted that it was often quite difficult to prepare bills of exceptions or reports without having a stenographic transcript of the trial proceedings.. Furthermore, indigent defendants sentenced to death were by law allowed free copies of all trial proceedings. Therefore, both those with money and indigents condemned to death could secure proper papers on appeal in error, while indigent, non-capital convicts could not be assured of such papers on appeal. The movants argued before the trial court that a denial of free bills of exceptions in their cases was a denial of the Fourteenth Amendment due process and equal protection of the law clauses (note the twin claims). The motion was denied without a hearing.

The prisoners then filed with the trial court a petition under the new Illinois Post-Conviction Act[21] (the provisions of which limited review to questions arising directly from constitutional law, state or federal). A companion law had provided for free transcripts to indigents in criminal appeals in constitutional matters only under the Post-Conviction Act; errors, such as those involved in admissibility or sufficiency of evidence would not "rate" free transcripts. The petitioners, insisted that there were "manifest" constitutional errors in the trial proceedings entitling them to have their conviction set aside, and that the denial of free stenographic transcripts and other papers was a denial of both protective clauses of the Fourteenth Amendment. The state trial court dismissed the petition and the State Supreme Court affirmed. The Supreme Court granted certiorari, indigent procedure, and appointed very able lawyers (if their briefs, supported by researches, were indications of ability).[22]

Justice Black, speaking for the majority, reversed and remanded the case. The basic reason was that indigent petitioners had been discriminated against in their effort to secure full criminal appellate procedure required by the State Supreme Court. Legal provisions that had been violated were the thrice-presented due process and equal protection clauses of the Fourteenth Amendment. The speaker did not distinguish sharply between the two clauses but asserted that both emphasized the central aim of the national judicial system, namely, that all people charged with crime must, so far as law was concerned, "stand in an equality before the bar of justice."[23] Citing race and color cases, he then made the all-important statement: in the field of discrimination, "Poverty stands with religion, race and color."[24] The Justice stated, in a more practical way, that the ability to pay costs (in advance) bore no rational relation to a defendant's guilt or innocence and could not be used as an excuse to deprive him of a fair trial, that is, of a free transcript for securing a a full appellate review.

Justice Black had been informed that most of the states had provided in some way for equalizing the opportunity of the indigent convict's chances for appeal in criminal cases with that of the convicted defendant who had money to pay his way to the final court. The fact that in Illinois those convicted of capital crimes had a "free ticket" on appeal did not excuse the state from denying the same advantages to the majority of prisoners who had committed lesser crimes. Therefore, on the basis of the ancient struggles between rich and poor, strong and weak, the majority of the Court placed the commandment of the Fourteenth Amendment upon the states (those which had not already done so) to equalize the position of the rich with that of the poor by subsidizing the latter. Of course, the state was not obligated by the federal Constitution to provide for appellate procedure in criminal or civil cases; if it did, equal access for rich and poor was a constitutional demand.

The petitioners' briefs had supplied the Court with statistics on the value of appeal, a value indicated by percentages running from 16% to 40% of reversals in criminal cases among the states. Justice Frankfurter agreed with the minority that the Fourteenth Amendment permitted of classification, but his separate opinion backed the majority on discrimination against the poor man on appellate opportunity. His objection was not to the new ruling, but to the "evil" of placing no limitation in time for the application. Obviously, he thought the new ruling had not always existed and should not be utilized by criminals who could claim relief by habeas corpus or other methods, regardless of the period of conviction.[25]

The minority disagreed, using the doctrine of division of powers (a highly eroded one), urging the wisdom of judicial self-restraint, arguing that the two protective clauses of the Fourteenth Amendment allowed classification, and insisting that social policy made up of whole cloth was for the legislature, not the judiciary.[26]

Soon after the 1956 Griffin ruling, a life-termer in a Washington State prison since 1935 started proceedings to upset his sentence on the strength of that ruling. The prisoner had discovered two things: 1) that the State Constitution allowed all persons convicted of crime to appeal as of right to the State Supreme Court, and 2) that a state statute gave the trial judge discretionary power to furnish a convicted indigent defendant, at the state's expense, a transcript sufficient to guarantee a full review of any errors contained in the trial proceedings. The prisoner petitioned for a writ of error but the final court dismissed the petition without a hearing. Certiorari was granted by the Supreme Court and in a per curiam opinion[27] the Court held that the prisoner was denied a constitutional right of the Fourteenth Amendment, since the state had allowed all convicted defendants to have appellate review except those who could not pay for the essential records of the trial.[28] Reversal and remand followed. Justices Harlan and Whittaker dissented on the ground that the Griffin rule was the law as of 1956 and could or should not be retroactive to 1935.

The result of the Griffin decision in Ohio was the promulgation by the State Supreme Court of a procedural rule to the effect that a convicted defendant who was without funds should be given free transcripts, if they were necessary to secure a full review. In 1935 a man named Burns had been convicted of a crime and he had appealed as a poor person to an intermediate court without getting relief. He gave notice of appeal and the final court so moved but dropped the whole matter until 1957. He then sought to file a copy of the earlier notice of appeal and motion for appeal in the State Supreme Court, attaching a certificate of poverty to the papers. The clerk of that court refused to file the papers unless the applicant paid a fee of $20, a requirement made by the State Supreme Court. Certiorari was granted for reviewing the refusal of the clerk (whose action was taken to be an action of the Supreme Court). The Court, citing the Griffin rule, limited review to whether a state may constitutionally require that an indigent defendant in a criminal case pay a filing fee before permitting him to file a motion for leave to appeal in one of its courts. Chief Justice Warren, speaking for the majority, brushed aside all arguments of the State's attorneys as being beside the point and ruled that, since in Ohio a non-indigent may have the final state court consider on its own merits his application for leave to appeal from a felony conviction, though as indigent petitioner may not under the court's rules of practice, the petitioner has been denied the rights of the Fourteenth Amendment. The decision was then reversed and remanded.[29]

The Eskridge and Burns cases have illustrated in two states the application of the Griffin rule by the pronouncement of the Supreme Court itself. It was noted in connection with the Burns decision that the Ohio State Court had issued, closely following the Griffin case, a new rule of procedure giving the state court judges discretionary power to grant free transcripts to indigent appellants where it was deemed necessary to prosecute fully a writ of error. A rather perceptive treatment of the impact of the Griffin ruling upon state courts appeared in 1959.[30] When the action of a federal court (or state court) affects that of a state court (or federal court), the relationship between the two jurisdictions may become serious, according to the judge. However, when a state litigant resorts to a federal court in an effort to overturn a state court decision, the potential for friction between the two judicial systems may not only become serious but dangerous.

At the time of the Griffin decision (1956) there were four different policies with respect to furnishing free transcripts to appellants in state criminal proceedings: 1) 7 states furnished none; 2) 8, only to indigents convicted of capital offenses; 3) 6, to all persons convicted of any crime; 4) 27, to all indigents.[31] Within a year of the great decision, either the legislature or rule-making state final courts were amending rules regarding free transcripts. By May, 1957, 7 states had changed to category 3 above, bringing this figure to 13.[32] Poverty was added to religion, race, and color as "items" that could not enter as part of criminal procedure under the equal protection and, likely, the due process clause of the Fourteenth Amendment. Should wealth be added to this list? Note 2 and the statistics support its inclusion.

To the author, the logic of the Griffin case calls for no discrimination among classes in criminal proceedings (later on, perhaps, in civil cases); and since the same minds were centered on the problem of no discrimination on appeals, this prohibition served as the basis in citing the Fifth Amendment for the elimination of discretion of the court in the Federal Indigent Code. Time and opportunity so indicated. Section 3 raised appeal to a constitutional right, an idea suggested by the statistics in the Griffin supporting material, and whatever applied to the states of constitutional proportions had to appear in the central Government. Of course, the reverse is also the case for there is only one authoritative agency on what the Constitution means, even when changed by the amending process. Doing away with appeals was a nonsensical suggestion by the Court as viewed from the perspective of 1964.

3. FEDERAL INDIGENT PRISONERS' RIGHT OF APPEAL

Between March, 1957, and May, 1958 the Supreme Court rendered three important per curiam opinions,[33] which both startled and confused most of the lower courts as regards the meaning of the first section of the Indigent Code, and which plainly set forth the procedure in *in forma pauperis* appeals, civil and criminal. So greatly did the rule of practice in applying the policy of Congress, as laid down in the statute, differ from the new gloss given by the High Court in the three cases, that the majority of the lower court judges could not readily adjust their minds to the new approach. One well-known judge of the Middle West agreed that the interpretation was not only new but so vaguely presented, both as to procedure and constitutional doctrine, that the lower appellate courts could not follow the High Court's philosophy or invent the procedures necessary to apply it.[34] Each of the three cases involved a serious crime; in each the trial judge, after the defendant had been convicted, refused direct appeal on the statutory ground that the appeal lacked good faith or some equivalent thereof. Furthermore, in each case the appellate court backed the discretion of the trial judge to block *in forma* appeal by certification of "lack of merit," provided there was no showing "that the trial judge had acted without warrant or not in good faith" (actions that would kill any kind of decision). The convicted defendant-appellant in each case alleged prejudicial error in procedure or the denial of rights known to be precious to a majority of the Supreme Court, and in each case the Supreme Court vacated and remanded or returned to the appellate court for consideration on one or more points.

The Johnson case[35] was the first of the three decisions referred to above. It came up from the 2nd Circuit Court, Judges Hincks, Medina, and Frank sitting.[36] The trial court had denied motions to appeal *in forma pauperis*, for the appointment of counsel, and by inference for the furnishing of free copies of the minutes and record of proceedings at the trial. The majority denied that a legislative privilege of appeal allowable to an indigent was a constitutional right,[37] and scorned the contention that the Griffin case, decided the year before,[38] could possibly have any application to the instant case. Judge Frank dissented. He admitted that the majority had a point but since the Griffin case (involving a violation of the due process and the equal protection clauses of the Fourteenth Amendment), the principle of due process of the Fifth Amendment elevated the appeal of and free service to the indigent in criminal cases to constitutional stature because appeal had been granted to non-indigent persons.[39]

The Johnson decision had an effect on the usual interpretation of the Indigent Code somewhat similar to that which the explosion of the bombs on Japan had on that nation's attitude toward the continuance of war. The defendant made a general allegation that the appeal was not frivolous, and then two specific ones. The High Court stated: 1) that a trial judge's certificate under the Indigent Code was not, and could not have been, conclusive of the convicted defendant's right to proceed as a poor person in the appellate court; 2) that the defendant had the right to be represented by appointed counsel, who were to aid in proving to the appellate court that the trial court's certificate should be displaced and

appeal allowed;[40] 3) that an agreed statement of facts for the
record,[41] or free transcript of the essentials of the official
minutes and record of the lower court, should be made in
order to support the allegations of the petitioner.

The Farley case was the second of the trio.[42] The defendant alleged the following: 1) that the evidence had not supported the conviction (general); 2) that the federal attorney
had committed reversible error in asking irrelevant and prejudicial questions; 3) that the prosecutor had failed to contro-
vert the second allegation in his answering affidavit; 4) that
a free transcript for defense counsel had been denied by the
trial court. The opinion was in harmony with Johnson v.
United States and hinted that the trial judge's discretionary
power to block *in forma* appeals should be further limited. The
Court remarked that if the petitioner and his counsel approved
the appeal, the chances were that it was not frivolous.

Then, there was the Ellis case.[43] It came up from the circuit court of the District of Columbia on a 4-3 split vote. The
attorneys appointed by the appellate court had to look two
ways: they were obliged to act as counsel for the petitioner
and they were directed to review the facts supporting the trial
judge's certificate of lack of merit and report their findings to
the appellate court as a basis for granting leave to appeal.
The two attorneys made a thorough investigation of the various facts of the allegation that the trial court had committed
reversible error in that the defendant had been arrested illegally. The attorneys, after careful research, reported to the
appellate court that the appeal was frivolous insofar as the
petitioner's allegation was concerned. However, the attorneys
had found, on hearing the record read, that there was possible
error in that the petitioner had been convicted chiefly on an
out-of-court confession which had not been properly corrobo-
rated, a point that the *pro se* petitioner did not catch and
could not have caught under the circumstances. The appellate
court affirmed.

The Supreme Court insisted that the court-appointed attorneys could not really "try" the trial court's action on
frivolity or lack of merit and at the same time act in an
advocatory manner for the petitioner. After asserting that the

Court of Appeals could disallow an appeal *in forma pauperis* to the extent that it could disallow a non-indigent appeal for frivolity under Rule 39 (a)[44] (an action which few if any of the appellate courts had ever performed), the High Court got down finally to its real meaning: indigent criminal cases were on a level with non-indigent criminal cases where effective counsel were concerned. The Court solved the problem in indigent cases by asserting that counsel should withdraw from cases which after diligent research clearly involved frivolity. If the trial judge believed that they were serious, he should allow withdrawal and might well indite a certificate of lack of merit.

In 1948 the Supreme Court, in the Adkins opinion,[45] had limited the discretion of the crusty old district judges regarding the meaning of poverty in Section 1 (a) of the Indigent Code. The result was that a person did not have to be a pauper to enjoy the *in forma pauperis* procedure. Ten years later the Supreme Court had practically destroyed the discretion, definitely authorized by the same section of the Indigent Code as to appeals, by substituting in criminal cases the opinion of defense counsel for the discretion of the trial judge. The Supreme Court gave the impression that its ideas regarding appeals for indigents would quickly find a response if the rural-minded lower court judge were removed rather than reversed.

Between 1957 and April 30, 1962 the Court had reviewed and remanded fourteen cases dealing with two short provisions of the Indigent Code, as amended: first, "An appeal may not be taken *in forma pauperis* if the trial court certifies in writing that it is not taken in good faith;"[46] second, "The court may request an attorney to represent any such person unable to employ counsel and may dismiss the case if...satisfied that the action is frivolous or malicious."[47]

The three cases discussed above had some elements that might go toward making a complete standard and were supplemented here and there by eleven cases following on the same subject, namely, the appeal of an indigent convicted of a crime. At the end of the period came the Coppedge case,[48] one in which the Court, the Chief Justice speaking, endeavored

to state a standard governing the application of the Indigent
Code in the particulars stated, a standard that the lower
federal courts could understand and easily apply. This Code
was written before the revolution in individual rights that
began in earnest about 1930. As a result, it did not *say* then
what it apparently now *means*.

In arriving at a standard the Court stated that all federal
law dealing with non-indigent criminal appeals (the special
rules found in the Federal Rules of Criminal Procedure),
some rules from the Civil Procedure dealing with habeas
corpus, other collateral attacks in which appeals were paid,
and political decisions had all definitely served to lift criminal appeals to the status of constitutional rights.[49] Further,
since the Court, in Griffin *v.* Illinois,[50] ruled that state
prisoners must have transcripts of all necessary material
for appellate procedures under the Fourteenth Amendment
equal protection clause, it was only good logic to apply
equality to federal indigent prisoners. There seems to be a
lack of clarity as to the meaning of this declaration in terms
of the Constitution. One can understand the rationale behind
it and perhaps give as its basis the Fifth Amendment due
process clause. But on the basis of logic, if the Fifth Amendment and the Fourteenth Amendment due process clause mean
the same, the Fourteenth Amendment equal protection clause
could readily be made to apply to the meaning of both
due process clauses where due process is made to cover
discrimination.

There were other elements in the decision, such as putting the burden of proof on the Government, but the important
result was that the Court, by declaring that both indigent
and other convicts had a general right to appeal, had raised
what Congress (and the Court itself at one time)[51] considered
a privilege to a constitutional right. Justice Stewart suggested that the provisions of the Code should grant in specific
words that indigent convicts should enjoy the right of appeal
and should give the Government the power to argue the questions of frivolity or maliciousness. Apparently the Justice
did not care too much to have Congressional privilege converted into constitutional rights by Court rule.[52]

NOTES TO CHAPTER XII

[1]304 U.S. 458, 1938; William M. Beaney, *The Right of Counsel in American Courts* (1955), gives a complete and thorough account of this development to 1953. Alpheus T. Mason, *Harlan Fiske Stone: Pillar of the Law* (1956), Chapter 31, illuminates certain aspects of the 1938 Johnson case. "Right to Counsel: Symposium," 45 *Minnesota Law Review* 693-875, 1960-61, gives a series of signed articles on the subject; both federal and state cases are discussed. The author will only touch on a few cases before 1956 in order to secure a background. See also Beaney's account of Attorney-General's Circular No. 2946, 1937; and Mason, *op. cit.*, p. 513, notes the comment of Justice Stone in Note 4 of United States *v.* Carolene Products Co., 304 U.S. 144, 151-154, 1938.

[2]Von Moltke *v.* Gillies, 332 U.S. 708, 724, 1948. In 1945 the Court had apparently established the rule that capital cases *must* have counsel under the Fourteenth Amendment; see Williams *v.* Kaiser, 323 U.S. 471, 1945.

[3]Powell *v.* Alabama, 287 U.S. 45, 1932.

[4]Smith *v.* O'Grady, 312 U.S. 329, 1941.

[5]Betts *v.* Brady, 316 U.S. 455, 1942.

[6]Cardozo, *The Nature of the Judicial Process* (1921), and applied in Palko *v.* Connecticut, 302 U.S. 519, 1937.

[7]335 U.S. 437, 1948 at 441. See also Cash *v.* Culver, 358 U.S. 633 at 636-637, 1959.

[8]Hamilton *v.* Alabama, 368 U.S. 62, 1961; McNeil v. Culver, 365 U.S. 109, 1961, second degree murder (proved almost fatal to the Betts case).

[9]371 U.S. 28, 1962.

[10]373 U.S. 59, 1963.

[11]Carnley *v.* Cochran, 369 U.S. 506, 1962. For comment on this case, see "Indigent Rights to Assigned Counsel in Non-capital

Cases," 14 *Western Reserve Law Review* 370, 1962.

[12]372 U.S. 335, 1963.

[13]375 U.S. 2, 1963.

[14]*Constitution of the United States of America* (1952 edition), E. S. Corwin, ed., p. 1141. Justice Brennan (in his contribution to *The Free Society*, "The Bill of Rights and the States," pamphlet, 1961) thinks that Fourteenth Amendment due process is lesser basis for curing the non-supplying by the state of counsel than is the Fourteenth Amendment equal protection, *infra*, Section 3.

[15]*Ibid.*, 1144-1145. In Coppedge *v.* United States, 369 U.S. 438, 446-447, 1959, the Court held its duty was to go beyond the Code to see that indigents were given equal protection before the courts. It cited Griffin *v.* Illinois in Note 2, elaborating on the philosophy. Does federal due process equal "equal protection"?

[16]Moore *v.* New York, 333 U.S. 565, 1948.

[17]Hernandez *v.* Texas, 347 U.S. 475, 1954 (not a formal IFP case).

[18]118 U.S. 356, 369, 1886.

[19]Dowd *v.* United States *ex rel.* Cook, 340 U.S. 306, 1951.

[20]351 U.S. 12, 1956.

[21]Albert E. Jenner, Jr., 9 *F.R.D.* 347-366, December, 1949, Illinois Post-Conviction Hearing Act.

[22]Free transcript service to indigent prisoners, law and practice: 29 states had full free appellate service for all felons; 7 states gave trial judge discretion to provide free service; 6 states provided free appeals to persons convicted of most serious crimes, such as first degree murder; 2 states had no help for indigents on appeal; other states unknown. The briefs gave the law and practice of Anglo-Saxon countries also. This was in 1956.

[23]Griffin *v.* Illinois, 351 U.S. 12, 17, 1956.

[24]*Ibid.*

[25]*Ibid.*, p. 26.

[26]*Ibid.*, pp. 26-29. Justice Harlan wrote a separate opinion (pp. 29-39) emphasizing aspects of the dissenting Justices Burton, Minton and Reed.

[27]Eskridge *v.* Washington State Prison Board, 357 U.S. 214, 1958.

[28]*Ibid.*, p. 216.

[29]Burns *v.* Ohio, 360 U.S. 252, 1959. This case and Smith *v.* Bennett, 360 U.S. 708, 1961, extended the Griffin principle from direct appeals to collateral appeals.

[30]Frank G. Hamley, "The Impact of Griffin *v.* Illinois on State Courts," 24 F.R.D. 75-83, 1959. Judge Hamley of the 9th U.S. Circuit was formerly Chief Justice of Washington State Supreme Court and a specialist in judicial administration.

[31]*Ibid.*, p. 78. Judge Hamley's article gives a different estimate from that of the defense attorney's set of facts noted *supra* in footnote 22.

[32]Council of State Governments, "The Effect of Griffin *v.* Illinois on the States' Administration of the Criminal Law," mimeograph (Chicago. 1957), p. 27. The article claims that the denial of free transcripts (or their equivalents) to any class of persons convicted of crime denies the effect of the equal protection clause concerning free transcripts on appeal. To avoid such a logical result, the Court turned to the due process clause of the Fourteenth Amendment, which has sufficiently large allowances to care for most needs.

[33]On June 13, 1945, Chief Justice Stone wrote that he had reserved to himself the writing of per curiam opinions, that he would do so where one question was to be decided, and that the opinion could readily be cited. See *Stone Papers*, L.C. His philosophy appeared in the per curiams.

[34]Judge Albert A. Ridge, "The Indigent Defendant: A Procedural Dilemma for the Courts," 24 F.R.D. 243, 295, 1960.

[35] Johnson *v.* United States, 352 U.S. 565, 1957.

[36] United States *v.* Johnson, 238 F. 2d 565, 1956; after vacation the Court of Appeals reversed itself, 254 F. 2d 175, 1958.

[37] Dorsey *v.* Gill, 325 U.S. 890, 1945, refusing certiorari to review *in forma pauperis* a decision of lower court, 148 F. 2d 857 at 878, 1945.

[38] Griffin *v.* Illinois, 351 U.S. 12, 1956; an unlimited principle, past and future.

[39] Judge Frank's opinion covered three times the space used by the majority. His notes included an excerpt from Butler's *Erehwon* emphasizing the moral obligation, numerous essays of his own and other non-legal writings.

[40] Johnson *v.* Zerbst, 304 U.S. 458, 1938, a decision that by inference threw *in forma* criminal appeals into the same category as non-indigent appeals and threatened loss of jurisdiction for failure to appoint counsel, if not intelligently refused.

[41] Miller *v.* United States, 317 U.S. 192, 1942.

[42] Farley *v.* United States, 354 U.S. 521, 1957; 238 F. 2d 575, 1956; 242 F. 2d 338, 1957.

[43] Ellis *v.* United States, 356 U.S. 674, 1958; 249 F. 2d 478, 1957.

[44] Federal Rules of Criminal Procedure.

[45] Adkins *v.* Dupont Company, 334 U.S. 331, 1948.

[46] 28 U.S.C.A., 1915 (a). See Appendix A-II.

[47] *Ibid.* (d).

[48] Coppedge *v.* United States, 369 U.S. 438, 1962.

[49] *Ibid.*, 441-446.

[50] 351 U.S. 14, 1956. A quotation from Coppedge (446-447), citing

this case; "In so holding we have been impelled by conditions beyond the corners of [the Indigent Code] that it is our duty to assure to the greatest degree possible within the statutory framework for appeals enacted by Congress, equal treatment for every litigant before the bar." See also Bollinger v. Sharpe, 347 U.S. 497, 1954.

[51]Dorsey v. Gill, 325 U.S. 890, 1945.

[52]Two recent cases of interest have been brought under this rule: Douglas and Meyer v. California, 372 U.S. 358, 1963, and Lane (Indiana Warden) v. Brown, 372 U.S. 477, 1963.

SUMMARY AND CONCLUSIONS

I

One often hears the remark that a biography of the Constitution is also that of the Supreme Court. From the facts presented in this monograph, it cannot be said that the entire history of the life of the Federal Code is a fractional bit of the biography of the Supreme Court, although that agency did appear occasionally to give its sanction to the principle involved in the Code. From 1789 until 1922 it was the more representative elements of the Constitution that began to create bits of what later became a Code giving free access to the hierarchy of the federal judicial system. Persons rich or poor charged with capital crimes led the way in 1790; soon the Sixth Amendment followed, permitting of free counsel to the poor charged with any crime. In both statute and Amendment the accused had to make request for aid. The enactment (in 1892) of the first Indigent Civil Code came about in response to the request of the lower economic class suffering from the consequences of the nationwide development of business and industry. The discretion of the trial courts caused trouble, even beyond 1922. But the outline of a Federal Indigent Code, including all types of cases and permitting appellate procedures, was provided by law in 1910 and, as amended in 1922, became the official Code.

The Supreme Court then used Congress as a handmaiden in perfecting the Code. One great Amendment passed in 1868, the Fourteenth, was of great value to the Court in giving it power to expand the indigent idea of free service wherever it was needed.

At the end of 1963 research had established the fact that a universal Code for the indigent had passed from a permissive privilege to practically a full constitutional right at all levels of government in the United States, insofar as criminal proceedings were involved. Civil matters were not so well covered but the philosophy of cooperation, even to the extent of a kind of socialism, had been adumbrated. The legal fraternity had not been able to agree on the method of furnishing free legal service in criminal proceedings. It seems that its members wanted pay for serving the indigent , but feared that the future might provide for moderately salaried legal aides. When and if the Court extended aid in civil cases to those with or without funds (under the equality principle) the economic welfare of that great fraternity of technicians of the law, who are needed at every turn, might become less attractive at the hands of the Government that had fostered the profession.

II

The author's main purpose in making this study was to find out what the federal judiciary, especially its topmost part, had done and is doing to promote legal justice for the poor. He is quite satisfied that social justice and the legal equivalent thereof have become more or less the same. His attention, however, has been called to the methods by which, for example, a special privilege granted by law has been transformed into a constitutional right without the aid of the formal amending power. To be sure, he could not feel quite safe in this semi-continental country to be governed through direct action of the voting masses nor through entire control of representatives of the mass of voters. He recognized that the separation of powers doctrine, checks and balances, could be real checks, even if the Supreme Court interpreted the constitutional powers in such a way as to make its notions of things — political, economic and social — prevail. The author recognizes that democracy has to have an authoritative element to serve as a balance wheel. That element could be either the President or the Supreme Court. But he cannot reconcile the idea that the chief judicial element, part of the intellectual aristocracy, should become a super-legislator whose conclusions on procedures and substantive law (both have been tied in with due process and equal protection of the law) have too often been political legislation little akin to any known provision of the Constitution. This practice has appeared in the development of the Indigent Code during the last twenty-five years.

A small group of Justices of the Court have exerted a powerful influence over a minority or majority of that body during the last quarter century. This group has doubtless played a part also in the selection of the new Court members. As a "majority-for-the-moment," the Court has been able to raise most rules to a Constitutional level—rules that control both national and state actions. Congress has been unable to agree on policies, even when they are pressing, and has allowed the Court to take the lead and fill in when Congress could not carry on.

This has been going on for years, but few have noticed it since the Court has screened its power by hiding behind the myth of passivity. The cure for this kind of political action is not the destruction of the Court or the attempt to discipline it by some Constitutional action. The cure must lie in the assertion of independence, under the leadership of the President, who at present is helping the Court by pushing Congress to implement in detail the Court's idea of the need for Constitutional reform to meet the four-barrelled revolution now in progress—including political, personal, social and economic rights of the less powerful classes. Franklin D. Roosevelt defied the Court and won out in interpreting the Constitution. A party-majority now can do the same or force some restraint on the free-wheeling that the Court has been carrying on—contrary to what the students of jurisprudence consider the judicial process as compared with the political process. An "intellectual authority" cannot rule for long over two hundred million people; and the power will shift to the alert President who is likely on horse-back now.

The late Justice Jackson, speaking of the will of the Court to control all legal activities of the Nation, remarked that thus far the authority of the Court had not been accepted because it was infallible, but because it was final.

APPENDICES

APPENDIX A

I. *In Forma Pauperis Law*[1]

Be it enacted..., That any citizen of the United States, entitled to commence *or defend*[2] any suit or action, *civil or criminal*,[3] commence and prosecute *or defend*[4] to conclusion any (such)[5] suit or action, *or a writ of error, or an appeal to the circuit court of appeals, or to the Supreme Court in such suit or action, including all appellate proceedings, unless the trial court shall certify in writing that in the opinion of the court such appeal or writ of error is not taken in good faith,*[6] without being required to prepay fees or costs *or for the printing of the record in the appellate court*[7] or give security therefor, before or after bringing suit or action, *or upon suing out a writ of error or appealing,*[8] upon filing in said court a statement under oath, in writing, that, because of his poverty, he is unable to pay the costs of said suit or action (which he is about to commence)[9] *or of such writ of error or appeal,*[10] or to give security for the same, and that he believes that he is entitled to the redress he seeks by such suit or action *or writ of error or appeal,*[11] and setting forth briefly the nature of his alleged cause of action, *or appeal:*[12] *Provided, That in any criminal case the court may, upon the filing in said court of the affidavit hereinbefore mentioned, direct that the expense of printing the record on appeal or writ of error be paid by the United States, and the same shall be paid when authorized by the Attorney General.*[13]

Sec. 2. That after any suit or action shall have been brought, or that is now pending, the plaintiff may answer and avoid a demand for fees or security for costs by filing a like affidavit, and willful false swearing in any affidavit provided for in this or the previous section, shall be punishable as perjury in other cases.

Sec. 3. That the officers of court shall issue, serve all process, and perform all duties in such cases, and witnesses shall attend as in other cases, and the plaintiff shall have the same remedies as are provided by law in other cases.

Sec. 4. That the court may request any attorney of the court to represent such poor person, if it deems the cause worthy of trial, and may dismiss any such cause so brought under this act if it be made to appear that the allegation of poverty is untrue, or if said court be satisfied that the alleged cause of action is frivolous or malicious.

Sec. 5. That judgment may be rendered for costs at the conclusion of the suit as in other cases: *Provided,* That the United States shall not be liable for any of the costs thus incurred.

II. U.S. Judicial Code of 1948 as Amended 1952, Sec. 1915.
Proceedings in forma pauperis.[14]

a) Any court of the United States may authorize the commencement, prosecution or defense of any suit, action or proceedings, civil or criminal, or appeal therein, without prepayment of fees and costs or security therefor, by a citizen[15] who makes affidavit that he is unable to pay such costs or give security therefor. Such affidavit shall state the nature of the action, defense or appeal and affiant's belief that he is entitled to redress.

An appeal may not be taken *in forma pauperis* if the trial court certifies in writing that it is not taken in good faith.

b) In any civil or criminal case the court may, upon the filing of a like affidavit, direct that the expense of printing the record on appeal, if such printing is required by the appellate court, be paid by the United States, and the same shall be paid when authorized by the Director of the Administrative Office of the United States Courts.

c) The officers of the court shall issue and serve all process, and perform all duties in such cases. Witnesses shall attend as in other cases, and the same remedies shall be available as are provided for by law in other cases.

d) The court may request an attorney to represent any such person unable to employ counsel and may dismiss the case if the allegation of poverty is untrue or if satisfied that the action is frivolous or malicious.

e) Judgment may be rendered for costs at the conclusion of the suit or action as in other cases, but the United States shall not be liable for any of the costs thus incurred. If the United States has paid the cost of a stenographic (record) transcript or printed record for the prevailing party, the same shall be taxed in favor of the United States.

NOTES TO APPENDIX A

[1]Original law, 27 Stat. 252, Ch. 209, Sec. 1-5, 1892; amendments are in italics.

[2]36 Stat. 866, 1910.

[3]*Ibid.*

[4]*Ibid.*

[5]Word or phrase appears in original law but not in revised versions of 1910 and 1922.

[6]See n. 2.

[7]*Ibid.*

[8]*Ibid.*

[9]See n. 3.

[10]See n. 2.

[11]*Ibid.*

[12]*Ibid.*

[13]42 Stat. 666, 1922.

[14]Sec. 1915 contains three other amendments, listed below:
6/25/48 Ch. 646, Sec. 1, 62 Stat. 954.
5/24/49 Ch. 139, Sec. 98, 63 Stat. 104.
11/31/51 Ch. 655, Sec. 51 (b and c), 65 Stat. 727.

[15]Sec. 1915 (a) of 28 U.S.C. of the 1948 Judicial Code, was amended by 73 Stat. 390, 1959, by deleting the word "citizen" and inserting in its place the word "person". All "natural" persons who can qualify, may sue or defend under the terms of the Indigent Code. An alien eligible to use the Code may on appeal have transcripts made at the expense of the United States Government, and by reference transcripts in criminal and habeas corpus proceedings

(28 U.S.C., Sec. 753 (f)) may be paid by the United States and in all other cases (non-criminal) the same may be paid by the United States on approval of the trial or circuit judges. The Judicial Conference approved this change and was supported by the Attorney-General. Interestingly enough, the Judicial Conference argued before the Senate Committee on the Judiciary that the then existing discrimination between citizens and aliens in cases before the courts might well have been unconstitutional, and that undoubtedly there were at least eight treaties with foreign countries the terms of which were violated by the discrimination against aliens. See *Congressional and Administrative News* (1959), pp. 3881-84.

I. *Appellate Jurisdiction of the Supreme Court*

1. Direct appeals to the Supreme Court:
Any party may appeal to the Supreme Court from an interlocutory or final judgment, decree, or order of any court of the
United States, or of its Territories and Possessions, holding
an Act of Congress unconstitutional in any civil action, suit,
or proceeding to which the United States or any of its agencies
or any officer or employee thereof, as such officer or employee,
is a party;[1] and any interlocutory or permanent injunction in
any civil action, suit or proceeding had in a three-judge
district court.[2]

2. Court of appeals cases:
(1)   By means of certiorari, granted upon petition, of any
civil or criminal case, before or after rendition of judgment
or decree;
(2)   By appeal to a party relying on a State statute held by
a circuit court of appeals to be invalid as repugnant to the
Constitution, treaties or laws of the United States, but such
appeal shall preclude review by writ of certiorari at the
instance of such appellant, and the review or appeal shall be
restricted to the federal question presented;
(3)   By certification at any time by a court of appeals of any
question of law in any civil or criminal case as to which
instructions are desired, and upon such certification the
Supreme Court may give binding instructions or require the
entire record to be sent up for decision of the entire matter
in controversy.[3]

3. Final judgments or decrees rendered by the highest
court of a State in which a decision could be had
may be reviewed by the Court:
(1)   By appeal (before 1928, writ of error and appeal), where
is drawn in question the validity of a treaty or statute of the
United States and the decision is *against* its validity; or by
appeal, where is drawn in question the validity of a statute
of any State on the ground of its being repugnant to the Constitution, treaties or laws of the United States, and the decision is *in favor* of its validity.   (Emphasis supplied)

(2)   By writ of certiorari, where the validity of a treaty or statute of the United States is drawn in question or where the validity of a State statute is drawn in question on the ground of its being repugnant to the Constitution, treaties or laws of the United States, or where any title, right, privilege or immunity is specially set up or claimed under the Constitution, treaties or statutes of, or commission held or authority exercised under, the United States.[4]

II. *Supreme Court Rules of Procedure, 1954: Jurisdiction*

1.   Original: Constitution, Art. III, Sec. 2, Par. 2, Rule 9.

2.   Appellate: Congress is source of
    i. On appeal: Rules 10-18
    ii. On writ of certiorari: Rules 19-27
    iii. On certified questions: Rules 28-29
    iv. To issue extraordinary writs: Rules 30-31

3.   Special proceedings: *in forma pauperis*
    i. Under 28 U.S.C. Sec. 1915:
        Party wishing to so proceed must file a motion to so proceed and together therewith an affidavit setting forth facts showing that he comes within the statutory requirement. Compliance with regular procedure, if possible.
    ii. File jurisdictional document, as in regular proceedings, except only one required, and need not be printed. He need not file a copy of the record below if he is unable to secure one without payment of fees and costs with his petition for cert. or motion for leave to file.
    iii. Papers required under i and ii will go to clerk and he will file them on misc. docket, without cost, provided there is proof that notice has been given to other parties.
    iv. Appellee or respondent *in forma pauperis* may file a single response, typewritten or otherwise duplicated, if applicant has filed unprinted papers.

v. *Pro se* parties must comply with all rules as far as possible, before the clerk will accept motion for proceeding IFP.

vi. If Court enters an order under this rule noting or postponing probable jurisdiction, or granting a writ of cert. and the case is set down for argument, it will be transferred to the appellate docket and the Court will make such order as to the printing of the record as it sees fit.

vii. When Court appoints a member of the bar to serve as counsel for an indigent party, the briefs prepared by such counsel shall be printed under the supervision of the clerk, unless counsel has other plans; at least the clerk will reimburse him for travel to and from Washington when he must appear for argument, all on a first-class basis.

4. Special proceedings in veterans' and seamen's cases: Rule 54

i. Under Veterans' Reemployment Act and other free service laws, the veteran may proceed under typewritten papers according to Rule 53. He then proceeds as he would otherwise in the case.

ii. A veteran, suing under 28 U.S.C. Sec. 1916, may proceed without payment or giving security, but he is not relieved of printing costs or entitled to proceed under typewritten papers, unless he by motion and affidavit brings himself under Rule 53.

NOTES TO APPENDIX B

[1]Title 28 U.S.C.A., 1252, 1948.

[2]*Ibid.*, 1253.

[3]*Ibid.*, 1264.

[4]*Ibid.*, 1257.

TABLE OF CASES

SUPREME COURT CASES

Gideon *v.* Wainwright, 372 U.S. 335, 1963.

Goldsby *v.* United States, 160 U.S. 70, 1895.

Good Shot *v.* United States, 179 U.S. 87, 1900.

Graves *v.* United States, 150 U.S. 118, 1893.

Griffin *v.* Illinois, 351 U.S. 12, 1956.

Hamilton *v.* Alabama, 368 U.S. 62, 1961.

Hawk, *Ex parte*, 321 U.S. 114, 1944.

Hawk *v.* O'Grady, 307 U.S. 645, 1940.

Heath, *In re*, 144 U.S. 92, 1892.

Heflin *v.* United States, 358 U.S. 415, 1959.

Hernandez *v.* Texas, 347 U.S. 475, 1954.

Hill *v.* Texas, 316 U.S. 400, 1942.

Holiday *v.* Johnston, 313 U.S. 342, 1941.

Holmes *v.* United States, 314 U.S. 583, 1941; 319 U.S. 776, 1943.

Horton *v.* United States, 175 U.S. 727, 1899.

Hull, *Ex parte*, 312 U.S. 546, 1941.

Irvin *v.* Dowd, 359 U.S. 394, 1959; 361 U.S. 717, 1961.

Johnson *v.* United States, 352 U.S. 565, 1957.

Johnson *v.* Zerbst, 304 U.S. 458, 1938.

Kearney, *Ex parte*, 3 Cr. 448, 1808.

Kinney *v.* Plymouth Rock Squab Co., 236 U.S. 43, 1915.

Ladner *v.* United States, 358 U.S. 169, 1958.

Lane *v.* Brown, 372 U.S. 477, 1963.

Logan *v.* United States, 144 U.S. 263, 1892.

McCann (Gene) *v.* Clark, 331 U.S. 813, 1947.

Ross *v.* Aguerre, 191 U.S. 60, 1903.

Sheppard *v.* Ohio, 352 U.S. 910, 1956.

Slaughter House Cases, 16 Wall. 36, 1873.

Smith *v.* Baldi, 343 U.S. 903, 1952; 344 U.S. 561, 1953.

Smith *v.* Bennett, 365 U.S. 708, 1961.

Smith *v.* O'Grady, 312 U.S. 329, 1941.

Steffler *v.* United States, 319 U.S. 38, 1943.

Stephen *v.* United States, 319 U.S. 423, 1943.

Stevenson *v.* United States, 162 U.S. 313, 1896.

Stonebreaker *v.* Smyth, 323 U.S. 754, 1944.

Storti *v.* Massachusetts, 183 U.S. 138, 1901.

Story *v.* United States, 337 U.S. 947, 1949.

Strauder *v.* West Virginia, 100 U.S. 303, 1879.

Struther *v.* United States, 171 U.S. 690, 1898.

Sunal *v.* Large, 332 U.S. 174, 1947.

Talton *v.* Mays, 163 U.S. 376, 1896.

Tennessee *v.* Davis, 100 U.S. 257, 1879.

Thompson *v.* Missouri, 171 U.S. 380, 1898.

Thompson *v.* United States, 159 U.S. 268, 1895.

Tinder *v.* United States, 345 U.S. 565, 1953.

Townsend *v.* Sain, 372 U.S. 293, 1963.

Tucker *v.* United States, 151 U.S. 164, 1894.

Twitchell *v.* The Commonwealth, 7 Wall. 321, 1868.

United States *v.* Alabama, 335 U.S. 252, 1948.

United States *v.* Allred, 155 U.S. 591, 1894.

United States *v.* Bevans, 3 Wheat. 336, 1818.

White *v*. Maryland, 373 U.S. 59, 1963.

White *v*. Ragen, 324 U.S. 760, 1945.

Williams *v*. Kaiser, 323 U.S. 471, 1945.

Wilson, *Ex parte*, 114 U.S. 417, 1885.

Withers *v*. Buckley, 20 How. 84, 1857.

Yick Wo *v*. Hopkins, 118 U.S. 356, 1885.

LOWER FEDERAL COURT CASES

American Mounting and Die Cutting Co., *In re*, 126 F.2d 419, 1942.

The Bella, 91 F. 540, 1899.

Bernstein *v*. United States, 195 F.2d 517, 1952 (cert. denied).

Boggan *v*. Provident Life and Accident Ins. Co., 79 F.2d 721, 1935.

Bolt *v*. Reynolds Metals Co., 42 F. Supp. 58, 1941.

Boyle *v*. Great Northern R.R. Co., 63 F. 539, 1894.

Bradford *v*. Bradford, 2 Flipp. 280, 281, 1879.

Brinkley *v*. L. and N. R.R. Co., 95 F. 345, 1899.

Carter *v*. Kurn, 120 F.2d 261, 1941.

Checkovitch *v*. United States, 47 F.2d 894, 1931.

Clark *v*. United States, 57 F.2d 214, 1932.

Clay *v*. Southern Ry., 90 F. 472, 1898.

Collier, *In re*, 97 F. 191, 1899.

Columb *v*. Webster Manufacturing Co., 84 F. 592, 1898.

Davita *v*. McCorkle, 248 F.2d 211, 1947.

DeHay *v*. Cline, 5 F. Supp. 630, 1933.

Robinson *v.* Swope, 197 F.2d 633, 1952 (cert. denied).

Rosier, *Ex parte*, 133 F.2d 316, 1943 (cert. denied).

Roy *v.* Louisville, N.O.T.T. R.R. Co., 34 F. 276, 1888.

Ruby *et Ux. v.* Federal Land Bank, 19 F.2d 549, 1937.

Silvas *v.* Arizona Copper Co., 213 F. 504, 1914.

Smith *v.* Johnston, 109 F.2d 152, 1940.

Stanley *v.* Swope, 99 F.2d 308, 1938.

Stewart *v.* St. Sure, 109 F.2d 162, 1940 (cert. denied).

Taylor *v.* Hudspeth, 113 F.2d 825, 1940.

Taylor *v.* Steele, 194 F.2d 864, 1952 (cert. denied).

United States ex rel. Bongiorno *v.* Ragen, 54 F. Supp. 973, 1944.

United States ex rel. Estabrook *v.* Otis, 18 F.2d 689, 1927.

United States *v.* Fair, 235 F. 1015, 1916.

United States *v.* Falshaw, 4 Arizona 330, 1895.

United States ex rel. Foley *v.* Ragen, 52 Supp. 265, 1943.

United States *v.* Holmes, 115 F.2d 528, 1940.

United States *v.* Johnson, 238 F.2d 565, 1956; 254 F.2d 175, 1958.

United States ex rel. Payne *v.* Call, 287 F. 520, 1923.

United States ex rel. Randolph *v.* Ross, 298 F. 64. 1924.

United States *v.* Shive, 27 Fed. Cases No. 16, 278, 1832.

United States *v.* Stevens, 244 F.2d 866, 1955.

United States *v.* Taylor, 11 F. 470, 1882.

Volk *v.* Sturtevant Co., 99 F. 532, 1900.

Waterman *v.* McMillan, 135 F.2d 807, 1943.

BOOKS

Beaney, Wm. M., *The Right to Counsel in American Courts*, Ann Arbor: University of Michigan Press, 1955.

Black, Charles L., Jr., *The People and the Court*, New York: Macmillan Co., 1960.

Burgess, John W., *Political Science and Comparative Constitutional Law*, Vols. I and II, Boston: Ginn and Co., 1893.

Cardozo, Benjamin, *The Nature of the Judicial Process*, New Haven: Yale University Press, 1921.

Cohn, Edmond (ed), *The Supreme Court and Supreme Law*, Bloomington: Indiana University Press, 1954.

Crosskey, Wm. W., *Politics and the Constitution in the History of the United States*, Vols. I and II, Chicago: University of Chicago Press, 1953.

Curtis, Charles P., *Lions Under the Throne*, Boston: Houghton-Mifflin, 1947.

Daniel, Hawthorne, *Judge Medina*, New York: W. Funk, 1952.

Doyle, Sir Arthur Conan, *The Complete Sherlock Holmes*, New York: Doubleday, 1952.

Fairman, Charles, *Mr. Justice Miller and the Supreme Court*, Cambridge: Harvard University Press, 1939.

Frankfurter, Felix and Landis, James M., *The Business of the Supreme Court*, New York: Macmillan Co., 1927.

Freund, Paul A., *On Understanding the Supreme Court*, Boston: Little, Brown, 1949.

Friedrick, Carl J., *The Philosophy of Law and Historical Perspective*, Chicago: University of Chicago Press, 1963.

Gerhart, Eugene C., *American Advocate: Robert H. Jackson*, Indianapolis: Bobbs-Merrill, 1958.

Hand, Learned (Judge), *The Bill of Rights*, Cambridge: Harvard University Press, 1958.

Hart, Henry M., Jr. and Wechsler, Herbert. *The Federal Courts and the Federal System*, Brooklyn: Foundation Press, 1953.

Holdsworth, W. S., *History of English Law*, Vols. IV, VI, IX. London: Methuen, 1924.

Hyneman, Chas. B., *Supreme Court on Trial*, New York: Atherton Press, 1963.

Jackson, Robert H., *The Supreme Court in the American System of Government*, Cambridge: Harvard University Press, 1955.

Kempin, Frederick G., Jr., *Legal History: Law and Social Change*, New York: Prentice Hall 1963.

Mason, Alpheus T., *Brandeis: A Free Man's Life*, New York: The Viking Press, 1946.

Mason, Alpheus T., *Harlan Fiske Stone: Pillar of the Law*, New York: The Viking Press, 1956.

Meiklejohn, Alexander, *Political Freedom*, New York: Harper, 1960 ed.

Mendelson, Wallace H., *Justices Black and Frankfurter; Conflict in the Court.* Chicago: University of Chicago Press, 1961.

Mendelson, Wallace H., *The Constitution and the Supreme Court*, New York: Dodd Mead and Co., 1959.

Murphy, Walter F., *Congress and the Court*, Chicago: University of Chicago Press, 1962.

Murphy, Walter F. and Pritchett, C. Herman, *Courts, Judges and Politics*, New York: Random House, 1961.

Pound, Roscoe, *Introduction to the Philosophy of Law*, New Haven: Yale University Press, 1953 ed.

Powell, Thomas Reed, *Vagaries and Varieties in Constitu-*

tional Interpretation, New York: Columbia University Press, 1956.

Pringle, Henry F., *Life and Times of Wm. Howard Taft*, Vols. I and II, New York: Farrar and Rinehart, 1939.

Pritchett, C. Herman, *The Roosevelt Court*, New York: Macmillan, 1948.

Pritchett, C. Herman, *Civil Liberties and the Vincent Court*, Chicago: University of Chicago Press, 1950.

Pusey, Marlo J., *Charles Evans Hughes*, Vols. I and II, New York: Macmillan, 1951.

Roosevelt, Franklin D., *The Public Papers and Addresses of Franklin D. Roosevelt*, New York: Random House, 1934, 1935, and Macmillan, 1937, 1938.

Seagle, William, *The Quest for Law*, New York: A. A. Knopf, 1941.

Stern, Robt. L. and Gressman, Eugene, *Supreme Court Practice*, Washington: Bureau of National Affairs, 2d ed., 1954.

Thorsen, Thomas L., *The Logic of Democracy*, New York: Holt, Rinehart and Winston, 1962.

Van Santvoord, G., *Lives and Services of the Chief Justices of the United States*, New York: C. Scribner, 1854.

PUBLIC DOCUMENTS

Attorney-General, Dept. of— Reports of Attorney General: Committee on Public Defender (1963).

Comptroller's Decisions; Comptroller-General's Decisions

Congressional Record

Director of Administrative Office of the United States Courts: Annual Reports

Federal Rules of Civil Procedure

Federal Rules of Criminal Procedure

Supreme Court: Minutes of the Supreme Court
                Rules of the Supreme Court
                Supreme Court Journal

U.S. Legislative Reference Service — "Constitution of the United States, Annotated to June 30, 1952," Gov. Printing Office, 1953

ARTICLES

Abernathy, Glenn. "Expansion of the State Action Concept Under the Fourteenth Amendment," 43 *Corn. L.Q.* (1958), 43.

Abrahams, Robert D., "The English Legal Assistance Plan...," 36 *A.B.A.J.* (1950), 31.

Allen Francis A., "The Supreme Court, Federalism and the States' Systems of Criminal Justice," 8 *De Paul L. Rev.* (1959), 213.

The Annals of the American Academy of Political and Social Science, "Lagging Justice," 328 *Annals* (1960), 163.

Blaustein, Albert P. and Field, Andrew H., "Overruling Opinions in the Supreme Court 1810-1959," 57 *Mich. L. Rev.* (1958-59), 151-183.

Bickel, Alexander M., "Supreme Court 1960 Term 'Foreward: The Passive Virtues,'" 75 *Harv. L. Rev.* (1961), 45, 69.

Boskey, Bennett and Pickering, John H., "Federal Restrictions on State Criminal Procedures," 13 *Univ. of Chi. L. Rev.* (1945-46), 266.

_____, "Mechanics of Supreme Court's Certiorari Jurisdiction," 46 *Col. L. Rev.* (March, 1946), 255-65.

Brennan, Wm. J., Jr. (Justice), "The Bill of Rights and the States," *Center for Study of Democratic Institutions*, Santa Barbara, Calif. (1956)

————, "Federal Habeas Corpus and State Powers: An Exercise in Federalism," 7 *Utah L. Rev.* (1960-61), 423-41.

Brown, Ernest J., "Supreme Court 1957 Term," 72 *Harv. L. Rev.* (1958-59), 77.

Clark, Tom C. (Justice), "The Supreme Court Conference," 19 *F.R.D.* (Nov. 1956), 303.

Comments: "Appointment of Counsel for Indigent Accused," by Niles Chubb, 28 *Tex. L. Rev.* (1949-1950), 236-257.

————; Docketry: Office of the Supreme Court, "On Docketry of the Supreme Court," 59 *Harv. L. Rev.* (1945-1956), 604-606.

————; Federal Habeas Corpus – State Prisoners, 55 *Col. L. Rev.* (1955), 196-209.

————; The Griffin Case, 55 *Mich. L. Rev.* (1956-57), 428-430.

————; Indigent Rights to Assigned Counsel in Non-Capital Cases, 14 *West. Res. L. Rev.* (1962), 370.

————: "International Due Process and the Law," by Justice Wm. J. Brennan, Jr., 48 *Va. L. Rev.* (1962), 1258.

————: Federal Habeas Corpus – State Prisoners, 55 *Col. L. Rev.* (1955), 196-209.

Conference of State Chief Justices – Report:
"Committee on Federal-State Relationships, As Affected by Judicial Decisions," (August 23, 1958)

Corbett, Percy E., "The Search for General Principles of Law," 47 *Va. L. Rev.* (1961), 811.

Dimock, Edward J. (Judge), "The Public Defender: A Step Toward the Police State," 42 *A.B.A.J.* (1956), 219-220.

Fairman, Charles, "Does the Fourteenth Amendment Incorporate the Bill of Rights? The Original Understanding," 2 *Stanford L. Rev.* (1951), 1.

Frank, John P. and Monroe, Robt. F., "The Original Understanding of the Equal Protection of the Laws," 50 *Col. L. Rev.* (1950), 151.

Goodhart, Arthur L., "Costs," 38 *Yale L.J.* (1928-29), 847.

Graham, Howard J., "Our 'Declaratory' Fourteenth Amendment," 7 *Stanford L. Rev.* (1954), 3.

Hamley, Hon. Frank G., "The Impact of Griffin *v.* Illinois on State Courts," 24 *F.R.D.* (1959), 75-83.

Harper, Fowler T. and Rosenthal, William S., "What the Supreme Court Did Not Decide in the 1949 Term," 99 *Univ. of Penn. L. Rev.* (1950), 293.

Holtzoff, Alexander, "Collateral Review," 25 *B.U.L. Rev.* (1945), 26.

Illinois, "Collateral Relief for Convictions in Violation of Due Process in Illinois," 42 *Ill. L. Rev.* (1947), 329.

Jenner, Albert E., Jr., "Illinois Post-Conviction Hearing Act," 9 *F.R.D.* (Dec. 1949), 347-366.

Judicial Conference of the U.S., "General Measures Affecting IFP:" Court Reporter System
          Public Defender Bills
          Habeas Corpus and Similar Proceedings

Kauper, Paul G., "The Supreme Court and the Rule of Law," 59 *Mich. L. Rev.* (1961), 531.

————, "Supreme Court Trends in Constitutional Interpretation," 24 *F.R.D.* (Oct. 1959), 155-185.

Latham, Earl, "The Supreme Court as a Political Institution," 31 *Minn. L. Rev.* (1947), 205.

Lewis, Anthony, "The Supreme Court and Its Critics," 45 *Minn. L. Rev.* (1960-1961), 305.

Longsdorf, G. G., "The Federal Habeas Corpus Act," 13 *F.R.D.* (1953), 407-424.

Lusky, Louis, "Minority Rights and the Public Interest," 52 *Yale L.J.* (1942), 1.

McElwain, Edwin, "The Business of the Supreme Court as Conducted by Chief Justice Hughes," 63 *Harv. L. Rev.* (1949-1950), 5-26.

Maguire, John M., "Poor Persons' Procedure in Civil Cases," 36 *Harv. L. Rev.* (1923-24), 361.

Malone, Albert C., Jr., "The Soviet Bar," 46 *Corn. L.Q.* (1961), 258-289.

Mason, Alpheus T., "Myth and Reality in Supreme Court Decisions," 48 *Va. L. Rev.* (1962), 1385.

Mendelson, Wallace H., "Mr. Justice Black and the Rule of Law," 4 *Mid. J. Pol. Sc.* (1961), 250.

Notes: Proceedings in State *In Forma Pauperis*, 31 *Harv. L. Rev.* (1917-1918), 485.

————: Proceedings in State *In Forma Pauperis*, 31 *Calif. L. Rev.* (1943), 207-210.

————: On Section 2255, 28 U.S.C., 59 *Yale L.J.* (1949-1950), 1183 ff.

Orfield, Lester B., "Appeals by Indigent Criminals," 3 *Univ. of Pitts. L. Rev.* (1936), 1.

————, "Criminal Appeals — Federal Courts," 45 *Yale L.J.* (1935-36), 1223.

Panda, N. N., "Justice and the Poor in India," 30 *J. Am. Judic. Soc.* (1947), 190-192.

Parker, John J. (Judge), "Limiting the Abuse of Habeas Corpus," 8 F.R.D. (1949), 171-177.

Pollak, Louis H., "Proposals to Curtail Federal Habeas Corpus to State Prisoners...," 66 *Yale L.J.* (Nov. 1956), 50-66.

Pound, Roscoe, "The Ideal Element in Law," *Encyclopedia of Social Sciences*, Vol. VIII, 477-92.

Rathner, Leonard G., "Congressional Power over the Appellate Jurisdiction of the Supreme Court," 109 *Univ. of Penn. L. Rev.* (Dec. 1960), 157.

Recent Decisions, "Indigent Right to Assigned Counsel in Non-Capital Cases: Carnley *v.* Cochran (369 U.S. 508, 1962), 14 *West Res. L. Rev.* (1962), 370.

Ridge, Albert A. (Judge), "The Indigent Defendant: A Procedural Dilemma for the Courts," 24 *F.R.D.* (1960), 243-295.

Rietz, Curtis R., "Federal Habeas Corpus: Impact on Abortive State Proceeding," 74 *Harv. L. Rev.* (1960-61), 1315.

Right to Counsel: A Symposium, 45 *Minn. L. Rev.* (1960-61), 693-874 (8 contributions, esp.).

Roche, John P., "Judicial Self-Restraint," 49 *Am. Pol. Sc. Rev.* (1955), 162, 193.

Rockwell, Landon G., "Justice Rutledge on Civil Liberties," 59 *Yale L.J.* (1949), 27.

Rostow, Eugene V., "The Court and Its Critics," 4 *So. Tex. L. Rev.* (1959), 160.

Rothe, E. W., Jr., "Exhaustion of State Remedies," 47 *Mich. L. Rev.* (1945), 720.

Schubert, Glendon, "Policy Without Law: An Extension of the Certiorari Game," 14 *Stanford L. Rev.* (1952), 284.

26 State Government (1953), "Report of the Special Committee on Habeas Corpus," 242-246.

Stewart, Wm. Scott, "The Public Defender Principle is Unsound in Principle," 32 *J. Am. Judic. Soc.* (1948), 115.

Stone, Harlan F., Address to Fourth Circuit Judicial Conference on Certiorari, 28 *A.B.A.J.* (1942), 519.

8 University of Chicago Law School Record: *Special Supplement* (Autumn 1958)